OXFORD READINGS IN PHILOSOPHY

Series Editor G. J. Warnock

PHILOSOPHY AND
ECONOMIC THEORY

D0781063

Also published in this series.

The Philosophy of Law, edited by Ronald M. Dworkin
Moral Concepts, edited by Joel Feinberg
Theories of Ethics, edited by Philippa Foot
The Philosophy of Mind, edited by Jonathan Glover
Knowledge and Belief, edited by A. Phillips Griffiths
The Philosophy of Mathematics, edited by Jaakko Hintikka
Reference and Modality, edited by Leonard Linsky
The Philosophy of Religion, edited by Basil Mitchell
The Philosophy of Science, edited by P. H. Nidditch
Aesthetics, edited by Harold Osborne
The Theory of Meaning, edited by G. H. R. Parkinson
The Philosophy of Education, edited by R. S. Peters
Political Philosophy, edited by Anthony Quinton
Practical Reasoning, edited by Joseph Raz
The Philosophy of Social Explanation, edited by Alan Ryan
The Philosophy of Language, edited by J. R. Searle
Semantic Syntax, edited by Pieter A. M. Seuren
Causation and Conditionals, edited by Ernest Sosa
Philosophical Logic, edited by P. F. Strawson
The Justification of Induction, edited by Richard Swinburne
Locke on Human Understanding, edited by I. C. Tipton
The Philosophy of Perception, edited by G. J. Warnock
The Philosophy of Action, edited by Alan R. White

Other volumes are in preparation

PHILOSOPHY AND ECONOMIC THEORY

Edited by
FRANK HAHN AND MARTIN HOLLIS

OXFORD UNIVERSITY PRESS
1979

Oxford University Press, Walton Street, Oxford OX2 6DP

OXFORD LONDON GLASGOW
NEW YORK TORONTO MELBOURNE WELLINGTON
KUALA LUMPUR SINGAPORE JAKARTA HONG KONG TOKYO
DELHI BOMBAY CALCUTTA MADRAS KARACHI
NAIROBI DAR ES SALAAM CAPE TOWN

Published in the United States by Oxford University Press, New York

© *Oxford University Press 1979*

All rights reserved. No part of this publication may be reproduced, stored in a retrieval system, or transmitted, in any form or by any means, electronic, mechanical, photocopying, recording, or otherwise, without the prior permission of Oxford University Press

This book is sold subject to the condition that it shall not, by way of trade or otherwise, be lent, re-sold, hired out, or otherwise circulated without the publisher's prior consent in any form of binding or cover other than that in which it is published and without a similar condition including this condition being imposed on the subsequent purchaser.

British Library Cataloguing in Publication Data

Philosophy and economic theory.—(Oxford readings in philosophy).
1. Economics—Addresses, essays, lectures
2. Philosophy—Addresses, essays, lectures
I. Hahn, Frank   II. Hollis, Martin   III. Series
330.1 HB72 79-41054
ISBN 0-19-875042-0

*Printed in Great Britain by
Fakenham Press Limited, London and Fakenham*

ACKNOWLEDGEMENTS

I   Friedman   From *Essays in Positive Economics* by Milton Friedman (University of Chicago Press, 1953) part I, sections 1, 2, 3, and 6 (Conclusion). Copyright 1953 by The University of Chicago. All rights reserved. Reprinted by permission of the author and the publishers.

II   Robbins   From *An Essay on the Nature and Significance of Economic Science* by L. Robbins, second edition (Macmillan, 1935) Chapter IV, pp. 72–9, 83–4, 86–9, 90–8, 100. Reprinted by permission of Macmillan, London and Basingstoke.

III   Hollis & Nell   From *Rational Economic Man* by M. Hollis and E. J. Nell (Cambridge University Press, 1975) appendix to Chapter 7. Reprinted by permission of the publishers.

IV   von Mises   From *Epistemological Problems of Economics* by L. von Mises translated by G. Reisman (D. Van Nostrand Co. Ltd., 1960) Chapter I, Sections 5 & 6. © 1960 by the William Volker Fund in the series Humane Studies. Reprinted by permission of the Institute for Humane Studies who will be publishing a new edition in 1979.

V   Simon   From S. Latsis (ed.) *Method and Appraisal in Economics* (Cambridge University Press, 1976). Reprinted by permission of the publishers.

VI   Sen   From H. Harris (ed.) *Scientific Models and Man. The Herbert Spencer Lectures 1976* (Oxford University Press, 1979). © Oxford University Press, 1979. Reprinted by permission of the publishers and the Herbert Spencer Fund.

VII   Arrow   From P. Laslett and W. G. Runciman (eds.) *Philosophy, Politics and Society*, Third Series (Basil Blackwell & Mott, 1967). Reprinted by permission of the author.

VIII Sen   From *The Journal of Political Economy*, Vol. 78, 1970, pp. 152–7. © 1970 by The University of Chicago. All rights reserved. Reprinted by permission of the author and The University of Chicago Press.

IX   Varian   From *Philosophy and Public Affairs*, Vol. 4, no. 3 (Spring 1975), pp. 223–47. Reprinted by permission of Princeton University Press.

X   Hammond   From *Econometrica*, Vol. 44, 1976, pp. 793–800 (omitting technical appendix). Reprinted by permission of The Econometric Society (U.S.A.), and the author.

XI   Rawls   From *A Theory of Justice* by John Rawls (Cambridge, Mass.: The Belknap Press of Harvard University Press and Oxford: The Clarendon Press). Copyright © 1971 by the President and Fellows of Harvard College. Section 41, pp. 258–65. Reprinted by permission of the publishers.

CONTENTS

INTRODUCTION

WHEN English-speaking philosophers think of economics, they usually have a particular kind of pure theory in mind. This is the class of theories predominantly taught in western universities and often called neo-Classical. Purity here is a matter of conceiving *homo economicus* in abstraction from his social setting and, more excusably, of forswearing the attempt to make economics part (or all) of a general theory of society. By contrast, political economy, as the term is now used, is just such an attempt and its champions insist that no economic theory can be as pure as neo-Classicals pretend. Marxian economics is a leading example but has no monopoly and there are heretics within the temple too. The point is less one about the fact–value distinction, although purity is indeed hard to maintain in welfare economics, than one about the proper uses of abstraction. So it raises issues of method and metaphysics, which will be stressed as we proceed. But let us start in innocence, with the claim of pure theory to state the general principles of an autonomous science of economics.

The most effective and subtle of the social sciences offers a fine array of topics for philosophers. Yet there is oddly little commerce at present. There used to be more, when economics was turning itself into a closed, technical discipline with the aid of Logical Positivism and against the wishes of those who valued its leadership of the moral sciences. Since then economists, absorbed in technical issues, have for the most part written little to surprise philosophers and philosophers have tackled economics rarely, nervously, and by way of example only. On the economists' side, Popper's picture of science as conjectures and refutations has been widely admired and endorsed but not seen as a threat to the hopes of a positive economics grounded on orthodox Positivist tenets. The upheaval caused by Quine's pragmatism, Kuhn's paradigms, and other more recent *bouleversements* has yet to send more than a tremor through the temple.

The topic most freely discussed is that of causal laws. Debate is within a broad assumption that progress comes by testing hypotheses against experience. In bald summary of the line handed out to beginners, a natural law is a regularity in nature holding in specifiable conditions; we have detected one when we have a well enough confirmed theory; a theory is a set of logically-linked, high-order generalizations; the only test of a theory is the success of its predictions; prediction and explanation are two sides of the same and only coin, in that explaining a fact is finding another from which it could have been predicted. Also, in keeping with this Positivist perspective, sciences are thought of as differing in subject-matter, not in method of validation, and there is a thorough distinction of 'is' from 'ought' (positive from normative). Admittedly so clear and simple a rubric is only for beginners and sits uneasily even in the introductory chapter to economics textbooks, whose later chapters are methodologically more involved and pragmatic. But economists are wont to blame their unsolved problems on the incompleteness of economic theory rather than on a philosophic virus and the search for empirical laws goes on.

One fierce, plainly philosophical argument is flourishing, however, and has long enlivened the pages of the *American Economic Review*. It was touched off by Milton Friedman's essay 'The Methodology of Positive Economics' and has to do with whether a good scientific theory needs realistic assumptions. Offhand one might suppose that theories of imperfect competition apply more widely and so are a clear advance on the theory of perfect competition as a guide to economic behaviour. To maintain the contrary, Friedman opens with a pithy and definitive statement of Positivism in economics and tries to use it to show that realism cannot be an independent criterion. He carves any sound economic theory into 'a language' and 'a body of substantive hypotheses'. The former is, he says, 'a set of tautologies' and 'its function is to act as a filing system'; the latter is 'designed to abstract essential features of a complex reality'. Since the only test of a theory is the success of its predictions, the theory of perfect competition enters the lists on equal terms and indeed proves the most useful. His critics have found it hard to escape the elenchus, since they too accept the picture of science, however much they wish to hymn the need for realism.

There is nothing peculiar to economics about this issue, when it is raised in a Positive setting, although the dispute about perfect competition is a notable example of it. But it also crops up elsewhere in economic theory, this time in a distinctive way. Pure theory is deeply committed to an assumption that economic behaviour is rational—not, one might think, a self-evidently realistic postulate to start from. Yet other social sciences are trying to borrow the assumption, together with its economic trappings, and it seems to us the current area of most philosophical interest. In what follows we shall introduce the economic notion of rationality, show how philosophically charged and perplexing it is, note its bearing on social choice and social justice, and indicate its relevance beyond economics. Since the philosophical topics in Positive economics will be aired in a more general manner, we shall not be neglecting our editorial duties by concentrating on this central assumption of pure economic theory.

In macro- no less than in micro-economics pure theory rests on propositions about individual action. To generalize, it needs to take the individual agent as typical or representative of others. Generality is achieved by conceiving the individual as a rational economic man and asserting that mankind at large is as rational as he. For instance the analysis of investment, savings and liquidity preference which occupies most of Keynes's *General Theory* takes just this form. Before low wages can be explained through the self-interest of capitalists as a group in keeping them low, it must be shown that each capitalist is acting rationally and in a way which, when aggregated, produces this effect. Before trades unions or shareholders can be treated as agencies, they are analysed as coalitions of individuals each with an interest in subscribing to rules which bind them together and in acting jointly. Throughout pure theory macro-movements are thus explained as the collective work of rational individuals and the pedagogic reasons why the pure economist starts with micro-analysis also reflect his deepest ontological commitments.

It is all too easy to suppose that pure theory equates rationality with self-interested action and hence applies only to rational egoists. There is every excuse. Edgeworth roundly declared, 'the first principle of economics is that every agent is actuated only by self-interest'[1] and countless economic models have been built on this principle. The stock distinction between economic and sociological theories of social action has been one between men as rational egoists versus men obedient to norms. Nevertheless egoism is only a special interpretation of the pure notion of rationality. To bring the point out and, at the same time, to guard against other ways in which the theory can easily be misunderstood, we have thought it best to give a technical (albeit incomplete) sketch. Despite the use of symbols, the careful novice should be able to follow.

The pure theory characterizes the agent independently of his environment. It is assumed that he has preferences and the characterization is by the kind of preferences he has. The domain of his preferences is the set of consequences of his possible actions. Let C, with elements c, c', c'', etc., be the domain of a given agent's preferences and let R be a relation among the elements of C, so that cRc' is read as 'c is at least as good as c''. The theory assigns three properties to R:

[1] F. Y. Edgeworth, *Mathematical Psychics: An Essay on the Application of Mathematics to the Moral Sciences* (Kegan Paul, London, 1881), p.16.

(1) *Completeness.* For all pairs (c, c') in C, either cRc' or $c'Rc$ or both. (When cRc' and *not* $c'Rc$, economists sometimes write cPc' (i.e. c is preferred to c'); when cRc' and $c'Rc$, they sometimes write cIc' (i.e. c is indifferent to c').)

(2) *Reflexivity.* For all c in C, cRc.

(3) *Transitivity.* For every triple (c, c', c'') in C, if cRc' and $c'Rc''$ then cRc''.

(We stress that this is not a complete account but it will serve.)

The interpretation of the theory depends on the domain specified. Where C is taken as the vector space an element of which gives the bundle of goods consumed by the agent himself, it is usual (although not obligatory) to regard this as postulating purely selfish preferences. Where C is taken as the vector space an element of which gives the consumption bundle of every agent in the economy, the matter is more open and the agent's preferences on C may or may not be selfish. If his ordering R can be fully specified independently of the consumption by other agents, we might want to call him prima facie selfish; if not, then his preferences may be selfless or they may be envious. Hence cPc' can mean 'c is more in the self-interest of the agent than c'' but it need not. The postulate that an agent is characterized by preferences rules out neither the saint nor Genghis Khan.

In an abstract way we may think of an agent as having available a set of mutually exclusive actions. The choice of one of these will have consequences, which are what interests the agent. In general a consequence need not be uniquely defined by an action but, whenever it is, a preference ordering over actions can be regarded as one over the consequences of actions and, for ease of exposition, we shall assume unique consequences of action.

The pure economist's definition of rational choice is now this: Given the set of available actions, the agent chooses rationally if there is no other action available to him the consequence of which he prefers to that of the chosen action. On the face of it, it looks very simple—even plausible; yet it has striking implications, as we shall next show by examples.

So let us consider an economy with only two goods—a restriction made for purposes of exposition only. Take an agent who owns some of both goods before the story starts and can trade at given prices. His action-set consists of all trades which he can make at these prices, given that (a) he can sell no more of any good than he owns and (b) that his receipts from a sale must not be less than the amount required for a purchase. The agent's preferences are defined over all possible consumption bundles of the two goods (all non-negative pairs).

Proposition A: The choice of the rational agent will be independent of the level of the two prices (i.e. will depend only on their ratio).

Proof: Consider two price situations which differ only in that each price in situation one is a positive multiple of the price in situation two. From the definition of the action-set of the agent it is clear that the sets are the same in both situations. But then the choice which was rational in one situation must also be rational in the other. For, if not, then one choice must be preferred to the other; but both are available in both situations.

This simple proposition plays an important role in the theory of inflation.

Proposition B: A rational agent will prefer to pay a given amount to the Government by means of an *ad valorem* tax to paying the same amount by means of a lump sum (poll) tax.

Proof: (a) Suppose the *ad valorem* tax on good one yields £T from the agent, good two being untaxed. Remove the *ad valorem* tax, thus lowering the price of good one, relative to good two, by the tax per unit. Impose a poll-tax of £T, thus making the agent pay £T whatever his choice. Check that the agent can now, if he wishes, buy as much of each good as he did when there was an *ad valorem* tax. Removing the *ad valorem* tax saves him the tax per unit of good one times the amount which he was buying; and that is exactly what is taken away from him by the poll-tax. Hence the *ad valorem* tax choice is in the action-set available under the poll-tax.

(b) If the agent now chooses a different action, it must, by the postulate of rational choice, be true that he prefers it to his *ad valorem* tax choice.

This proposition is closely related to the economist's prescription that price should equal marginal cost and is of wide practical interest.

Proposition C: Suppose there are *n* agents. Define a *competitive equilibrium* as a price system and a pair of trades, one for each agent, such that (a) at these prices, given preferences and the ownership of goods, the trade of each agent is a rational choice, (b) the total amount of each good supplied is equal to the total amount demanded. Assume that these prices are both positive and assume that each agent in this equilibrium would prefer to have more of any good (if possible) than he has—i.e. agents are not satiated. Then there is no way for a central authority to reallocate the existing stock of goods so as to ensure that each agent obtains an allocation at least as highly preferred as his equilibrium allocation and at least one agent receives an allocation which he prefers to his equilibrium allocation. The equilibrium is Pareto-efficient.

Proof: Suppose the proposition is false. Consider agent i, who obtains an allocation which he prefers to his equilibrium allocation. Since he was choosing rationally in the equilibrium, the newer allocation was not in his action-set at equilibrium prices. It must then be that at these prices the new allocation would violate the condition that receipts from sales should equal amount spent. (Non-satiation ensures that in equilibrium the agent will not spend less than he receives.) On the other hand all those agents to whom the central authority allocates a bundle which they consider indifferent to their equilibrium bundle will find that at equilibrium prices the centrally allocated bundle either violates or just meets the condition that receipts equal outgoings. For, if receipts were less than outgoings, when the central allocation is indifferent to the equilibrium one, the agent was not rational in his choice of equilibrium trades. That is because he could have traded to get a bundle as good as his equilibrium one and still have something left over to buy more or sell less. But non-satiation then leads to the result that the equilibrium choice was not rational— a contradiction.

So now we have shown that to obtain the centrally allocated bundle at equilibrium prices each agent would spend as much as or more than he receives and at least one agent would have to spend more than he receives. So if agent i is allocated the consumption (c_1^i, c_2^i) and owns (x_1^i, x_2^i), we have, when (p_1, p_2) are equilibrium prices:

$$p_1(c_1^i - x_1^i) + p_2(c_2^i - x_2^i) \geqslant 0, \qquad \text{for all } i.$$

$$p_1(c_1^i - x_1^i) + p_2(c_2^i - x_2^i) > 0, \qquad \text{for some } i.$$

Adding over agents and recalling that $p_1 > 0$, $p_2 > 0$, we conclude that the allocation would use more of at least one good than is available:

i.e.
$$\sum_i c_j^i > \sum_i x_j^i$$
for either $j = 1$ or $j = 2$ or both.

Hence Proposition C is not false.

This proposition has played a central role in economics and it can be made more significant by its 'dual', which asserts (roughly speaking) that any

Pareto-efficient allocation can, under certain conditions, be decentralized into a competitive equilibrium. But this and the many other applications would take us too far afield. The examples already given suffice to show that the rational-choice postulate is indeed powerful and useful.

To complete our brief account, and because some of the contributors later are concerned with it, we shall now sketch the notion of collective rational action.

Consider an economy of n agents and let there be a number of possible alternatives. Let $\mathscr{R}$ be the set of all possible orderings of the alternatives, where the orderings are complete, reflexive, and transitive. For instance, if there are two alternatives a and b, then either a is preferred to b, or b is preferred to a, or a and b are indifferent. The problem posed by Arrow[2] is this: does there exist an ordering which is complete, reflexive, and transitive (i.e. in $\mathscr{R}$) which is derived (a map) from any preference profile $R^1 \cdots R^n$ of the n agents with R^i in $\mathscr{R}$, for all i? That is, can we get an ordering of the alternatives which depends on the orderings of the agents?

The answer is of course yes. We need only to make the ordering of any one individual into our social ordering, so that his preferences *are* the social preferences. But that is too easy and also undesirable. So we exclude this solution by imposing a *non-dictatorship* condition.

Next it seems reasonable to require that, if alternative b is higher in the preferences of every agent than is alternative a, then the social order should put b as socially preferred to a. So we write this in by imposing the *Pareto-condition* on the social order which we will accept.

Lastly one imposes the plausible, but none the less problematic, condition that social preferences between b and a should depend only on agents' preferences between b and a and not at all on their preferences between any other pair. This is the condition of *Independence of Irrelevant Alternatives*.

Arrow proved a remarkable theorem: if we allow any preferences in $\mathscr{R}$ (unrestricted domain) and require non-dictatorship, the Pareto-condition, and Independence of Irrelevant Alternatives, then a social preference cannot be constructed from agents' preferences.

A vast literature has grown up on this theorem. Without trying to pass any judgements, we would like four points to be noted. Firstly, the problem has been formulated at a high level of generality. In particular we are asked to find a derivation or 'map' which will work for *any* admissible preference profile ('unrestricted domain'). Thus the agnosticism concerning the origin or social determination of preferences is carried very far. Secondly, in conformity with the theory of rational choice of the agent only orderings of

---

[2] K. J. Arrow, *Social Choice and Individual Values* (New York, 1951). See also his article in the present volume.

alternatives are considered. In particular we are not allowed to consider intensities of preferences. If we were allowed to do so, then in deriving a social order we could either take account of them or not. If we do not, nothing is gained. If we do, it implies that we can compare intensities. Thirdly, the Pareto property may not in fact be desirable. It may conflict with the view that there are 'private domains' for each agent over which his ordering should be decisive. Fourthly, the requirement of the independence of irrelevant alternatives rules out considerations of intensity of preferences and is not a self-evidently acceptable axiom. The large literature notwithstanding, however, Arrow's result shows that there are great difficulties in extending the notion of individual rationality found in economic theory to one of collective rationality.[3]

This concludes the brief exposition and we next consider two obvious objections to the postulate in a summary way. One is to using unexplained preferences as explanans, the other to supposing that agents do or can act rationally on the preferences ascribed. Both objections look formidable but, we think, neither is decisive.

Firstly, then, it seems plain that preferences are determined in part by the very process which they are meant to explain, and not given independently as the theory requires; nor, granted that they are not all of equal permanence, importance, or worth, can they be relied on to yield any social optimum when aggregated.

As far as explanation goes, the pure economist replies that preferences, although mutable, change slowly in relation to the endogenous variables of economic models. Hence it does no harm to the rest of the analysis to treat them as exogenous (and unexplained). That they do change more slowly is a falsifiable hypothesis which is confirmed by experience. For instance much, in our view vulgar, criticism of the theory has turned on the effects of advertising, by which firms are allegedly able to engineer whatever preferences suit them. The pure economist might, of course, retort by disputing the power of advertising to affect tastes directly. But, more subtly, he will probably answer by pointing out that the domain of preferences may very well not be the space of goods but the space of characteristics of goods—the speed and comfort of travel, for example, rather than the motor cars which

---

[3] It is plain that this account leaves much of interest undiscussed. In particular it is not made clear what interpretation to put on agents' preferences. Do they reflect just choice or judgement or consideration of their own welfare? Certainly these are matters for investigation (witness the work of A. K. Sen) but they do not, in our view, much affect the formal apparatus. For it would seem on close examination that it is satisfactory to endow agents with single preferences but to make their domain large enough. For instance the domain includes not only butter but also 'freedom' and so forth, and the agents' preferences give us trade-offs between all the elements.

embody these characteristics in varying proportions. Advertising, he will argue, is more to do with getting us to ascribe these virtues to particular cars than with changing what we ask of a car. By affecting the (perceived) map from actions to consequences, it can change actions without changing tastes. In general to perceive something under a fresh description is not necessarily to alter the criteria for evaluating it against other things and hence it is no blow to the theory to recognize that preferences alter. Whether he is right is an empirical matter but he does have at least some answers to the objection.

This retort is too quick, however, when it comes to aggregating preferences for purposes of Welfare economics. If we want to order social states by the relation '*a* is socially no worse than *b*', we must know why preferences of agents have a claim on our attention at all and which preferences are to count for how much. Whether or not we can significantly ask if *A*'s preferences are rational, we can certainly ask if they are good or indeed if they are no worse than *B*'s.

The general answer is that pure economists are democrats enough to try for a measure of welfare which respects what people actually want. But, believing that some wants are more transitory or antisocial than others, they are also ready to weight preferences in arriving at social preferences. By adopting some moralist's preferences over preferences, they can assign zero or even negative weights in some cases. If this seems to sully the purity of a theory of rational action, it at least permits them to escape Arrow's theorem by introducing intensity of preferences and a suitable notion of comparability.[4] Also they do not propose their own moral calculus and have been content to axiomatize various moral ideas supplied by others. For instance Rawls's theory of justice as fairness has given rise to much recent work in economics, one result of which has been to convert the criterion of ordering social states by the welfare of the worst-off person in each into a lexicographical maximin on the grounds that, if *a* and *b* leave the worst-off equally well-off, while *b* does better for everyone else, *b* should be socially preferred to *a*. Yet the economist thinks of himself in transactions like these not as solving problems but as helping to clarify possible solutions. (We shall ask presently whether he is being disingenuous.)

Where preferences are being weighted by their social worth, economists can try leaving the choice of weights to others. Where weights are used because preferences are transitory they cannot. The fact that the agent's preferences will change with learning, ageing and circumstance should reasonably limit what he can prefer today, if he is not to regret it tomorrow. The point has been studied recently and a new, but not deeply different,

[4] A. K. Sen, *Collective Choice and Social Welfare* (Oliver and Boyd, 1970).

axiomatization of rationality has been proposed to allow for it.[5] But more than technicality is involved, since orthodox pure theory cannot admit any serious sense in which preferences may be irrational. Indeed there is difficulty even in the unproblematic thought that it is irrational to hold inconsistent preferences or to be unwarrantably mistaken about the consequences of enacting a preference (for instance that one will not regret doing so). For the theory takes preferences to range over well-defined states (consequences of actions) and it is not obvious where to locate these possibilities.

That brings us to the second blunt objection, which doubts whether agents do or can act rationally on the preferences ascribed. It is all too plain that no one in fact has a complete ordering of relevant alternative states for every, or indeed any, occasion—nor could he have one without spending his life in hypothetical comparisons. Nor will it do to postulate consistency without ascribing to everyone a degree of computational skill which no one in fact possesses. We are thus led back to the question left hanging at the start—whether a theory needs realistic assumptions if it is to have explanatory merit. A possible, if blunt, answer is that pure economic theory works well enough when it is used for rational choice over a more or less small subset of available choices. Certainly there is no denying that modest empirical studies have been successful. But, finding this a craven reply and the issues it shirks interesting for all the social sciences, we urge even the pure to have the courage of its assumptions.

Perhaps, then, it is not irrational to act on incomplete preferences, even when the agent makes a choice which, had he made the effort, he would have discovered to be inferior to another choice available. After all, the exploration of his preferences or environment takes time, trouble, and expense (buying *Which?*, for example) and so is an activity which should itself feature among his preferences. Admittedly this thought threatens to make nonsense of the very idea of complete preferences, since the agent cannot know whether he rationally prefers to rest content with what he knows already unless he knows already what he would discover if he continued searching. But it suggests that it can be rational to act on a consistent subset of one's preferences even if it would be found inconsistent with some larger set. Thus Simon has long advocated an approach through 'bounded rationality', where agents behave as in the theory which we have outlined but only over a subset of alternatives and of their environment.[6] The subset is determined by the agent's 'aspiration level', which in turn has social and

[5] B. Peleg and M. Yaari, 'On the Existence of a Consistent Course of Action when Tastes are Changing', *Review of Economic Studies* (1973).

[6] H. Simon, *Models of Man* (J. Wiley and Sons, 1957).

psychological determinants. It is only when outcomes fall below aspiration levels that the agent will institute search of his environment or of his preferences.

This way out is descriptively plausible but has not so far proved theoretically useful, since the aspiration levels and the search activities are ill-defined.[7] But it offers a tempting answer to the question whether it is preferences and correct computation which constitute rationality. The answer is, in effect, that there is no 'correct' definition of rationality but that different applications of the theory call for different definitions, each leaving a fringe of actions whose rationality is undecidable.

At any rate we think this a much better line than that of restoring completeness by making the consequence space merely subjective. It may seem promising to say that, even if the agent would have changed his mind, had he discovered more, nevertheless he chose rationally what he perceived to be best at the time. Indeed it is hard to deny that a man can act rationally on false beliefs about consequences, including those of satisfying his present desires. Hence it looks as if the objective notion of rationality which we have used in sketching the theory should be recast in terms of how an agent's world looks and works from within. The change would be more than local. For instance it would no longer follow that a competitive equilibrium is Pareto-efficient relative to the true possibility of the economy; Welfare economics would have to judge social states on the basis not just of preferences but also of varying perceptions and computational skills, with great loss of persuasiveness. But it looks as if it could and indeed should be done. In truth, however, pure economic theory has found it hard to make the change. Pure theory rests on an assumption that R is a fixed relation, present in all economic agents. The typical or representative individual, with whom we began, has to have complete, reflexive, transitive preferences, if the first, essential theorems are to sustain a scheme of explanation. The theory has had to ignore the source of preferences[8] and to construct everything from their implications. It is not enough that each man does what seems to him required by what he thinks his preferences are in what he takes to be the circumstances. Yet plainly there is an unrealism about the universal assumption of R and, we submit, a notion of 'bounded' or restricted, but still objective, rationality is the best way to face up to it.

That, we agree, does not finally dispose of the doubt that whether the rationality postulate is realistic enough. Nor does it prove that pure theory

[7] R. Radner, 'Aspirations, Bounded Rationality and Control', Berkeley Discussion Paper, 1975.

[8] But see C. C. von Weizsäcker, 'Notes on Endogenous Changes in Taste', *Journal of Economic Theory*, iii (1971).

has, or else does not need, a correct definition of rationality. Nor does it do more than show that the question whether a sound theory needs realistic assumptions is still alive and relevant. So our summing up must be tentative and provisional, not least because the authors of this introduction find themselves in genial disagreement.

To Hahn (the economist), the position is this. Economics probably made a mistake when it adopted the nomenclature of 'rational' when all it meant is correct calculations and an orderly personality. The term invites philosophers and others to invest the whole theory with too much significance. Even so the hypothesis of the economist is wrong for the reasons sketched and the question, which the reader will see discussed in this volume, is whether a wrong hypothesis can yield a correct theory. At a proper level of generality the answer to this, Friedman's persuasiveness notwithstanding, must surely be no. But a hypothesis may be generally wrong yet right in properly specified applications. Thus it is doubtful that any of the criticisms we have considered are very important when one studies the response of a consumer to a rise in the price of butter relative to that of margarine. Or consider again the proposition concerning lump sum taxes and ask whether it is seriously at risk from the likely limitations on the 'rationality hypothesis'. What is at risk is a good deal of grand (as opposed to small) Welfare economics and almost certainly much of the social choice programme. But that is the nature of the beast and Hahn foresees no profitable or interesting answer to the question: what does it really mean to say that a has been rationally chosen?

Hollis (the philosopher) thinks that Hahn is altogether too modest. The rationality postulate cannot be construed as a tentative empirical postulate which experience confirms in particular areas; nor is it incidental that what it postulates happens to be labelled 'rationality'. On the first point, even in the charting of a man's preferences between butter and margarine it regulates and explains the data. It regulates them in that it lets the econometrician so specify and identify discrete, unadjusted, raw observations that he can treat them as instancing R and hence within the theory's scope—a function yet more visible when producing a market demand curve from individual preferences. It explains them in that it authorizes statements of how the agent *would* respond to changes in price. Without such authority there is no telling the law-like from the merely accidental. There was always this much truth in the slogan that prediction and explanation are two sides of the same coin. Moreover it is no mere empirical matter how widely the postulate applies. To decide whether an agent or group is rational enough, the economist must identify their preferences and he has some choice of the descriptions under which he is to assign characteristics of goods to the vector space. Even with bounded rationality, the descriptions must be recognizable to the agents and the characteristics he can warrantably impute will vary with the degree of accurate perception and computational skill which he possesses. He is not a modest under-labourer but a judge.

On the point about labels, what is at risk is the rationality of the economist. He is offering to find rational solutions for economic problems. The promise is explicit (if not always kept) in Welfare economics, cost–benefit analysis, and other areas of public policy but it is also there in every analysis of the rational allocation of resources. What the rational man would do, the plain man should do. Hence the more modest the economist is about the actual scope of his theory, the less modest he is committed to being about its value. Where it does not explain, it shows men how to do better. So, whenever actual agents are found not to be as the theory implies, it is a criticism not of the theory but of the agents. The theory is the measure of the agent's performance and, if it is entitled to the immunity from refutation which it thus acquires, it can only be because it is a true measure. Of what? Presumably of what it is to be a rational economic agent. The term 'rational' occurs essentially in *a priori* statements whose truth is crucial to the descriptive, explanatory, and prescriptive uses of the theory. So it does matter that the theory is concerned with the concept of rationality and whether it is right about it. Otherwise the pure economist is rational neither in his choice of assumptions nor in his advice.

In this editorial disagreement the reader is not, of course, obliged to side with either of us. But we would like it granted that much is at stake for economics in particular and for the social sciences in general. By treating rational action as the central topic of pure economic theory we are not trying to bypass the old argument about laws in economics or to set a divide between natural and social sciences. We leave it to others to decide whether the rational explanation of action is a form of causal explanation and, as noted, the rationality postulate raises questions of realism squarely enough. But we do recommend that analogies between economics and natural science be taken coolly. Economists have been greatly under the influence of a majestic image of the Laws of Physics and have sometimes been led to hope for a set of Laws of Economic Motion as forceful as Newton's laws. We suggest that these are the wrong images to rely on. Aerodynamics, for instance, is a tightly constructed, highly developed theory yet it is quite impossible to design an aeroplane on paper and then go straight into production. The design will need testing with mock-ups and wind-tunnels and may require *ad hoc*, imperfectly understood modifications. Theories have to simplify and then have to patch. The most it is worth insisting on in advance is agreed rules of evidence and argument. Keynes urged economists to be 'like dentists' and, although he did not take the advice himself, we think it excellent.

It may sound as if we think dentists merely pragmatic and humble. Once again, however, we do not mean to deny the larger questions. What is to be taken coolly is the image of natural science as rigid deductions from simple general laws and the idea of the relation between theory and reality as one of simplified map-making. Larger questions remain but we cannot go into them here. Instead we shall say a little about pure theory in political economy and other social sciences.

We began by distinguishing pure theory from political economy by its way of conceiving *homo economicus* in abstraction from his social setting and by its belief in the clear division between positive and normative. By focusing on rationality we have made the distinction hard to uphold. The rational man of pure theory is an ideal type in the sense not only of being an idealization where the theory holds without qualification but also of being a model to copy, a guide to action. In pointing out the way to satisfy a given set of ordered preferences, the theorist gives reasons for action. Initially these reasons apply only to agents with the same preferences but, in showing up hidden costs and complications, the theorist also gives reasons for overhauling the preferences. He is operating not only with but also on the agent's preference order over preferences, by pointing out changes which would result in a more satisfiable set of preferences. Such calculations will have to allow for the wants and actions of other agents, who will in turn have reason to pay attention to the theory. Meanwhile the theory is being developed in order to be able to say what is rational for several agents at the same time. Here again it is a source of reasons not only for pursuing social strategies appropriate to existing social preferences but also for changing preferences for the sake of more widespread satisfaction. In brief the theory holds out the prospect of a general analysis of social choice and of guidance on the old problem of distribution. Hence it is hard to resist the conclusion that pure economic theory is implicitly in competition with what rides openly under the banner of normative science. It is, despite itself, political economy, done in the traditional way by taking, in Rousseau's words, 'men as they are and laws as they might be'. Also in the traditional way, it ends by showing how it would be most convenient to reshape men too.

With or without implications for ethics, the pure notion of *homo economicus* is of great interest to other social sciences. It offers an analysis of agency which yields a systematic macro-theory and yet can be interpreted voluntaristically. This may seem an odd description on both counts to anyone who reflects on the notorious snags of getting micro-theory to deal with institutional behaviour or who regards it as a virtue of revealed preference theory that it dispenses with mental events. Also the orthodox account of rational economic man was developed under the influence of a Positive view of natural science and cannot easily be detached from these origins. Yet, as we have already noted, many economists seem to rub along nicely without trying too hard to find natural laws of the kind which Positivism insists on. There are, moreover, other epistemologies worth looking to for a systematic notion of rational choice. At any rate the social sciences have been changing character lately in ways inimical to Positivism but increasingly well disposed to economic models of rationality.

In sociology, for instance, the social world is being presented not as the product of social forces but as human handiwork. In role theory the dramaturgical analogy is being used to show how men are not *dramatis personae* created and controlled by the script but actors who interpret or even create the play. In phenomenological and cognitive sociology men construct and reconstruct their world by self-definition and negotiation. Similar thoughts inform the self-styled 'radical' moves in politics, psychology, and elsewhere. The catch-phrase is that human beings are, somehow and to some degree, autonomous. The large snag, however, is that any explanation of an autonomous action threatens to explain its autonomy away. For example, if explaining is still showing how actions result from initial conditions and covering laws, then the actor is lost in the explanation. Equally, if social explanation works by identifying the rules and meanings embodied in actions, the actor is prone to become in consequence the creature of these bearers of significance. Yet, if autonomous action is the unpredictable expression of an existential will, social science becomes impossible. That is doubtless too dogmatic but the threat, coupled with the lack of other modes of explanation, is proving awkward. The air is loud with cries of search but it may perhaps be that this missing mode has been in full view all along. It may be that in showing why an autonomous action was *rationally* done, the inquirer can both demonstrate the autonomy and explain the action.

The hope has not gone unnoticed and rational economic man has already entered sociology. In social exchange theory social life is seen very much as a market in varying states of co-operation and competition. The giving of gifts, for instance, can be interestingly explored on the assumption that recipients always reciprocate somehow to the same amount. The forming of friend-ships, the working of charities, the conduct of elections, the basis of coalitions, the stockpiling of weapons, the diplomacy of nations have all been treated as neo-Classical transactions. The medium of exchange varies from one realm to another but the constant aim of each agent is to enact his highest preference at lowest cost, calculated with regard to risk and uncertainty. What started as a protest against an 'oversocialised conception of man' continued with a case for 'bringing men back in' with the aid of psychological assumptions, which turned out to be the principles of marginalist economics.[9] If that makes men passive after all, by placing them in a social market where they adjust almost automatically to fixed rules and prices, it is easy to go further. In 'radical' versions the market is constantly renegotiated, rules, prices, and all. What might look at first like mere romantic assertion becomes sharp and forceful, when the economic theory of games is pressed into service.

If there is to be a link between autonomy and rationality, then the best grounded theories of rational choice are those by neo-Classical economists. But they must be disentangled from their usual Positive context. Yet that job needs doing in any case, now that Positivist epistemology has lost its charms. It seems to us that the pure theory of rational economic action can be construed neither as a mere filing system nor as a body of substantive hypotheses (Friedman's only alternatives). If the core of neo-Classical economics is here, then what are its epistemological warrant and function? We suggest that pure theory, once it is recognized as a version of political economy after all, contains a sophisticated yet un-Marxian notion of agency, able perhaps to fill an evident gap in the understanding of social life.

Our purpose is less to endorse these hopes than to air them, just as our choice of a broadly neo-Classical frame for the anthology is not meant to decry other and radically different approaches to economics. With so little space we have thought it best not to seek philosophy everywhere but to concentrate on issues raised by the kind of pure economic theories most familiar in Western universities. Even so, we have had to be selective and the pieces which follow can be grouped roughly under three headings.

The first is Explanation, the traditional topic for philosophers and the one most discussed by students of methodology. Here there was no resisting Friedman's essay 'The Methodology of Positive Economics', which continues to give its many critics an uncomfortable ride, especially with its provoking first half, which is all we have had room for. Next come some of Robbins's older but evergreen thoughts on economic generalizations and a critical note on both theorists from Hollis and Nell. Lastly von Mises supplies a whiff of the Austrian School with his insistence on the *a priori* character of economic science. Two classic pieces missing are E. Nagel's 'Assumptions in Economic Theory' and T. C. Koopmans's discussion of Friedman and Robbins in *Three Essays on the State of Economic Science*, but the former appears in Alan Ryan's volume in this series and the latter proved too

---

[9] See, for example, G. E. Homans, 'Bringing Men Back In', *American Sociological Review*, xxix (1964), reprinted in A. Ryan (*ed.*), *The Philosophy of Social Explanation* (Oxford, 1973).

lengthy. Readers wishing to pursue the debate about Friedman's 'F-twist' in the *American Economic Review* will find references in our bibliography.

The second heading is Rationality, represented here by two substantial essays. In 'From Substantive to Procedural Rationality' Simon endorses the recent trend of concern towards the latter and urges a shift in scientific style from deductive reasoning to empirical exploration of algorithms of thought. Sen's 'Rational Fools' is a delightful plea for an economic psychology which makes 'a bit more room up top' for the kind of motives which actually move men to economic decision. Both pieces dissect the stock economists' ideas of rationality—a matter on which it is oddly hard for the layman to get information—and offer themes which connect with much that is discussed in other terms by philosophers of mind.

The third section can be called Questions of Value and is of current interest to philosophers owing to Rawls's *Theory of Justice*. Much of the most striking work is highly technical and we have hesitated over the editorial problem thus set. The pieces chosen hint at deeper intricacies but should be accessible enough to the layman. In 'Values and Collective Decision-Making' Arrow argues that every individual decision involves the participation of a whole society and obligingly expounds his Impossibility theorem, which has fathered a huge literature. Sen makes a brief second appearance in order to put Paretian liberals in an impossible position and we regret having had no space for his later article in *Economica* (1976) where he replies to critics. Varian in 'Distributive Justice, Welfare Economics, and the Theory of Fairness' sets off from Nozick's *Anarcy, State, and Utopia* and presents his own theory of distributive justice. Hammond comments with technical elegance on Arrow and Rawls, and finally there is a terse reflection by Rawls on the concept of justice in political economy.

Although the pieces included need no trumpet, we are very conscious of our exclusions. The choice of framework and limits of space have driven much tempting work into the bibliography. In balancing competing claims we have been greatly helped by Amartya Sen, who has kindly given us much valued advice. We are also grateful to him and to Angus Ross for comments on our Introduction. Responsibility remains ours, of course, and finally we would like to thank each other for the unfinished intellectual disagreements which have enlivened our task.

I

THE METHODOLOGY OF
POSITIVE ECONOMICS*

MILTON FRIEDMAN

IN his admirable book on *The Scope and Method of Political Economy* John Neville Keynes distinguishes among 'a *positive science* ... [,] a body of systematized knowledge concerning what is; a *normative* or *regulative science* ... [,] a body of systematized knowledge discussing criteria of what ought to be ...; an *art* ... [,] a system of rules for the attainment of a given end'; comments that 'confusion between them is common and has been the source of many mischievous errors'; and urges the importance of 'recognizing a distinct positive science of political economy'.[1]

This paper is concerned primarily with certain methodological problems that arise in constructing the 'distinct positive science' Keynes called for—in particular, the problem how to decide whether a suggested hypothesis or theory should be tentatively accepted as part of the 'body of systematized knowledge concerning what is'. But the confusion Keynes laments is still so rife and so much of a hindrance to the recognition that economics can be, and in part is, a positive science that it seems well to preface the main body of the paper with a few remarks about the relation between positive and normative economics.

1. THE RELATION BETWEEN POSITIVE AND NORMATIVE ECONOMICS

Confusion between positive and normative economics is to some extent inevitable. The subject matter of economics is regarded by almost everyone

From *Essays in Positive Economics* (Chicago: University of Chicago Press, 1953), Part I, sections 1, 2, 3, and 6.

* I have incorporated bodily in this article without special reference most of my brief 'Comment' in *A Survey of Contemporary Economics*, vol. II, ed. B. F. Haley (Chicago: Richard D. Irwin, Inc., 1952), pp. 455–7.

I am indebted to Dorothy S. Brady, Arthur F. Burns, and George J. Stigler for helpful comments and criticism.

[1] (London: Macmillan & Co., 1891), pp. 34–5 and 46.

as vitally important to himself and within the range of his own experience and competence; it is the source of continuous and extensive controversy and the occasion for frequent legislation. Self-proclaimed 'experts' speak with many voices and can hardly all be regarded as disinterested; in any event, on questions that matter so much, 'expert' opinion could hardly be accepted solely on faith even if the 'experts' were nearly unanimous and clearly disinterested.[2] The conclusions of positive economics seem to be, and are, immediately relevant to important normative problems, to questions of what ought to be done and how any given goal can be attained. Laymen and experts alike are inevitably tempted to shape positive conclusions to fit strongly held normative preconceptions and to reject positive conclusions if their normative implications—or what are said to be their normative implications—are unpalatable.

Positive economics is in principle independent of any particular ethical position or normative judgements. As Keynes says, it deals with 'what is', not with 'what ought to be'. Its task is to provide a system of generalizations that can be used to make correct predictions about the consequences of any change in circumstances. Its performance is to be judged by the precision, scope, and conformity with experience of the predictions it yields. In short, positive economics is, or can be, an 'objective' science, in precisely the same sense as any of the physical sciences. Of course, the fact that economics deals with the interrelations of human beings, and that the investigator is himself part of the subject-matter being investigated in a more intimate sense than in the physical sciences, raises special difficulties in achieving objectivity at the same time that it provides the social scientist with a class of data not available to the physical scientist. But neither the one nor the other is, in my view, a fundamental distinction between the two groups of sciences.[3]

---

[2] Social science or economics is by no means peculiar in this respect—witness the importance of personal beliefs and of 'home' remedies in medicine wherever obviously convincing evidence for 'expert' opinion is lacking. The current prestige and acceptance of the views of physical scientists in their fields of specialization—and, all too often, in other fields as well—derives, not from faith alone, but from the evidence of their works, the success of their predictions, and the dramatic achievements from applying their results. When economics seemed to provide such evidence of its worth, in Great Britain in the first half of the nineteenth century, the prestige and acceptance of 'scientific economics' rivalled the current prestige of the physical sciences.

[3] The interaction between the observer and the process observed that is so prominent a feature of the social sciences, besides its more obvious parallel in the physical sciences, has a more subtle counterpart in the indeterminacy principle arising out of the interaction between the process of measurement and the phenomena being measured. And both have a counterpart in pure logic in Gödel's theorem, asserting the impossibility of a comprehensive self-contained logic. It is an open question whether all three can be regarded as different formulations of an even more general principle.

Normative economics and the art of economics, on the other hand, cannot be independent of positive economics. Any policy conclusion necessarily rests on a prediction about the consequences of doing one thing rather than another, a prediction that must be based—implicitly or explicitly—on positive economics. There is not, of course, a one-to-one relation between policy conclusions and the conclusions of positive economics; if there were, there would be no separate normative science. Two individuals may agree on the consequences of a particular piece of legislation. One may regard them as desirable on balance and so favour the legislation; the other, as undesirable and so oppose the legislation.

I venture the judgement, however, that currently in the Western world, and especially in the United States, differences about economic policy among disinterested citizens derive predominantly from different predictions about the economic consequences of taking action—differences that in principle can be eliminated by the progress of positive economics—rather than from fundamental differences in basic values, differences about which men can ultimately only fight. An obvious and not unimportant example is minimum-wage legislation. Underneath the welter of arguments offered for and against such legislation there is an underlying consensus on the objective of achieving a 'living wage' for all, to use the ambiguous phrase so common in such discussions. The difference of opinion is largely grounded on an implicit or explicit difference in predictions about the efficacy of this particular means in furthering the agreed-on end. Proponents believe (predict) that legal minimum wages diminish poverty by raising the wages of those receiving less than the minimum wage as well as of some receiving more than the minimum wage without any counterbalancing increase in the number of people entirely unemployed or employed less advantageously than they otherwise would be. Opponents believe (predict) that legal minimum wages increase poverty by increasing the number of people who are unemployed or employed less advantageously and that this more than offsets any favourable effect on the wages of those who remain employed. Agreement about the economic consequences of the legislation might not produce complete agreement about its desirability, for differences might still remain about its political or social consequences; but, given agreement on objectives, it would certainly go a long way towards producing consensus.

Closely related differences in positive analysis underlie divergent views about the appropriate role and place of trade unions and the desirability of direct price and wage controls and of tariffs. Different predictions about the importance of so-called 'economies of scale' account very largely for divergent views about the desirability or necessity of detailed government regulation of industry and even of socialism rather than private enterprise.

And this list could be extended indefinitely.[4] Of course, my judgement that the major differences about economic policy in the Western world are of this kind is itself a 'positive' statement to be accepted or rejected on the basis of empirical evidence.

If this judgement is valid, it means that a consensus on 'correct' economic policy depends much less on the progress of normative economics proper than on the progress of a positive economics yielding conclusions that are, and deserve to be, widely accepted. It means also that a major reason for distinguishing positive economics sharply from normative economics is precisely the contribution that can thereby be made to agreement about policy.

2. POSITIVE ECONOMICS

The ultimate goal of a positive science is the development of a 'theory' or 'hypothesis' that yields valid and meaningful (i.e., not truistic) predictions about phenomena not yet observed. Such a theory is, in general, a complex intermixture of two elements. In part, it is a 'language' designed to promote 'systematic and organized methods of reasoning'.[5] In part, it is a body of substantive hypotheses designed to abstract essential features of complex reality.

Viewed as a language, theory has no substantive content; it is a set of tautologies. Its function is to serve as a filing system for organizing empirical material and facilitating our understanding of it; and the criteria by which it is to be judged are those appropriate to a filing system. Are the categories clearly and precisely defined? Are they exhaustive? Do we know where to file each individual item, or is there considerable ambiguity? Is the system of headings and subheadings so designed that we can quickly find an item we want, or must we hunt from place to place? Are the items we shall want to consider jointly filed together? Does the filing system avoid elaborate cross-references?

---

[4] One rather more complex example is stabilization policy. Superficially, divergent views on this question seem to reflect differences in objectives; but I believe that this impression is misleading and that at bottom the different views reflect primarily different judgements about the source of fluctuations in economic activity and the effect of alternative countercyclical action. For one major positive consideration that accounts for much of the divergence see 'The Effects of a Full-Employment Policy on Economic Stability: A Formal Analysis', pp. 117–32 [of Friedman, 1953]. For a summary of the present state of professional views on this question see 'The Problem of Economic Instability', a report of a subcommittee of the Committee on Public Issues of the American Economic Association, *American Economic Review*, vol. xl (September 1950), pp. 501–38.

[5] Final quoted phrase from Alfred Marshall, 'The Present Position of Economics' (1885), reprinted in *Memorials of Alfred Marshall*, ed. A. C. Pigou (London: Macmillan & Co., 1925), p. 164. See also 'The Marshallian Demand Curve', pp. 56–7, 90–1 [of Friedman, 1953].

The answers to these questions depend partly on logical, partly on factual, considerations. The canons of formal logic alone can show whether a particular language is complete and consistent, that is, whether propositions in the language are 'right' or 'wrong'. Factual evidence alone can show whether the categories of the 'analytical filing system' have a meaningful empirical counterpart, that is, whether they are useful in analysing a particular class of concrete problems.[6] The simple example of 'supply' and 'demand' illustrates both this point and the preceding list of analogical questions. Viewed as elements of the language of economic theory, these are the two major categories into which factors affecting the relative prices of products or factors of production are classified. The usefulness of the dichotomy depends on the 'empirical generalization that an enumeration of the forces affecting demand in any problem and of the forces affecting supply will yield two lists that contain few items in common'.[7] Now this generalization is valid for markets like the final market for a consumer good. In such a market there is a clear and sharp distinction between the economic units that can be regarded as demanding the product and those that can be regarded as supplying it. There is seldom much doubt whether a particular factor should be classified as affecting supply, on the one hand, or demand, on the other; and there is seldom much necessity for considering cross-effects (cross-references) between the two categories. In these cases the simple and even obvious step of filing the relevant factors under the headings of 'supply' and 'demand' effects a great simplification of the problem and is an effective safeguard against fallacies that otherwise tend to occur. But the generalization is not always valid. For example, it is not valid for the day-to-day fluctuations of prices in a primarily speculative market. Is a rumour of an increased excess-profits tax, for example, to be regarded as a factor operating primarily on today's supply of corporate equities in the stock-market or on today's demand for them? In similar fashion, almost every factor can with about as much justification be classified under the heading 'supply' as under the heading 'demand'. These concepts can still be used and may not be entirely pointless; they are still 'right' but clearly less useful than in the first example because they have no meaningful empirical counterpart.

Viewed as a body of substantive hypotheses, theory is to be judged by its predictive power for the class of phenomena which it is intended to 'explain'. Only factual evidence can show whether it is 'right' or 'wrong' or, better, tentatively 'accepted' as valid or 'rejected'. As I shall argue at greater length below, the only relevant test of the *validity* of a hypothesis is comparison of its

[6] See 'Lange on Price Flexibility and Employment: A Methodological Criticism', pp. 282–9 [of Friedman, 1953].

[7] 'The Marshallian Demand Curve', p. 57 [of Friedman, 1953].

predictions with experience. The hypothesis is rejected if its predictions are contradicted ('frequently' or more often than predictions from an alternative hypothesis); it is accepted if its predictions are not contradicted; great confidence is attached to it if it has survived many opportunities for contradiction. Factual evidence can never 'prove' a hypothesis; it can only fail to disprove it, which is what we generally mean when we say, somewhat inexactly, that the hypothesis has been 'confirmed' by experience.

To avoid confusion, it should perhaps be noted explicitly that the 'predictions' by which the validity of a hypothesis is tested need not be about phenomena that have not yet occurred, that is, need not be forecasts of future events; they may be about phenomena that have occurred but observations on which have not yet been made or are not known to the person making the prediction. For example, a hypothesis may imply that such and such must have happened in 1906, given some other known circumstances. If a search of the records reveals that such and such did happen, the prediction is confirmed; if it reveals that such and such did not happen, the prediction is contradicted.

The validity of a hypothesis in this sense is not by itself a sufficient criterion for choosing among alternative hypotheses. Observed facts are necessarily finite in number; possible hypotheses, infinite. If there is one hypothesis that is consistent with the available evidence, there are always an infinite number that are.[8] For example, suppose a specific excise tax on a particular commodity produces a rise in price equal to the amount of the tax. This is consistent with competitive conditions, a stable demand curve, and a horizontal and stable supply curve. But it is also consistent with competitive conditions and a positively or negatively sloping supply curve with the required compensating shift in the demand curve or the supply curve; with monopolistic conditions, constant marginal costs, and stable demand curve, of the particular shape required to produce this result; and so on indefinitely. Additional evidence with which the hypothesis is to be consistent may rule out some of these possibilities; it can never reduce them to a single possibility alone capable of being consistent with the finite evidence. The choice among alternative hypotheses equally consistent with the available evidence must to some extent be arbitrary, though there is general agreement that relevant considerations are suggested by the criteria 'simplicity' and 'fruitfulness', themselves notions that defy completely objective specification. A theory is 'simpler' the less the initial knowledge needed to make a prediction within a given field of phenomena; it is more 'fruitful' the more precise the resulting

[8] The qualification is necessary because the 'evidence' may be internally contradictory, so there may be no hypothesis consistent with it. See also 'Lange on Price Flexibility and Employment', pp. 282–3 [of Friedman, 1953].

prediction, the wider the area within which the theory yields predictions, and the more additional lines for further research it suggests. Logical completeness and consistency are relevant but play a subsidiary role; their function is to assure that the hypothesis says what it is intended to say and does so alike for all users—they play the same role here as checks for arithmetical accuracy do in statistical computations.

Unfortunately, we can seldom test particular predictions in the social sciences by experiments explicitly designed to eliminate what are judged to be the most important disturbing influences. Generally, we must rely on evidence cast up by the 'experiments' that happen to occur. The inability to conduct so-called 'controlled experiments' does not, in my view, reflect a basic difference between the social and physical sciences both because it is not peculiar to the social sciences—witness astronomy—and because the distinction between a controlled experiment and uncontrolled experience is at best one of degree. No experiment can be completely controlled, and every experience is partly controlled, in the sense that some disturbing influences are relatively constant in the course of it.

Evidence cast up by experience is abundant and frequently as conclusive as that from contrived experiments; thus the inability to conduct experiments is not a fundamental obstacle to testing hypotheses by the success of their predictions. But such evidence is far more difficult to interpret. It is frequently complex and always indirect and incomplete. Its collection is often arduous, and its interpretation generally requires subtle analysis and involved chains of reasoning, which seldom carry real conviction. The denial to economics of the dramatic and direct evidence of the 'crucial' experiment does hinder the adequate testing of hypotheses; but this is much less significant than the difficulty it places in the way of achieving a reasonably prompt and wide consensus on the conclusions justified by the available evidence. It renders the weeding-out of unsuccessful hypotheses slow and difficult. They are seldom downed for good and are always cropping up again.

There is, of course, considerable variation in these respects. Occasionally, experience casts up evidence that is about as direct, dramatic, and convincing as any that could be provided by controlled experiments. Perhaps the most obviously important example is the evidence from inflations on the hypothesis that a substantial increase in the quantity of money within a relatively short period is accompanied by a substantial increase in prices. Here the evidence is dramatic, and the chain of reasoning required to interpret it is relatively short. Yet, despite numerous instances of substantial rises in prices, their essentially one-to-one correspondence with substantial rises in the stock of money, and the wide variation in other circumstances that might appear to be relevant, each new experience of inflation brings forth vigorous contentions, and not only by the lay public, that the rise in the stock of money is either an incidental effect of a rise in prices produced by other factors or a purely fortuitous and unnecessary concomitant of the price rise.

One effect of the difficulty of testing substantive economic hypotheses has been to foster a retreat into purely formal or tautological analysis.[9] As already noted, tautologies have an extremely important place in economics and other sciences as a specialized language or 'analytical filing system'. Beyond this, formal logic and mathematics, which are both tautologies, are essential aids in checking the correctness of reasoning, discovering the implications of hypotheses, and determining whether supposedly different hypotheses may not really be equivalent or wherein the differences lie.

But economic theory must be more than a structure of tautologies if it is to be able to predict and not merely describe the consequences of action; if it is to be something different from disguised mathematics.[10] And the usefulness of the tautologies themselves ultimately depends, as noted above, on the acceptability of the substantive hypotheses that suggest the particular categories into which they organize the refractory empirical phenomena.

A more serious effect of the difficulty of testing economic hypotheses by their predictions is to foster misunderstanding of the role of empirical evidence in theoretical work. Empirical evidence is vital at two different, though closely related, stages: in constructing hypotheses and in testing their validity. Full and comprehensive evidence on the phenomena to be generalized or 'explained' by a hypothesis, besides its obvious value in suggesting new hypotheses, is needed to assure that a hypothesis explains what it sets out to explain—that its implications for such phenomena are not contradicted in advance by experience that has already been observed.[11] Given that the hypothesis is consistent with the evidence at hand, its further testing involves deducing from it new facts capable of being observed but not previously known and checking these deduced facts against additional empirical evidence. For this te st to be relevant, the deduced facts must be about the class of phenomena the hypothesis is designed to explain; and they must be well enough defined so that observation can show them to be wrong.

The two stages of constructing hypotheses and testing their validity are related in two different respects. In the first place, the particular facts that enter at each stage are partly an accident of the collection of data and the

---

[9] See 'Lange on Price Flexibility and Employment' [in Friedman, 1953], *passim*.

[10] See also Milton Friedman and L. J. Savage, 'The Expected-Utility Hypothesis and the Measurability of Utility', *Journal of Political Economy*, vol. lx (December 1952), pp. 463–74, esp. pp. 465–7.

[11] [We have omitted a long, technical footnote discussing a possible distinction between a 'model' and a 'structure'—eds.]

knowledge of the particular investigator. The facts that serve as a test of the implications of a hypothesis might equally well have been among the raw material used to construct it, and conversely. In the second place, the process never begins from scratch; the so-called 'initial stage' itself always involves comparison of the implications of an earlier set of hypotheses with observation; the contradiction of these implications is the stimulus to the construction of new hypotheses or revision of old ones. So the two methodologically distinct stages are always proceeding jointly.

Misunderstanding about this apparently straightforward process centres on the phrase 'the class of phenomena the hypothesis is designed to explain'. The difficulty in the social sciences of getting new evidence for this class of phenomena and of judging its conformity with the implications of the hypothesis makes it tempting to suppose that other, more readily available, evidence is equally relevant to the validity of the hypothesis—to suppose that hypotheses have not only 'implications' but also 'assumptions' and that the conformity of these 'assumptions' to 'reality' is a test of the validity of the hypothesis *different from* or *additional to* the test by implications. This widely held view is fundamentally wrong and productive of much mischief. Far from providing an easier means for sifting valid from invalid hypotheses, it only confuses the issue, promotes misunderstanding about the significance of empirical evidence for economic theory, produces a misdirection of much intellectual effort devoted to the development of positive economics, and impedes the attainment of consensus on tentative hypotheses in positive economics.

In so far as a theory can be said to have 'assumptions' at all, and in so far as their 'realism' can be judged independently of the validity of predictions, the relation between the significance of a theory and the 'realism' of its 'assumptions' is almost the opposite of that suggested by the view under criticism. Truly important and significant hypotheses will be found to have 'assumptions' that are widely inaccurate descriptive representations of reality, and, in general, the more significant the theory, the more unrealistic the assumptions (in this sense).[12] The reason is simple. A hypothesis is important if it 'explains' much by little, that is, if it abstracts the common and crucial elements from the mass of complex and detailed circumstances surrounding the phenomena to be explained and permits valid predictions on the basis of them alone. To be important, therefore, a hypothesis must be descriptively false in its assumptions; it takes account of, and accounts for, none of the many other attendant circumstances, since its very success shows them to be irrelevant for the phenomena to be explained.

---

[12] The converse of the proposition does not of course hold: assumptions that are unrealistic (in this sense) do not guarantee a significant theory.

To put this point less paradoxically, the relevant question to ask about the 'assumptions' of a theory is not whether they are descriptively 'realistic', for they never are, but whether they are sufficiently good approximations for the purpose in hand. And this question can be answered only by seeing whether the theory works, which means whether it yields sufficiently accurate predictions. The two supposedly independent tests thus reduce to one test.

The theory of monopolistic and imperfect competition is one example of the neglect in economic theory of these propositions. The development of this analysis was explicitly motivated, and its wide acceptance and approval largely explained, by the belief that the assumptions of 'perfect competition' or 'perfect monopoly' said to underlie neoclassical economic theory are a false image of reality. And this belief was itself based almost entirely on the directly perceived descriptive inaccuracy of the assumptions rather than on any recognized contradiction of predictions derived from neoclassical economic theory. The lengthy discussion on marginal analysis in the *American Economic Review* some years ago is an even clearer, though much less important, example. The article on both sides of the controversy largely neglect what seems to me clearly the main issue—the conformity to experience of the implications of the marginal analysis—and concentrate on the largely irrelevant question whether businessmen do or do not in fact reach their decisions by consulting schedules, or curves, or multivariable functions showing marginal cost and marginal revenue.[13] Perhaps these two examples, and the many others they readily suggest, will serve to justify a more extensive

[13] See R. A. Lester, 'Shortcomings of Marginal Analysis for Wage-Employment Problems', *American Economic Review*, vol. xxxvi (March 1946), pp. 62–82; Fritz Machlup, 'Marginal Analysis and Empirical Research', *American Economic Review*, vol. xxxvi (September 1946), pp. 519–54; R. A. Lester, 'Marginalism, Minimum Wages, and Labor Markets', *American Economic Review*, vol. xxxvii (March 1947), pp. 135–48; Fritz Machlup, 'Rejoinder to an Antimarginalist', *American Economic Review*, vol. xxxvii (March 1947), pp. 148–54; G. J. Stigler, 'Professor Lester and the Marginalists', *American Economic Review*, vol. xxxvii (March 1947), pp. 154–7; H. M. Oliver, Jr., 'Marginal Theory and Business Behavior', *American Economic Review*, vol. xxxvii (June 1947), pp. 375–83; R. A. Gordon, 'Short-Period Price Determination in Theory and Practice', *American Economic Review*, vol. xxxviii (June 1948), pp. 265–88.

It should be noted that, along with much material purportedly bearing on the validity of the 'assumptions' of marginal theory, Lester does refer to evidence on the conformity of experience with the implications of the theory, citing the reactions of employment in Germany to the Papen plan and in the United States to changes in minimum-wage legislation as examples of lack of conformity. However, Stigler's brief comment is the only one of the other papers that refers to this evidence. It should also be noted that Machlup's thorough and careful exposition of the logical structure and meaning of marginal analysis is called for by the misunderstandings on this score that mar Lester's paper and almost conceal the evidence he presents that is relevant to the key issue he raises. But, in Machlup's emphasis on the logical structure, he comes perilously close to presenting the theory as a pure tautology, though it is evident at a number of points that he is aware of this danger and anxious to avoid it. The papers by Oliver and Gordon are the most extreme in the exclusive concentration on the conformity of the behaviour of businessmen with the 'assumptions' of the theory.

discussion of the methodological principles involved than might otherwise seem appropriate.

3. CAN A HYPOTHESIS BE TESTED BY THE REALISM OF ITS ASSUMPTIONS?

We may start with a simple physical example, the law of falling bodies. It is an accepted hypothesis that the acceleration of a body dropped in a vacuum is a constant—g, or approximately 32 feet per second per second on the earth—and is independent of the shape of the body, the manner of dropping it, etc. This implies that the distance travelled by a falling body in any specified time is given by the formula $s = \frac{1}{2}gt^2$, where s is the distance travelled in feet and t is time in seconds. The application of this formula to a compact ball dropped from the roof of a building is equivalent to saying that a ball so dropped behaves *as if* it were falling in a vacuum. Testing this hypothesis by its assumptions presumably means measuring the actual air pressure and deciding whether it is close enough to zero. At sea-level the air pressure is about 15 pounds per square inch. Is 15 sufficiently close to zero for the difference to be judged insignificant? Apparently it is, since the actual time taken by a compact ball to fall from the roof of a building to the ground is very close to the time given by the formula. Suppose, however, that a feather is dropped instead of a compact ball. The formula then gives wildly inaccurate results. Apparently, 15 pounds per square inch is significantly different from zero for a feather but not for a ball. Or, again, suppose the formula is applied to a ball dropped from an airplane at an altitude of 30,000 feet. The air pressure at this altitude is decidedly less than 15 pounds per square inch. Yet, the actual time of fall from 30,000 feet to 20,000 feet, at which point the air pressure is still much less than at sea-level, will differ noticeably from the time predicted by the formula—much more noticeably than the time taken by a compact ball to fall from the roof of a building to the ground. According to the formula, the velocity of the ball should be gt and should therefore increase steadily. In fact, a ball dropped at 30,000 feet will reach its top velocity well before it hits the ground. And similarly with other implications of the formula.

The initial question whether 15 is sufficiently close to zero for the difference to be judged insignificant is clearly a foolish question by itself. Fifteen pounds per square inch is 2,160 pounds per square foot, or 0·0075 ton per square inch. There is no possible basis for calling these numbers 'small' or 'large' without some external standard of comparison. And the only relevant standard of comparison is the air pressure for which the formula does or does not work under a given set of circumstances. But this raises the same problem at a second level. What is the meaning of 'does or does not work'? Even if we could eliminate errors of measurement, the measured time of fall would seldom if ever be precisely equal to the computed time of fall. How large must the difference between the two be to justify saying that the theory 'does not work'? Here there are two important external standards of comparison. One is the accuracy achievable by an alternative theory with which this theory is being compared and which is equally acceptable on all other grounds. The other arises when there exists a theory that is known to yield better predictions but only at a greater cost. The gains from greater accuracy, which depend on the purpose in mind, must then be balanced against the costs of achieving it.

This example illustrates both the impossibility of testing a theory by its assumptions and also the ambiguity of the concept 'the assumptions of a theory'. The formula $s = \frac{1}{2}gt^2$ is valid for bodies falling in a vacuum and can be derived by analysing the behaviour of such bodies. It can therefore be stated: under a wide range of circumstances, bodies that fall in the actual atmosphere behave *as if* they were falling in a vacuum. In the language so common in economics this would be rapidly translated into: the formula assumes a vacuum. Yet it clearly does no such thing. What it does say is that in many cases the existence of air pressure, the shape of the body, the name of the person dropping the body, the kind of mechanism used to drop the body, and a host of other attendant circumstances have no appreciable effect on the distance the body falls in a specified time. The hypothesis can readily be rephrased to omit all mention of a vacuum: under a wide range of circumstances, the distance a body falls in a specified time is given by the formula $s = \frac{1}{2}gt^2$. The history of this formula and its associated physical theory aside, is it meaningful to say that it assumes a vacuum? For all I know there may be other sets of assumptions that would yield the same formula. The formula is accepted because it works, not because we live in an approximate vacuum—whatever that means.

The important problem in connection with the hypothesis is to specify the circumstances under which the formula works or, more precisely, the general magnitude of the error in its predictions under various circumstances. Indeed, as is implicit in the above rephrasing of the hypothesis, such a specification is not one thing and the hypothesis another. The specification is itself an essential part of the hypothesis, and it is a part that is peculiarly likely to be revised and extended as experience accumulates.

In the particular case of falling bodies a more general, though still incomplete, theory is available, largely as a result of attempts to explain the errors of the simple theory, from which the influence of some of the possible disturbing factors can be calculated and of which the simple theory is a special case. However, it does not always pay to use the more general theory because the extra accuracy it yields may not justify the extra cost of using it, so the question under what circumstances the simpler theory works 'well enough' remains important. Air pressure is one, but only one, of the variables that define these circumstances; the shape of the body, the velocity attained, and still other variables are relevant as well. One way of interpreting the variables other than air pressure is to regard them as determining whether a particular departure from the 'assumption' of a vacuum is or is not significant. For example, the difference in shape of the body can be said to make 15 pounds per square inch significantly different from zero for a feather but not for a compact ball dropped a moderate distance. Such a statement must, however, be sharply distinguished from the very different statement that the theory does not work for a feather because its assumptions are false. The relevant relation runs the other way: the assumptions are false for a feather because the theory does not work. This point needs emphasis, because the entirely valid use of 'assumptions' in *specifying* the circumstances for which a theory holds is frequently, and erroneously, interpreted to mean that the assumptions can be used to *determine* the circumstances for which a theory holds, and has, in this way, been an important source of the belief that a theory can be tested by its assumptions.

Let us turn now to another example, this time a constructed one designed to be an analogue of many hypotheses in the social sciences. Consider the density of leaves around a tree. I suggest the hypothesis that the leaves are positioned as if each leaf deliberately sought to maximize the amount of sunlight it receives, given the position of its neighbours, as if it knew the physical laws determining the amount of sunlight that would be received in various positions and could move rapidly or instantaneously from any one position to any other desired and unoccupied position.[14] Now some of the more obvious implications of this hypothesis are clearly consistent with experience: for example, leaves are in general denser on the south than on the north side of trees but, as the hypothesis implies, less so or not at all on the northern slope of a hill or when the south side of the trees is shaded in some other way. Is the hypothesis rendered unacceptable or invalid because, so far as we know, leaves do not 'deliberate' or consciously 'seek', have not been to school and learned the relevant laws of science or the mathematics required to calculate the 'optimum' position, and cannot move from position to position? Clearly, none of these contradictions of the hypothesis is vitally relevant; the phenomena involved are not within the 'class of phenomena the

---

[14] This example, and some of the subsequent discussion, though independent in origin, is similar to and in much the same spirit as an example and the approach in an important paper by Armen A. Alchian, 'Uncertainty, Evolution, and Economic Theory', *Journal of Political Economy*, vol. lviii (June 1950), pp. 211–21.

hypothesis is designed to explain'; the hypothesis does not assert that leaves do these things but only that their density is the same *as if* they did. Despite the apparent falsity of the 'assumptions' of the hypothesis, it has great plausibility because of the conformity of its implications with observation. We are inclined to 'explain' its validity on the ground that sunlight contributes to the growth of leaves and that hence leaves will grow denser or more putative leaves survive where there is more sun, so the result achieved by purely passive adaptation to external circumstances is the same as the result that would be achieved by deliberate accommodation to them. This alternative hypothesis is more attractive than the constructed hypothesis not because its 'assumptions' are more 'realistic' but rather because it is part of a more general theory that applies to a wider variety of phenomena, of which the position of leaves around a tree is a special case, has more implications capable of being contradicted, and has failed to be contradicted under a wider variety of circumstances. The direct evidence for the growth of leaves is in this way strengthened by the indirect evidence from the other phenomena to which the more general theory applies.

The constructed hypothesis is presumably valid, that is, yields 'sufficiently' accurate predictions about the density of leaves, only for a particular class of circumstances. I do not know what these circumstances are or how to define them. It seems obvious, however, that in this example the 'assumptions' of the theory will play no part in specifying them: the kind of tree, the character of the soil, etc., are the types of variables that are likely to define its range of validity, not the ability of the leaves to do complicated mathematics or to move from place to place.

A largely parallel example involving human behaviour has been used elsewhere by Savage and me.[15] Consider the problem of predicting the shots made by an expert billiard player. It seems not at all unreasonable that excellent predictions would be yielded by the hypothesis that the billiard player made his shots *as if* he knew the complicated mathematical formulas that would give the optimum directions of travel, could estimate accurately by eye the angles, etc., describing the location of the balls, could make lightning calculations from the formulas, and could then make the balls travel in the direction indicated by the formulas. Our confidence in this hypothesis is not based on the belief that billiard players, even expert ones, can or do go through the process described; it derives rather from the belief that, unless in some way or other they were capable of reaching essentially the same result, they would not in fact be *expert* billiard players.

[15] Milton Friedman and L. J. Savage, 'The Utility Analysis of Choices Involving Risk', *Journal of Political Economy*, vol. lvi (August 1948), p. 298. Reprinted in American Economic Association, *Readings in Price Theory* (Chicago: Richard D. Irwin, Inc., 1952), pp. 57–96.

It is only a short step from these examples to the economic hypothesis that under a wide range of circumstances individual firms behave *as if* they were seeking rationally to maximize their expected returns (generally if misleadingly called 'profits')[16] and had full knowledge of the data needed to succeed in this attempt; *as if*, that is, they knew the relevant cost and demand functions, calculated marginal cost and marginal revenue from all actions open to them, and pushed each line of action to the point at which the relevant marginal cost and marginal revenue were equal. Now, of course, businessmen do not actually and literally solve the system of simultaneous equations in terms of which the mathematical economist finds it convenient to express this hypothesis, any more than leaves or billiard players explicitly go through complicated mathematical calculations or falling bodies decide to create a vacuum. The billiard player, if asked how he decides where to hit the ball, may say that he 'just figures it out' but then also rubs a rabbit's foot just to make sure; and the businessman may well say that he prices at average cost, with of course some minor deviations when the market makes it necessary. The one statement is about as helpful as the other, and neither is a relevant test of the associated hypothesis.

Confidence in the maximization-of-returns hypothesis is justified by evidence of a very different character. This evidence is in part similar to that adduced on behalf of the billiard-player hypothesis—unless the behaviour of businessmen in some way or other approximated behaviour consistent with the maximization of returns, it seems unlikely that they would remain in business for long. Let the apparent immediate determinant of business behaviour be anything at all—habitual reaction, random chance, or whatnot. Whenever this determinant happens to lead to behaviour consistent with rational and informed maximization of returns, the business will prosper and acquire resources with which to expand; whenever it does not, the business will tend to lose resources and can be kept in existence only by the addition of

---

[16] It seems better to use the term 'profits' to refer to the difference between actual and 'expected' results, between *ex post* and *ex ante* receipts. 'Profits' are then a result of uncertainty and, as Alchian (op. cit., p. 212), following Tintner, points out, cannot be deliberately maximized in advance. Given uncertainty, individuals or firms choose among alternative anticipated probability distributions of receipts or incomes. The specific content of a theory of choice among such distributions depends on the criteria by which they are supposed to be ranked. One hypothesis supposes them to be ranked by the mathematical expectation of utility corresponding to them (see Friedman and Savage, 'The Expected-Utility Hypothesis and the Measurability of Utility', op. cit.). A special case of this hypothesis or an alternative to it ranks probability distributions by the mathematical expectation of the money receipts corresponding to them. The latter is perhaps more applicable, and more frequently applied, to firms than to individuals. The term 'expected returns' is intended to be sufficiently broad to apply to any of these alternatives.

The issues alluded to in this note are not basic to the methodological issues being discussed, and so are largely bypassed in the discussion that follows.

resources from outside. The process of 'natural selection' thus helps to validate the hypothesis—or, rather, given natural selection, acceptance of the hypothesis can be based largely on the judgement that it summarizes appropriately the conditions for survival.

An even more important body of evidence for the maximization-of-returns hypothesis is experience from countless applications of the hypothesis to specific problems and the repeated failure of its implications to be contradicted. This evidence is extremely hard to document; it is scattered in numerous memorandums, articles, and monographs concerned primarily with specific concrete problems rather than with submitting the hypothesis to test. Yet the continued use and acceptance of the hypothesis over a long period, and the failure of any coherent, self-consistent alternative to be developed and be widely accepted, is strong indirect testimony to its worth. The evidence *for* a hypothesis always consists of its repeated failure to be contradicted, continues to accumulate so long as the hypothesis is used, and by its very nature is difficult to document at all comprehensively. It tends to become part of the tradition and folklore of a science revealed in the tenacity with which hypotheses are held rather than in any textbook list of instances in which the hypothesis has failed to be contradicted.

* * * * * * * * *

4. CONCLUSION

Economics as a positive science is a body of tentatively accepted generalizations about economic phenomena that can be used to predict the consequences of changes in circumstances. Progress in expanding this body of generalizations, strengthening our confidence in their validity, and improving the accuracy of the predictions they yield is hindered not only by the limitations of human ability that impede all search for knowledge but also by obstacles that are especially important for the social sciences in general and economics in particular, though by no means peculiar to them. Familiarity with the subject-matter of economics breeds contempt for special knowledge about it. The importance of its subject matter to everyday life and to major issues of public policy impedes objectivity and promotes confusion between scientific analysis and normative judgement. The necessity of relying on uncontrolled experience rather than on controlled experiment makes it difficult to produce dramatic and clear-cut evidence to justify the acceptance of tentative hypotheses. Reliance on uncontrolled experience does not affect the fundamental methodological principle that a hypothesis can be tested only by the conformity of its implications or predictions with observable phenomena; but it does render the task of testing hypotheses more difficult and gives greater scope for confusion about the methodological principles involved. More than other scientists, social scientists need to be self-conscious about their methodology.

One confusion that has been particularly rife and has done much damage is confusion about the role of 'assumptions' in economic analysis. A meaningful scientific hypothesis or theory typically asserts that certain forces are, and other forces are not, important in understanding a particular class of phenomena. It is frequently convenient to present such a hypothesis by stating that the phenomena it is desired to predict behave in the world of observation *as if* they occurred in a hypothetical and highly simplified world containing only the forces that the hypothesis asserts to be important. In general, there is more than one way to formulate such a description—more than one set of 'assumptions' in terms of which the theory can be presented. The choice among such alternative assumptions is made on the grounds of the resulting economy, clarity, and precision in presenting the hypothesis; their capacity to bring indirect evidence to bear on the validity of the hypothesis by suggesting some of its implications that can be readily checked with observation or by bringing out its connection with other hypotheses dealing with related phenomena; and similar considerations.

Such a theory cannot be tested by comparing its 'assumptions' directly with 'reality'. Indeed, there is no meaningful way in which this can be done. Complete 'realism' is clearly unattainable, and the question whether a theory is realistic 'enough' can be settled only by seeing whether it yields predictions that are good enough for the purpose in hand or that are better than predictions from alternative theories. Yet the belief that a theory can be tested by the realism of its assumptions independently of the accuracy of its predictions is widespread and the source of much of the perennial criticism of economic theory as unrealistic. Such criticism is largely irrelevant, and, in consequence, most attempts to reform economic theory that it has stimulated have been unsuccessful.

The irrelevance of so much criticism of economic theory does not of course imply that existing economic theory deserves any high degree of confidence. These criticisms may miss the target, yet there may be a target for criticism. In a trivial sense, of course, there obviously is. Any theory is necessarily provisional and subject to change with the advance of knowledge. To go beyond this platitude, it is necessary to be more specific about the content of 'existing economic theory' and to distinguish among its different branches; some parts of economic theory clearly deserve more confidence than others. A comprehensive evaluation of the present state of positive economics, summary of the evidence bearing on its validity, and assessment of the relative confidence that each part deserves is clearly a task for a treatise or a set of treatises, if it be possible at all, not for a brief paper on methodology.

About all that is possible here is the cursory expression of a personal view. Existing relative price theory, which is designed to explain the allocation of resources among alternative ends and the division of the product among the co-operating resources and which reached almost its present form in Marshall's *Principles of Economics*, seems to me both extremely fruitful and deserving of much confidence for the kind of economic system that characterizes Western nations. Despite the appearance of considerable controversy, this is true equally of existing static monetary theory, which is designed to explain the structural or secular level of absolute prices, aggregate output, and other variables for the economy as a whole and which has had a form of the quantity theory of money as its basic core in all of its major variants from David Hume to the Cambridge School to Irving Fisher to John Maynard Keynes. The weakest and least satisfactory part of current economic theory seems to me to be in the field of monetary dynamics, which is concerned with the process of adaptation of the economy as a whole to changes in conditions and so with short-period fluctuations in aggregate activity. In this field we do not even have a theory that can appropriately be called 'the' existing theory of monetary dynamics.

Of course, even in relative price and static monetary theory there is enormous room for extending the scope and improving the accuracy of existing theory. In particular, undue emphasis on the descriptive realism of 'assumptions' has contributed to neglect of the critical problem of determining the limits of validity of the various hypotheses that together constitute the existing economic theory in these areas. The abstract models corresponding to these hypotheses have been elaborated in considerable detail and greatly improved in rigour and precision. Descriptive material on the characteristics of our economic system and its operations have been amassed on an unprecedented scale. This is all to the good. But, if we are to use effectively these abstract models and this descriptive material, we must have a comparable exploration of the criteria for determining what abstract model it is best to use for particular kinds of problems, what entities in the abstract model are to be identified with what observable entities, and what features of the problem or of the circumstances have the greatest effect on the accuracy of the predictions yielded by a particular model or theory.

Progress in positive economics will require not only the testing and elaboration of existing hypotheses but also the construction of new hypotheses. On this problem there is little to say on a formal level. The construction of hypotheses is a creative act of inspiration, intuition, invention; its essence is the vision of something new in familiar material. The process must be discussed in psychological, not logical, categories; studied in autobiographies and biographies, not treatises on scientific method; and promoted by maxim and example, not syllogism or theorem.

II

THE NATURE OF ECONOMIC GENERALIZATIONS

LIONEL ROBBINS

2. THE most fundamental propositions of economic analysis are the propositions of the general theory of value. No matter what particular 'school' is in question, no matter what arrangement of subject-matter is adopted, the body of propositions explaining the nature and the determination of the relation between given goods of the first order will be found to have a pivotal position in the whole system. It would be premature to say that the theory of this part of the subject is complete. But it is clear that enough has been done to warrant our taking the central propositions as established. We may proceed, therefore, to inquire on what their validity depends.

It should not be necessary to spend much time showing that it cannot rest upon a mere appeal to 'History'. The frequent concomitance of certain phenomena in time may suggest a problem to be solved. It cannot by itself be taken to imply a definite causal relationship. It might be shown that, whenever the conditions postulated in any of the simple corollaries of the theory of value have actually existed, the consequences deduced have actually been observed to follow. Thus, whenever the fixing of prices in relatively free markets has taken place it has been followed either by evasion or by the kind of distributive chaos which we associate with the food queues of the late war or the French or Russian Revolutions. But this would not prove that the phenomena in question were causally connected in any intimate sense. Nor would it afford any safe ground for predictions with regard to their future relationship. In the absence of rational grounds for supposing intimate connection, there would be no sufficient reason for

From *An Essay on the Nature and Significance of Economic Science* (London: Macmillan, 2nd edition, 1935), chapter IV, pp. 72–9, 83–4, 86–9, 90–8, 100.

supposing that history 'would repeat itself'. For if there is one thing which *is* shown by history, not less than by elementary logic, it is that historical induction, unaided by the analytical judgement, is the worst possible basis of prophecy. 'History shows', commences the bore at the club, and we resign ourselves to the prediction of the improbable. It is one of the great merits of the modern philosophy of history that it has repudiated all claims of this sort, and indeed makes it the *fundamentum divisionis* between history and natural science that history does not proceed by way of generalizing abstraction.

It is equally clear that our belief does not rest upon the results of controlled experiment. It is perfectly true that the particular case just mentioned has on more than one occasion been exemplified by the results of government intervention carried out under conditions which might be held to bear some resemblance to the conditions of controlled experiment. But it would be very superficial to suppose that the results of these 'experiments' can be held to justify a proposition of such wide applicability, let alone the central propositions of the general theory of value. Certainly it would be a very fragile body of economic generalizations which could be erected on a basis of this sort. Yet, in fact, our belief in these propositions is as complete as belief based upon any number of controlled experiments.

But on what, then, does it depend?

It does not require much knowledge of modern economic analysis to realize that the foundation of the theory of value is the assumption that the different things that the individual wants to do have a different importance to him, and can be arranged therefore in a certain order. This notion can be expressed in various ways and with varying degrees of precision, from the simple want systems of Menger and the early Austrians to the more refined scales of relative valuations of Wicksteed and Schönfeld and the indifference systems of Pareto and Messrs. Hicks and Allen. But in the last analysis it reduces to this, that we can judge whether different possible experiences are of equivalent or greater or less importance to us. From this elementary fact of experience we can derive the idea of the substitutability of different goods, of the demand for one good in terms of another, of an equilibrium distribution of goods between different uses, of equilibrium of exchange, and of the formation of prices. As we pass from the description of the behaviour of the single individual to the discussion of markets we naturally make other subsidiary assumptions—there are two individuals or many, the supply is in the hands of a monopoly or of a multiplicity of sellers, the individuals in one part of the market know or do not know what is going on in other parts of the market, the legal framework of the market prohibits this or that mode of acquisition or exchange, and so on. We assume, too, a given initial distribution of property. But always the main underlying assumption is the assumption of the schemes of valuation of the different economic subjects. But this, we have seen already, is really an assumption of one of the conditions which must be present if there is to be economic activity at all. It is an essential constituent of our conception of conduct with an economic aspect.

The propositions so far mentioned all relate to the theory of the valuation of given goods. In the elementary theory of value and exchange no inquiry is made into the conditions of continuous production. If we assume that production takes place, a new set of problems arises, necessitating new principles of explanation. We are confronted, e.g., with the problem of explaining the relation between the value of the products and the value of the factors which produced them—the so-called problem of imputation. What is the sanction here for the solutions which have been put forward?

As is well known, the main principle of explanation, supplementary to the principles of subjective valuation assumed in the narrower theory of value and exchange, is the principle sometimes described as the Law of Diminishing Returns. Now the Law of Diminishing Returns is simply one way of putting the obvious fact that different factors of production are imperfect substitutes for one another. If you increase the amount of labour without increasing the amount of land the product will increase, but it will not increase proportionately. To secure a doubling of the product, if you do not double both land and labour, you have to more than double either one of the factors. This is obvious. If it were not so, then all the corn in the world could be produced from one acre of land. It follows, too, from considerations more intimately connected with our fundamental conceptions. A class of scarce factors is to be defined as consisting of those factors which are perfect substitutes. That is to say, difference in factors is to be defined essentially as imperfect substitutability. The Law of Diminishing Returns, therefore, follows from the assumption that there is more than one class of scarce factors of production. The supplementary principle that, within limits, returns may increase, follows equally directly from the assumption that factors are relatively indivisible. On the basis of these principles and with the aid of subsidiary assumptions of the kind already mentioned (the nature of markets and the legal framework of production, etc.), it is possible to build up a theory of equilibrium of production.

Let us turn to more dynamic considerations. The theory of profits, to use the word in the rather restricted sense in which it has come to be used in recent theory, is essentially an analysis of the effects of uncertainty with regard to the future availability of scarce goods and scarce factors. We live in a world in which, not only are the things that we want scarce, but their exact occurrence is a matter of doubt and conjecture. In planning for the future we have to choose, not between certainties, but rather between a range of estimated probabilities. It is clear that the nature of this range itself may vary, and accordingly there must arise not only relative valuation of the different kinds of uncertainties between themselves, but also of different ranges of uncertainty similarly compared. From such concepts may be deduced many of the most complicated propositions of the theory of economic dynamics.

And so we could go on. We could show how the use of money can be deduced from the existence of indirect exchange and how the demand for money can be deduced from the existence of the same uncertainties that we have just examined. We could examine the propositions of the theory of capital and interest, and reduce them to elementary concepts of the type we have been here discussing. But it is unnecessary to prolong the discussion further. The examples we have already examined should be sufficient to establish the solution for which we are seeking. The propositions of economic theory, like all scientific theory, are obviously deductions from a series of postulates. And the chief of these postulates are all assumptions involving in some way simple and indisputable facts of experience relating to the way in which the scarcity of goods which is the subject-matter of our science actually shows itself in the world of reality. The main postulate of the theory of value is the fact that individuals can arrange their preferences in an order, and in fact do so. The main postulate of the theory of production is the fact that there is more than one factor of production. The main postulate of the theory of dynamics is the fact that we are not certain regarding future scarcities. These are not postulates the existence of whose counterpart in reality admits of extensive dispute once their nature is fully realized. We do not need controlled experiments to establish their validity: they are so much the stuff of our everyday experience that they have only to be stated to be recognized as obvious. Indeed, the danger is that they may be thought to be so obvious that nothing significant can be derived from their further examination. Yet in fact it is on postulates of this sort that the complicated theorems of advanced analysis ultimately depend. And it is from the existence of the conditions they assume that the general applicability of the broader propositions of economic science is derived.

* * * * * * * *

4. If the argument which has been developed above is correct, economic analysis turns out to be as Fetter has emphasized, the elucidation of the implications of the necessity of choice in various assumed circumstances. In pure Mechanics we explore the implication of the existence of certain given properties of bodies. In pure Economics we examine the implication of the

existence of scarce means with alternative uses. As we have seen, the assumption of relative valuations is the foundation of all subsequent complications.

It is sometimes thought, even at the present day, that this notion of relative valuation depends upon the validity of particular psychological doctrines. The borderlands of Economics are the happy hunting-ground of minds averse to the effort of exact thought, and, in these ambiguous regions, in recent years, endless time has been devoted to attacks on the alleged psychological assumptions of Economic Science. Psychology, it is said, advances very rapidly. If, therefore, Economics rests upon particular psychological doctrines, there is no task more ready to hand than every five years or so to write sharp polemics showing that, since psychology has changed its fashion, Economics needs 'rewriting from the foundations upwards'. As might be expected, the opportunity has not been neglected. Professional economists, absorbed in the exciting task of discovering new truth, have usually disdained to reply: and the lay public, ever anxious to escape the necessity of recognizing the implications of choice in a world of scarcity, has allowed itself to be bamboozled into believing that matters, which are in fact as little dependent on the truth of fashionable psychology as the multiplication table, are still open questions on which the enlightened man, who, of course, is nothing if not a psychologist, must be willing to suspend judgement.

*   *   *   *   *   *   *   *   *

All that we need to assume as economists is the obvious fact that different possibilities offer different incentives, and that these incentives can be arranged in order of their intensity. The various theorems which may be derived from this fundamental conception are unquestionably capable of explaining a manifold of social activity incapable of explanation by any other technique. But they do this, not by assuming some particular psychology, but by regarding the things which psychology studies as the data of their own deductions. Here, as so often, the founders of Economic Science constructed something more universal in its application than anything that they themselves claimed.

But now the question arises how far even this procedure is legitimate. It should be clear from all that has been said already that although it is not true that the propositions of analytical economics rest upon any particular psychology, yet they do most unquestionably involve elements which are of a psychological—or perhaps better said a psychical—nature. This, indeed, is explicitly recognized in the name by which they are sometimes known—the subjective or psychological theory of value; and, as we have seen, it is clear that the foundation of this theory is a psychical fact, the valuations of the individual. In recent years, however, partly as a result of the influence of Behaviourism, partly as a result of a desire to secure the maximum possible austerity in analytical exposition, there have arisen voices urging that this framework of subjectivity should be discarded. Scientific method, it is urged, demands that we should leave out of account anything which is incapable of direct observation. We may take account of demand as it shows itself in observable behaviour in the market. But beyond this we may not go. Valuation is a subjective process. We cannot *observe* valuation. It is therefore out of place in a scientific explanation. Our theoretical constructions must assume observable data. Such, for instance, is the attitude of Professor Cassel, and there are passages in the later work of Pareto which permit of a similar interpretation. It is an attitude which is very frequent among those economists who have come under the influence of Behaviourist psychology or who are terrified of attack from exponents of this queer cult.

At first sight this seems very plausible. The argument that we should do nothing that is not done in the physical sciences is very seductive. But it is doubtful whether it is really justified. After all, our business is to explain certain aspects of conduct. And it is very questionable whether this can be done in terms which involve no psychical element. It is quite certain that whether it be pleasing or no to the desire for the maximum austerity, we do in fact *understand* terms such as choice, indifference, preference, and the like in terms of inner experience. The idea of an end, which is fundamental to our conception of the economic, is not possible to define in terms of external behaviour only. If we are to explain the relationships which arise from the existence of a scarcity of means in relation to a multiplicity of ends, surely at least one-half of the equation, as it were, must be psychical in character.

* * * * * * * * *

5. But now the question arises whether the generalizations of economics, in addition to being based on this fundamental assumption of relative valuations, do not also depend upon a more general psychological assumption—upon the assumption of completely rational conduct. Is it not correct to describe the subject-matter of Economics as the *rational* disposal of goods? And in this sense cannot Economics be said to depend upon another, and more contentious, kind of psychological assumption than any we have yet examined? This is a matter of some intricacy which deserves attention,

not only for its own sake, but for the light it casts upon the methods of Economics in general.

Now in so far as the idea of rational action involves the idea of *ethically appropriate* action, and it certainly is sometimes used in this sense in everyday discussion, it may be said at once—there will be more to be said about it later—that no such assumption enters into economic analysis. As we have just seen, economic analysis is *wertfrei* in the Weber sense. The values of which it takes account are valuations of individuals. The question whether in any further sense they are *valuable* valuations is not one which enters into its scope. If the word rationality is to be construed as in any way implying this meaning, then it may be said that the concept for which it stands does not enter into economic analysis.

But in so far as the term rational is taken to mean merely 'consistent', then it is true that an assumption of this sort does enter into certain analytical constructions. The celebrated generalization that in a state of equilibrium the relative significance of divisible commodities is equal to their price, does involve the assumption that each final choice is consistent with every other, in the sense that if I prefer A to B and B to C, I also prefer A to C: in short, that in a state of perfect equilibrium the possibility of advantage from further 'internal arbitrage operations' is excluded.

There is a wider sense, too, in which the conception of rationality as equivalent to consistency can be understood as figuring in discussions of the conditions of equilibrium. It may be irrational to be completely consistent as between commodities, in the sense just described, just because the time and attention which such exact comparisons require are (in the opinion of the economic subject concerned) better spent in other ways. In other words, there may be an opportunity cost of 'internal arbitrage' which, beyond a certain point, outweighs the gain. The marginal utility of not bothering about marginal utility is a factor of which account has been taken by the chief writers on the subjective theory of value from Böhm-Bawerk onwards. It is not a recent discovery. It can be taken into account in a formal sense by permitting a certain margin (or structure of margins) of inconsistency between particular valuations.

It is perfectly true that the assumption of perfect rationality figures in constructions of this sort. But it is not true that the generalizations of economics are limited to the explanation of situations in which action is perfectly consistent. Means may be scarce in relation to ends, even though the ends be inconsistent. Exchange, production, fluctuation—all take place in a world in which people do not know the full implications of what they are doing. It is often inconsistent (i.e., irrational in this sense) to wish at once for the fullest satisfaction of consumers' demands, and at the same time to impede the import of foreign goods by tariffs or such-like obstacles. Yet it is frequently done: and who shall say that economic science is not competent to explain the situation resulting?

Of course there is a sense in which the word rationality can be used which renders it legitimate to argue that at least some rationality is assumed before human behaviour has an economic aspect—the sense, namely, in which it is equivalent to 'purposive'. As we have seen already, it is arguable that if behaviour is not conceived of as purposive, then the conception of the means–end relationships which economics studies has no meaning. So if there were no purposive action, it could be argued that there were no economic phenomena. But to say this is not to say in the least that all purposive action is completely consistent. It may indeed be urged that the more that purposive action becomes conscious of itself, the more it necessarily becomes consistent. But this is not to say that it is necessary to assume *ab initio* that it always is consistent or that the economic generalizations are limited to that, perhaps, tiny section of conduct where all inconsistencies have been resolved.

The fact is, of course, that the assumption of perfect rationality in the sense of complete consistency is simply one of a number of assumptions of a psychological nature which are introduced into economic analysis at various stages of approximation to reality. The perfect foresight, which it is sometimes convenient to postulate, is an assumption of a similar nature. The purpose of these assumptions is not to foster the belief that the world of reality corresponds to the constructions in which they figure, but rather to enable us to study, in isolation, tendencies which, in the world of reality, operate only in conjunction with many others, and then, by contrast as much as by comparison, to turn back to apply the knowledge thus gained to the explanations of more complicated situations. In this respect, at least, the procedure of pure economics has its counterpart in the procedure of all physical sciences which have gone beyond the stage of collection and classification.

6. Considerations of this sort enable us to deal also with the oft-reiterated accusation that Economics assumes a world of economic men concerned only with money-making and self-interest. Foolish and exasperating as this may appear to any competent economist, it is worth some further examination. Although it is false, yet there is a certain expository device of pure analysis which, if not explained in detail, might give rise to strictures of this nature.

The general absurdity of the belief that the world contemplated by the economist is peopled only by egotists or 'pleasure machines' should be sufficiently clear from what has been said already. The fundamental concept of economic analysis is the idea of relative valuations; and, as we have seen, while we assume that different goods have different values at different margins, we do not regard it as part of our problem to explain why these particular valuations exist. We take them as data. So far as we are concerned, our economic subjects can be pure egoists, pure altruists, pure ascetics, pure sensualists, or—what is much more likely—mixed bundles of all these impulses. The scales of relative valuation are merely a convenient formal way of exhibiting certain permanent characteristics of man as he actually is. Failure to recognize the primacy of these valuations is simply a failure to understand the significance of the last sixty years of Economic Science.

Now the valuations which determine particular transactions may be of various degrees of complexity. In my purchase of bread I may be interested solely in the comparison between the bread and the other things in the circle of exchange on which I might have spent the money. But I may be interested too in the happiness of my baker. There may exist between us certain liens which make it preferable for me to buy bread from him, rather than procure it from his competitor who is willing to sell it a little cheaper. In exactly the same way, in my sale of my own labour or the hire of my property, I may be interested only in the things which I receive as a result of the transaction; or I may be interested also in the experience of labouring in one way rather than another, or in the prestige or discredit, the feeling of virtue or shame in hiring out my property in this line rather than in that.

All these things are taken into account in our conception of scales of relative valuation. And the generalizations descriptive of economic equilibrium are couched in a form which explicitly brings this to the fore. Every first-year student since the days of Adam Smith has learnt to describe equilibrium in the distribution of particular grades of labour in terms of a tendency, *not* to the maximization of *money gains*, but to the maximization of *net advantages* in the various alternatives open. As we have seen already, the theory of risk, too, and its influence on the capital market depends essentially on assumptions of this kind. But sometimes for purposes of exposition it is convenient to start from the first approximation that the valuation is of a very simple order, and that, on the one side is a thing desired or offered, and on the other is the money to be got or given in exchange for it. For the elucidation of certain complicated propositions, such as the theory of costs or marginal productivity analysis, it permits an economy of terms. It is not in the least difficult, at the appropriate stage, to remove these assumptions and to pass to analysis couched in terms of complete generality.

This, then, is all that lies behind the *homo economicus*—the occasional assumption that in certain exchange relationships all the means, so to speak, are on one side and all the ends on the other. If, e.g., for purposes of demonstrating the circumstances in which a single price will emerge in a limited market, it is assumed that in my dealings in that market I always buy from the cheapest seller, it is not assumed at all that I am necessarily actuated by egotistical motives. On the contrary, it is well known that the impersonal relationship postulated is to be seen in its purest form when trustees, not being in a position to allow themselves the luxury of more complicated relationships, are trying to make the best terms for the estates they administer: your business man is a much more complicated fellow. All that it means is that my relation to the dealers does not enter into my hierarchy of ends. For me (who may be acting for myself or my friends or some civic or charitable authority) they are regarded merely as means. Of, again, if it is assumed—which in fact is usually done for purposes of showing *by contrast* what the total influences in equilibrium bring about—that I sell my labour always in the dearest market, it is not assumed that money and self-interest are my ultimate objects—I may be working entirely to support some philanthropic institution. It is assumed only that, so far as that transaction is concerned, my labour is only a means to an end; it is not to be regarded as an end in itself.

If this were commonly known, if it were generally realized that Economic Man is only an expository device—a first approximation used very cautiously at one stage in the development of arguments which, in their full development, neither employ any such assumption nor demand it in any way for a justification of their procedure—it is improbable that he would be such a universal bogey. But of course it is generally thought that he has a wider significance, that he lurks behind all those generalizations of the 'Laws of Supply and Demand' better described as the theory of comparative statics, whose elucidation so often is inimical to the desire to be able to believe it to be possible both to have your cake and to eat it. And it is for this reason that he is so furiously attacked. If it were Economic Man who barred the gates of Cloud-cuckooland, then it might well seem that a little psychology—it would not matter much of what brand—might be expected to burst them open. What prestige, what repute for really *deep* insight into human motivation might be expected to accrue from so spectacular an exposure!

Unfortunately this belief rests upon misapprehension. The propositions of the theory of variations do not involve the assumption that men are actuated *only* by considerations of money gains and losses. They involve only the assumption that money plays *some* part in the valuation of the given alternatives. And they suggest only that if from any position of equilibrium the money incentive is *varied* this must tend to alter the equilibrium valuations. Money may not be regarded as playing a predominant part in the situation contemplated. So long as it plays some part then the propositions are applicable.

* * * * * * * * *

7. In the light of all that has been said the nature of economic analysis should now be plain. It consists of deductions from a series of postulates, the chief of which are almost universal facts of experience present whenever human activity has an economic aspect, the rest being assumptions of a more limited nature based upon the general features of particular situations or types of situations which the theory is to be used to explain.

III

TWO ECONOMISTS

MARTIN HOLLIS and EDWARD J. NELL

After more than a century of intensive activity in scientific economics, two economists who have made outstanding substantive contributions to our science and whose positions on questions of economic policy are moreover not far apart, seek the ultimate basis of economic knowledge in considerations which (*a*) contradict each other and (*b*) are each subject to strong objections. One is led to conclude that economics as a scientific discipline is still somewhat hanging in the air.

T. C. KOOPMANS wrote these words in 1957,[1] the economists referred to being Milton Friedman and Lionel Robbins. Fifteen years later economics still seems to us to lack visible means of support, which is why we have written this book. In partial 'proof of the pudding', we propose here to show how Friedman and Robbins contradict each other about the answers to our earlier questions and then to argue that the deductive model of explanation just given will meet some of the strong objections mentioned by Koopmans. We shall take as texts Friedman's essay, 'The methodology of Positive economics', and Robbins's *An Essay on the Nature and Significance of Economic Science*.[2] There is more recent literature, but those works have weathered well and, particularly in the case of Friedman, raise points which have not been met. Indeed, we shall argue that Friedman, though in our view wholly wrong, has seen the issues far more clearly than most of his critics.

Friedman writes as an empiricist in general and as a positivist in particular. Robbins is harder to classify. His original version of 1932 is, on the whole, Rationalist but by 1935 he was readier to think of economics in empiricist

From *Rational Economic Man: A Philosophical Critique of Neo-Classical Economics* by M. Hollis and E. J. Nell (Cambridge: C.U.P., 1975), the appendix to ch. 7.

[1] T. C. Koopmans, *Three Essays on the State of Economic Science* (McGraw-Hill, 1957), p. 141.

[2] Our page references are to the 1966 Phoenix edition of Friedman's *Essays in Positive Economics* and to the 1932 and 1935 Macmillan editions of Robbins. [Where a page number in square brackets follows, it refers to the present volume. Eds.]

terms by playing up its psychological content. We shall argue that his earlier line is preferable. Both authors confront what we have called the Inductive and Deductive problems,* arriving at very different solutions. Ignoring the historical order of writing, we shall first follow Friedman from Positivism, through Pragmatism, to an impasse and then trace the interplay of Empiricism and Rationalism in Robbins. We shall read rather more philosophy into the texts than is made explicit there and our account of them will be selective; but we hope to have been true to their epistemological intent.

The task of Positive economics, Friedman opens, 'is to provide a system of generalizations that can be used to make correct predictions about the consequences of any change in circumstances' (p. 4) [p. 19]. This is to be done by 'the development of a "theory" or "hypothesis" that yields valid and meaningful (i.e. not truistic) predictions about phenomena not yet observed' (p. 7) [p. 21]. The theory is to be a blend of two elements, a 'language' and 'a body of substantive hypotheses designed to abstract essential features of a complex reality' (p. 7). In its former role 'theory has no substantive content; it is a set of tautologies. Its function is to act as a filing system ...' (p. 7) [p. 21]. In its latter role, 'theory is to be judged by its predictive power for the class of phenomena which it is intended to "explain"' (p. 8) [p. 22].

The distinction between 'language', and 'substantive hypothesis' is the Positivist one between 'analytic' and 'synthetic'. So, when the Inductive problem arises, there can be no appeal to the filing system as grounds for preferring one hypothesis to another. Nor does Friedman wish to make one—'the only relevant test of the *validity* of a hypothesis is comparison of its predictions with experience' (p. 8, his italics) [p. 22].

With admirable consistency, he then proceeds to saw off any other branch which he might be tempted to sit on. It would be an error, he says 'to suppose that hypotheses have not only "implications" but also "assumptions" and that the conformity of these "assumptions" to "reality" is a test of the validity of the hypothesis *different from* and *additional to* the test by implications (p. 14, his italics) [p. 26]. Hence he argues that it is no weakness of perfect competition models and no strength of imperfect ones, that the former have less 'realistic' assumptions than the latter. For, if the only question is which predict better, then that is the only question!

Nor should this move be underestimated. Imperfect competition models are often claimed to be superior because they are more realistic. But, once the

---

*[See the Introduction to *Rational Economic Man*, where the authors define the Inductive problem as that of why it strengthens a hypothesis to survive testing and why we are warranted in adopting some survivors, while rejecting others; and the Deductive problem as that of accounting for the necessity of necessary truths and of explaining their place in scientific knowledge. Eds.]

realism of assumptions is admitted to matter, they too are open to heavy attack. Do supply curves really rise? How are marginal costs to be determined for joint production? Are outputs and costs really continuously variable? Do firms in fact know their marginal revenue curves? And the questions grow more awkward, when we go behind the cost curves to the true basis of supply, the production function. Can inputs really be much varied in the way supposed, without altering the characteristics of the product or the specification of jobs offered by the firm? Yet, if we cease to assume wide substitution in production, rising supply price, continuous variability, calculation of marginal revenue and so forth, we abandon traditional neo-Classical market behaviour theory. Admittedly there can be other be-havioural theories,[3] even incorporating some neo-Classical insights. But, so long as the aim is to preserve and defend the core of modern economic thinking, 'the grand neo-classical synthesis', as Samuelson calls it, the usual assumptions are needed. So Friedman's neo-Classical critics are well advised to agree with him that the realism of assumptions does not matter.

Without going into his own reasons, we can see why Friedman is bound to take this line on philosophical grounds. For a positivist, general synthetic statements can be known true only if they are reached inductively by comparison of their implications with experience. So there is simply no room for distinguishing between 'realistic assumptions' and 'predictive hy-potheses'.[4] 'Realism' has to be a matter of confirmation through the testing of implications. Consequently recent critics who accept Friedman's Positivist tenets, while arguing for the greater realism of imperfect competition models, as distinct from their predictive power, are certainly wrong. The same applies to critics who argue that Friedman, in saying that success in prediction validates the hypothesis tested, has committed the fallacy of affirming the consequent. Friedman does not, in any case, say that, where H implies P and P is true, then H is true. He says that, where H implies P and P is true, then H is confirmed. And neither he nor they can possibly say anything else.

We now have a fine case of the inductive problem. Any particular statement is implied by many and mutually incompatible hypotheses. Which are we to prefer, when a prediction is confirmed? Friedman does not pose himself this question directly but his essay has the bones of what is perhaps his answer. Having earlier dismissed the analytic aspects of theory as a mere filing system, he now begins to claim that some filing systems are better than others. On further consideration of the notion of 'realism', he suggests that

[3] Cf. R. M. Cyert and J. G. March, *A Behavioral Theory of the Firm*, Prentice-Hall, 1963.

[4] This remark does not conflict with Nagel's distinctions of senses of 'realism', which we judge to be fair comment but addressed to parts of Friedman's case which do not concern us here. See E. Nagel, 'Assumptions in economic theory', *American Economic Review*, vol. i, 54, no. 2 (May 1963).

one hypothesis is to be preferred to another 'not because its "assumptions" are more "realistic" but rather because it is part of a more general theory that applies to a wider variety of phenomena . . . has more implications capable of being contradicted, and has failed to be contradicted under a wider variety of circumstances' (p. 20) [p. 31]. Generality, he explains, involves abstraction and analogy. Assumptions are best simplified to a point where it is '*as if*' they were true (pp. 18, [p. 29] 40), even when interpreted literally, they are not true at all. For instance, apropos of the formula $s = \frac{1}{2}gt^2$, he writes, '. . . bodies that fall in the actual atmosphere behave *as if* they were falling in a vacuum. In the language so common in economics this would be rapidly translated into 'the formula assumes a vacuum'. Yet it clearly does no such thing. The formula is accepted because it works, not because we live in an approximate vacuum—whatever that means' (p. 18) [p. 29].[5] The analytic part of theory contains ' "ideal types" ' (p. 35). 'The ideal types are not intended to be descriptive; they are designed to isolate the features that are crucial for a particular problem' (p. 36).

Now, we could see in this an answer to the Inductive problem, if Friedman were to claim that a hypothesis was strengthened by being expressed in a forceful 'ideal type'. But he cannot do so, while remaining loyal to Positivism. He does claim two merits for a forceful ideal type, its 'economy, clarity and precision in presenting the hypothesis' and, more ambitiously, that abstraction is a fruitful technique. 'A fundamental hypothesis of science is that appearances are deceptive and that there is a way of looking at or interpreting or organising the evidence that will reveal superficially disconnected and diverse phenomena to be manifestations of a more fundamental and relatively simple structure' (p. 33). But, since 'economy, clarity and precision' have no epistemological value and since his reason for appealing to this 'fundamental hypothesis of science' is that it has borne fruit in the past, he is still without any solution to the Inductive problem. The economist is to pick the most abstract, elegant and general theory, on the grounds that that technique has worked in the past. Our argument of earlier chapters that Positivism has no epistemological basis for induction is so far unshaken.

In any case, perfect competition models need more of a defence than this, since they do not predict better than a full cost 'classical' theory, in which prices are set by costs and normal profits in the standard range of operation, and output is regulated by demand. (That is, demand does not influence price nor do supply conditions influence output.) Having forsworn direct appeal to realism, Friedman tries to evade the consequences of relying exclusively on

---

[5] He goes on to compare the assumption of Frictionless Motion with the assumption of perfect competition. Cf. our appendix to Chapter 1, [of *Rational Economic Man*] where we rejected the comparison.

the criterion of predictive success—which would, as Schoeffler shows, undercut much conventional theory[6]—by stressing the importance of elegant and general basic theoretical structures. As already argued, such a move carries no epistemological weight within Positivism. But it does suggest that a well-entrenched and approved theory can be maintained against some vagaries of experience and so hints that Pragmatism has something to offer.

The hint soon becomes explicit. Since realism, when properly understood according to Friedman, is a matter of testing implications against experience, there is after all a requirement that assumptions be realistic. But they 'cannot possibly be thoroughly "realistic" in the immediate descriptive sense so often assigned to this term' (p. 32). For that kind of realism would include such characteristics as 'the colour of each trader's hair and eyes, his antecedents and education, the number of members of his family, their characteristics, antecedents and education etc.' (p. 32). The right kind of realism is the abstract or 'as if' variety mentioned earlier. Since there is no difference between assumptions and general implications, the two can be interchanged (p. 27). It is an easy step from this to denying that theory and facts are independent. When the merits of abstraction are combined with the idea that diverse phenomena are 'manifestations of a more fundamental and relatively simple structure', then Pragmatism is imminent.

There may seem no need for Friedman to go so far, especially since it means dropping Positivism. Nevertheless he does so. 'If a class of "economic phenomena" appears varied and complex, it is, we must suppose, because we have no adequate theory to explain them. Known facts cannot be set on one side; a theory to apply "closely to reality" on the other. A theory is the way we perceive "facts" and we cannot perceive "facts" without a theory' (p. 34). This strikingly conflicts with his Positivism but it is no mere careless flourish. 'There are many different ways of describing the model completely—many different "postulates" which both imply and are implied by the model as a whole. These are all logically equivalent: what are regarded as axioms or postulates of a model from one point of view can be regarded as theorems from another, and conversely' (p. 26). Since this line blurs the distinction between general statements and particular ones and also between analytic statements and synthetic ones, the seeds have already been sown. He is at once faced with the Deductive problem and with the snags of Pragmatism. The Deductive problem is lurking, in any case, but Friedman can no doubt avoid considering it by arguing that he is no worse off than any positivist. As soon as he makes this new and bold claim for theory, however, he must tackle it. If theory is only a filing system of tautologies and a body of hypotheses

[6] S. Schoeffler, *The Failures of Economics: A Diagnostic Study* (Harvard, 1955).

which confront the tribunal of experience, how can it be 'the way we perceive "facts" '?

Here, we suggest, Friedman must choose. If he sticks to Positivism, facts are given and concepts are optional. No sense can be given to the notion of more fundamental structures in reality and there is no room for interplay between pure model building, seen as logic and mathematics, and experience, seen as fact. Prediction remains the final criterion, with the consequences indicated by Schoeffler. If he prefers a pragmatist relation of theory to fact, he must withdraw his earlier account both of the filing system and of the substantive hypotheses. He can then defend theories which predict indifferently, on the pragmatist ground that any statement can be preserved in the face of experience and can defend 'unrealistic' assumptions, provided they are useful.

Friedman's Positivism runs him aground on the Inductive problem. He can edge himself off by claiming that theory plays an epistemological part in validating hypotheses. This beguiles him into Pragmatism. Yet, if our reflections in Chapter 6 are cogent, Pragmatism is simply another mudbank and the only exit is by dropping Empiricism. With this cheering thought, we turn to Robbins.

Robbins's *Essay* is an attempt 'to make clear what it is that economists discuss and what may legitimately be expected as a result of their discussions' (1932, Preface). He wishes to distinguish between analytical or theoretical economics on the one hand and descriptive or historical economics on the other. In so doing, he is denying that economists should try to limit themselves to the projection of historical trends by induction from observed patterns. Indeed they could not, even if they wished. For economic generalizations have no claim in themselves to be regarded as laws. 'However accurately they describe the past, there is no presumption that they will describe the future' (1932, p. 101; 1935, p. 109 is almost identical). For 'there is no reason to suppose that their having been so in the past is the result of the operation of homogeneous causes, nor that their changes in the future will be due to the causes which have operated in the past' (1932, p. 101; 1935, p. 109).

He thus sets himself the Inductive problem in a fresh form. What is a 'homogeneous cause' and when have we reason to suppose we have found one? He gives two answers, both present in both editions but with different emphasis. The one emphasized in 1932 is in the spirit of von Mises's remark that 'in the concept of money all the theorems of monetary theory are already implied'.[7] This is the solution which we ourselves proposed in the last chapter, neatly put by Robbins in these terms: 'In pure Mechanics we explore

---

[7] L. von Mises, *Human Action* (William Hodge, 1949), p. 38. Robbins pays tribute to von Mises in his 1932 Preface.

the implication of the existence of certain given properties of bodies. In pure Economics we examine the implication of the existence of scarce means with alternative uses' (p. 83 in both editions) [p. 39]. 'Economic laws describe inevitable implications' (1932, p. 110; 1935, p. 121). It is definitions which have the 'inevitable implications' and that is why Robbins begins his *Essay* by discussing rival definitions. Any behaviour involving the allocation of scarce resources to competing ends is economic behaviour and all economic theory describes the inevitable implications of this.

That answer is absurd as soon as any concession is made to Positivism. If definitions are arbitrary, nothing of epistemological interest depends on them. Between 1932 and 1935 Logical Positivism gained its ascendancy. Robbins remained unrepentant but did give more weight to his other answer. Economic analysis, he says, 'consists of deductions from a series of postulates, the chief of which are almost universal facts of experience present whenever human activity has an economic aspect' (1935, p. 99) [p. 46]. 'If the premises relate to reality the deduction from them must have a similar point of reference' (1935, p. 104). 'In Economics, as we have seen, the ultimate constituents of our fundamental generalizations are known to us by immediate acquaintance. In the natural sciences they are known only inferentially' (1935, p. 105).

Here 'real definitions' are supplemented, and perhaps replaced, by 'postulates'. The key three postulates are that there is more than one factor of production, that we are not certain about future scarcities, and that consumers have orders of preference. They 'do not need controlled experiments to establish their validity: they are so much the stuff of our everyday experience that they have only to be stated to be recognized as obvious . . . yet in fact it is on postulates of this sort that the complicated theorems of advanced analysis ultimately depend' (1935, p. 179). Economics thus comes to differ radically from mechanics, in that its postulates are qualitative and known by introspection. These postulates are synthetic and so economic theory can be conducted by the hypothetico-deductive method. Theory applies to reality because the postulates happen to be true, not because they are necessarily true. So, if a discreet silence is kept about the status of logic and mathematics, we can discern an empiricism in Robbins's second answer.

The second answer, we contend, concedes too much. We began from Robbins's objection to historical generalizations that 'however accurately they describe the past, there is no presumption that they will describe the future'. His postulates face the same charge. They are, he says, 'the stuff of our everyday experience', 'qualitative and known by introspection'. But there is nothing here to explain why this means more than 'very highly confirmed'. Introspection is a fallible way of arriving at generalities and exactly Robbins's claim has been made for now suspect postulates like 'We are all tainted with origin sin' or 'Man is born free'.

Nor are his postulates evidently true.[8] There are few more contentious areas than the 'theory of value'. Socialists and Marxists have never bowed to marginalism; and modern growth theory reckons with prices, rates of return, and capital values more reminiscent of Ricardo and Marx than of Menger and Marshall and determined without reference to preference scales. Engels Law is the best-confirmed empirical generalization in household budget studies but does not necessarily follow from the usual theory of consumer behaviour. The Law of Demand itself is as riddled with exceptions as it is well-confirmed. Nor is there a shortage of rival approaches. American institutionalists from Veblen and Commons to Galbraith have steadily denied that individual scales of relative valuation are independent para-meters of the system, which in part determine the configuration of the other variables. On the contrary, they hold, such scales are determined, at least in part, by economic forces. They have denied, in other words, precisely what Robbins takes as a basic and self-evident postulate.

Nor, indeed, can we take it for granted that consumers order their preferences as traditionally supposed. Lexicographic orderings, for instance, have seemed to some thinkers to make better sense of household budget data, at the expense of certain theorems which then ceased to be derivable. Recently Lancaster has suggested that preferences range not over goods but over characteristics of goods,[9] a proposal supported by reflection on the famous diet problem in linear programming, as we showed in Chapter 5. Consequences for the theory of consumer behaviour are striking and, right or wrong, are enough to show Robbins's postulate less than self-evident.

Again, the past fifteen years have dealt unkindly with Robbins's belief that no one can 'really question' the existence of different factors of production. Joan Robinson, Sraffa, Pasinetti, and others of the new Cambridge persuasion[10] have really questioned whether 'capital', construed as a quantity of resources measurable independently of the distribution of income, can have any empirical sense. Admittedly there is no questioning the

---

[8] Cf. Koopmans, *Three Essays*, pp. 135–7, where another set of doubts is given.

[9] Lancaster, *Consumer Demand* (New York: Columbia, 1971).

[10] See J. Robinson, 'The production function and the theory of capitals', *Review of Economic Studies*, vol. 21 (1953), pp. 81–106, and many other papers—cf. her *Collected Economic Papers*, vols. II and III (Basil Blackwell, 1965). See also P. Sraffa, *Production of Commodities by Means of Commodities* (Cambridge, 1960), and the articles by L. Pasinetti in the *Review of Economic Studies*, vol. 27, no. 73 (1960), the *Quarterly Journal of Economics*, vol. lxxx, no. 4 (1966), and the *Economic Journal*, vol. 79, no. 315 (1969).

existence of different inputs in the manufacturing process. But 'inputs' are not to be equated with 'factors'. An input is a commodity or service, a precisely defined product. A factor of production is the recipient of some category of income. Robbins says (and means) 'factors of production', inviting the objection that nothing can be both a produced input in the production process and, defined in the same way, a category of recipient of income. 'Capital' is a vector of material goods and services, from the first point of view, and a sum of value upon which income is computed, from the second. It is not self-evident that the two views can be combined; and, if Marx and the Cambridge critics are right, they demonstrably cannot be.[11]

The postulate about uncertainty is less open to question. But it is also indefinite. Depending on how it is made explicit, a battery of models can be constructed, each with different informational postulates. So it can hardly be true that any particular set of theorems can be derived from the postulate as Robbins states it.

We therefore object to Robbins's postulates, not because they are false but because they will not function as postulates. Since they are open to more than one interpretation, they do not entail a particular set of theorems. Since they are disputable, they are not self-evident. Since they can be reasoned about, they are not introspectible. We therefore maintain that 'real definitions' make a better basis than introspected postulates.

We should perhaps guard against a riposte to our claim that what is disputable is not self-evident. 'Self-evidence' can be defined psychologically, so that what is self-evident is written, so to speak, in capital letters on the surface of the mind. In this case it is a sufficient objection that children, savages, and idiots do not perceive the allegedly self-evident feature of experience. But 'self-evident' can also have an epistemological sense, in which it means 'known without proof or evidence'. Here it matters not whether all mankind assents but whether it can be proved self-evident. This is less paradoxical than it sounds, if the argument we gave in Chapter 7 for the existence of real definitions and true axioms is sound. For instance, the law of non-contradiction is self-evident, in the sense that any proof can be proved to presuppose it. Similarly, if economic theory can be axiomatized, then its axioms will have to be self-evidently true. There will still be room for dispute about which the basic axioms are to be. But that does not cancel the search for those axioms which state the real definitions of the basic concepts of economics. Robbins's postulates are disputable, in that there is no pressing reason to accept them. This does not show them false but it does show that Robbins has no right to claim to know they are true.

[11] G. C. Harcourt, 'Some Cambridge Controversies in the Theory of Capital', *Journal of Economic Literature*, vol. 7, no. 2 (June 1969).

That leaves us with Robbins's first answer, that economic theory consists of the logical consequences of conceptual definitions. There is an ambiguity in the claim that economic laws are 'necessities to which human action is subject' (1935, p. 135). What sort of necessity? In our view not psychological nor physical necessity but *a priori* should be meant. Once again we return to real definitions and true axioms, repeating the caveat that real definitions are reached only after close observation and analysis. But here we finally part company with Robbins. Although committed to some kind of positivist analytic–synthetic distinction, he places little reliance on empirical and econometric studies. To concede the importance of statistical work would put his principal targets (Wesley, Mitchell, Kalecki, Frisch, and the early econometricians) out of range and rob his work of its main point. His notion of necessity is a psychological and subjective one. So, while agreeing that economic laws are 'necessities to which human action is subject', we finally disagree with Robbins. Without scope for real definitions and true axioms, economics as a scientific discipline is still somewhat hanging in the air.

IV

THE SCIENCE OF HUMAN ACTION

LUDWIG VON MISES

5. THE STANDPOINT OF EMPIRICISM

IT is indisputable that there is and must be an aprioristic theory of human action. And it is equally indisputable that human action can be the subject matter of historical investigation. The protest of the consistent representatives of historicism, who do not want to admit the possibility of a theory that would be independent of time and place, need disturb us no more than the contention of naturalism, which wants to challenge the scientific character of history so long as it has not reached the point where it can establish historical laws.

Naturalism presupposes that empirical laws could be derived *a posteriori* from the study of historical data. Sometimes it is assumed that these laws are valid without respect to time or place, sometimes that they have validity only for certain periods, countries, races, or nationalities. The overwhelming majority of historians reject both varieties of this doctrine. Indeed, it is generally rejected even by those who are in accord with historicism and who do not want to admit that, without the aid of the aprioristic theory of human action, the historian would be completely at a loss to deal with his material and would be unable to solve any of his problems. Such historians generally maintain that they are able to carry on their work completely free of theory.

We need not enter here into the investigation of whether historicism must lead necessarily to the one or to the other of these two views. Whoever is of the opinion that the doctrine of historicism cannot be consistently thought through to its conclusion will consider it futile to undertake such an investigation. The only point worth noting is that a sharp opposition exists

From *Epistemological Problems of Economics* (Princeton, 1960), ch. 1 'The Nature and Development of the Social Sciences', sections 5 and 6.

between the view of the adherents of the Historical School and that of the majority of historians. Whereas the former believe that they can discover empirical laws from the data of history and want to call the compilation of such laws sociology and economics, most historians would not be willing to agree that this can be done.

The thesis of those who affirm the possibility of deriving empirical laws from historical data we shall call empiricism. Historicism and empiricism are, consequently, not the same thing. As a rule, though certainly not always, if they take any position on the problem at all, historians profess their adherence to historicism. With few exceptions (Buckle, for example) they are opponents of empiricism. The adherents of the Historical and the Institutionalist Schools take the point of view of historicism, although they find it impossible to maintain this doctrine in its purity as soon as they attempt to state it in a logically and epistemologically coherent manner; they are almost always in accord with empiricism. Thus, a sharp contrast of view generally exists between the historians and the economists and sociologists of the Historical School.

The question with which we are now concerned is no longer whether a prevailing regularity can be discovered in human action, but whether the observation of facts without any reference to a system of aprioristic knowledge of human action can be considered a method capable of leading us to the cognition of such a regularity. Can economic history furnish 'building stones' for an economic theory, as Schmoller maintains? Can the 'findings of economic history's specialized description become elements of theory and lead to universal truths'? In this connection we shall not take up the question of the possibility of universal 'historical laws' (which would therefore not be economic laws) that has often been exhaustively discussed. We shall limit ourselves to examining whether, by means of the observation of facts, that is, by an *a posteriori* method, we could arrive at statements of the kind sought for by the system of economic theory.

The method used by the natural sciences for the discovery of the laws of phenomena begins with observation. However, the decisive step is taken only with the construction of an hypothesis: a proposition does not simply emerge from observation and experience, for these always present us only with complex phenomena in which various factors appear so closely connected that we are unable to determine what role should be attributed to each. The hypothesis is already an intellectual elaboration of experience, above all in its claim to universal validity, which is its decisive characteristic. The experience that has led to the construction of the proposition is always limited to the past; it is always an experience of a phenomenon that occurred in a particular place and at a particular time. However, the universal validity claimed for the proposition also implies applicability to all other past and future occur-rences. It is based on an imperfect induction. (No universal theorems emerge from perfect induction, but only descriptions of an event that occurred in the past.)

Hypotheses must be continually verified anew by experience. In an experiment they can generally be subjected to a particular method of examination. Various hypotheses are linked together into a system, and everything is deduced that must logically follow from them. Then experi-ments are performed again and again to verify the hypotheses in question. One tests whether new experience conforms to the expectations required by the hypotheses. Two assumptions are necessary for these methods of verification: the possibility of controlling the conditions of the experiment, and the existence of experimentally discoverable constant relations whose magnitudes admit of numerical determination. If we wish to call a proposition of empirical science true (with whatever degree of certainty or probability an empirically derived proposition can have) when a change of the relevant conditions in all observed cases leads to the results we have been led to expect, then we may say that we possess the means of testing the truth of such propositions.

With regard to historical experience, however, we find ourselves in an entirely different situation. Here we lack the possibility not only of performing a controlled experiment in order to observe the individual determinants of a change, but also of discovering numerical constants. We can observe and experience historical change only as the result of the combined action of a countless number of individual causes that we are unable to distinguish according to their magnitudes. We never find fixed relationships that are open to numerical calculation. The long cherished assumption that a proportional relationship, which could be expressed in an equation, exists between prices and the quantity of money has proved fallacious; and as a result the doctrine that knowledge of human action can be formulated in quantitative terms has lost its only support.

Whoever wants to derive laws of human action from experience would have to be able to show how given situations influence action quantitatively and qualitatively. It is psychology that generally has sought to provide such a demonstration, and for that reason all those who assign this task to sociology and economics are prone to recommend to them the psychological method. What is more, by the psychological method they understand not what was called psychological—in a rather inappropriate and even misleading sense—in the method of the Austrian School, but rather the procedures and discoveries of scientific psychology itself.

However, psychology has failed in this sphere. With the use of its methods it can, of course, observe unconscious reactions to stimuli in the manner of the biological sciences. Beyond this it can accomplish nothing that could lead to the discovery of empirical laws. It can determine how definite men have behaved in definite situations in the past, and it infers from its findings that conduct will be similar in the future if similar men are placed in a similar situation. It can tell us how English school boys behaved in the last decades when confronted with a definite situation, for example, when they encountered a crippled beggar. Such information tells us very little about the conduct of English school children in the coming decades or about the conduct of French or German school children. Psychology can establish nothing more than the occurrence of an historical incident: the cases observed have shown such and such; but the conclusions drawn from the observed cases, which refer to English school children of a definite period, are not logically justified when applied to other cases of the same historical and ethnological character that have not been observed.

All that observation teaches us is that the same situation has a different effect on different men. The attempt to arrange men in classes whose members all react in the same way has not been successful because even the same men react differently at different times, and there is no means of ascribing unequivocally definite modes of reaction to different ages or other objectively distinguishable periods or conditions of life. Consequently, there is no hope of achieving knowledge of a regularity in the phenomena by this method. This is what one has in mind when one speaks of free will, of the irrationality of what is human, spiritual, or historical, of individuality in history, and of the impossibility of rationally comprehending life in its fullness and diversity. One expresses the same idea in pointing out that it is not possible for us to grasp how the action of the external world influences our minds, our will, and, consequently, our action. It follows from this that psychology, in so far as it deals with such things, is history or, in the terminology of current German philosophy, a moral science.

Whoever declares that the method of historical understanding used by the moral sciences is appropriate also for economics should be aware of the fact that this method can never lead to the discovery of empirical laws. Understanding is precisely the method that the historical sciences (in the broadest sense of the term) employ in dealing with the unique, the non-repeatable, that is, in treating what is simply historical. Understanding is the mental grasp of something that we are unable to bring under rules and explain through them. This is true not only of the field traditionally designated as that of universal history, but also of all special fields, above all that of economic history. The position taken by the empiricist school of German economics in the struggle against economic theory is untenable also from the standpoint of the logic of the historical sciences as developed by Dilthey, Windelband, Rickert, and Max Weber.

In the empirical sciences the controlled experiment is indispensable for the *a posteriori* derivation of propositions whenever experience presents only complex phenomena in which the effect is produced by several interlinked causes. In historical experience we can observe only complex phenomena, and an experiment is inapplicable to such a situation. Sometimes it is said that a mental experiment (*Gedankenexperiment*) could take its place. However, a mental experiment, logically considered, has an entirely different meaning from a real experiment. It involves thinking through the implications of a proposition in the light of its compatibility with other propositions that we accept as true. If these other propositions are not derived from experience, then the mental experiment makes no reference to experience.

6. THE LOGICAL CHARACTER OF THE UNIVERSALLY VALID SCIENCE OF HUMAN ACTION

The science of human action that strives for universally valid knowledge is the theoretical system whose hitherto best elaborated branch is economics. In all of its branches this science is *a priori*, not empirical. Like logic and mathematics, it is not derived from experience; it is prior to experience. It is, as it were, the logic of action and deed.

Human thought serves human life and action. It is not absolute thought, but the forethought directed toward projected acts and the afterthought that reflects upon acts done. Hence, in the last analysis, logic and the universally valid science of human action are one and the same. If we separate them, so as to contrast logic and practice, we must show at what point their paths diverge and where the special province of the science of action is to be found.

One of the tasks with which thought must cope in order to fulfil its function is that of comprehending the conditions under which human action takes place. To treat these in their concrete detail is the work of the natural sciences and, in a certain sense, also of history and the other historical sciences. Our science, on the other hand, disregarding the accidental, considers only the essential. Its goal is the comprehension of the universal, and its procedure is formal and axiomatic. It views action and the conditions under which action takes place not in their concrete form, as we encounter them in everyday life, nor in their actual setting, as we view them in each of the sciences of nature and of history, but as formal constructions that enable us to grasp the patterns of human action in their purity.

Only experience makes it possible for us to know the particular conditions of action in their concrete form. Only experience can teach us that there are lions and microbes and that their existence can present definite problems to acting man; and it would be absurd, without experience, to indulge in speculations about the existence or nonexistence of some legendary beast. The existence of the external world is given through experience; and if we pursue definite plans, only experience can teach us how we must act *vis-à-vis* the external world in concrete situations.

However, what we know about our action under given conditions is derived not from experience, but from reason. What we know about the fundamental categories of action—action, economizing, preferring, the relationship of means and ends, and everything else that, together with these, constitutes the system of human action—is not derived from experience. We conceive all this from within, just as we conceive logical and mathematical truths, *a priori*, without reference to any experience. Nor could experience ever lead anyone to the knowledge of these things if he did not comprehend them from within himself.

As an *a priori* category the principle of action is on a par with the principle of causality. It is present in all knowledge of any conduct that goes beyond an unconscious reaction. 'In the beginning was the deed'. In our view the concept of man is, above all else, also the concept of the being who acts. Our consciousness is that of an ego which is capable of acting and does act. The fact that our deeds are intentional makes them actions. Our thinking about men and their conduct, and our conduct toward men and toward our surroundings in general, presuppose the category of action.

Nevertheless, we are quite incapable of thinking of this fundamental category and the system deduced from it without also thinking, at the same time, of the universal prerequisites of human action. For example, we are unable to grasp the concept of economic action and of economy without implying in our thought the concept of economic quantity relations and the concept of an economic good. Only experience can teach us whether or not these concepts are applicable to anything in the conditions under which our life must actually be lived. Only experience tells us that not all things in the external world are free goods. However, it is not experience, but reason, which is prior to experience, that tells us what is a free and what is an economic good.

Consequently, it would be possible to construct, by the use of the axiomatic method, a universal praxeology so general that its system would embrace not only all the patterns of action in the world that we actually encounter, but also patterns of action in worlds whose conditions are purely imaginary and do not correspond to any experience. A theory of money would still be meaningful even if throughout history there had never been any indirect exchange. That such a theory would have no practical importance in a world that did not use money would in no way detract from the truth of its statements. Because we study science for the sake of real life—and, it should be remembered, the desire for pure knowledge for its own sake is also a part of life—and not as a form of mental gymnastics, we generally do not mind forgoing the gratification that could be offered by a perfect, comprehensive system of the axioms of human action, a system so universal that it would comprise all thinkable categories of the conditions of action. Instead, we are satisfied with the less universal system that refers to the conditions given in the world of experience.

Nevertheless, this reference to experience in no way changes the aprioristic character of our knowledge. In this connection, experience is of absolutely no concern to our thinking. All that we owe to experience is the demarcation of those problems that we consider with interest from problems that we wish to leave aside because they are uninteresting from the point of view of our desire for knowledge. Hence, experience by no means always refers to the existence or nonexistence of the conditions of action, but often only to the presence of an interest in the treatment of a problem. In experience there is no socialist community; nevertheless, the investigation of the economy of such a community is a problem that in our age arouses the greatest of interest.

A theory of action could conceivably be constructed on the assumption that men lacked the possibility of understanding one another by means of symbols, or on the assumption that men—immortal and eternally young— were indifferent in every respect to the passage of time and therefore did not consider it in their action. The axioms of the theory could conceivably be framed in such universal terms as to embrace these and all other possibilities; and it would be conceivable to draw up a formal praxeological system patterned after the science of logic or the science built upon the axioms of, for example, Hilbertian geometry. We forgo these possibilities because conditions that do not correspond to those we encounter in our action interest us only in so far as thinking through their implications in imaginary constructions enables us to further our knowledge of action under given conditions.

The method actually employed by economists in the treatment of their problems can be seen with particular clarity in the case of the problem of imputation. Conceivably it would be possible to formulate the theory of the appraisement and pricing of the factors of production (goods of higher order, producers' goods) in the broadest generality so that, for one thing, we would work only with an unqualified concept, viz., means of production. We could then elaborate the theory in such a way that the three factors of production that are enumerated in the customary presentation would appear as special cases. But we proceed differently. We do not bother to furnish a universal imputation theory of the means of production as such, but proceed immediately to the treatment of the three categories of means of production: land, labour, and capital. This practice is altogether warranted by the object of our investigation, of which we must never lose sight.

However, the renunciation of axiomatic universality and precision also conceals many dangers, and it has not always been possible to avoid them. It is not only the Marxist theory of classes that has failed to grasp the categorial character of each of these specific groups of factors of production. To be sure, it was noted that the peculiarity of land as a factor of production lies in the difference in the usefulness of individual pieces of land from the point of view of the goals of action; the theory of ground rent never lost sight of the fact that land is appraised differently according to its quality and location. However, the theory of wages did overlook the fact that labour too is of different quality and intensity and that on the market there is never a supply of or a demand for 'labour' as such, but only a supply of and a demand for labour of a definite kind. Even after this fact was recognized, an attempt was made to evade its consequences by assuming that what forms the bulk of the supply and is chiefly in demand is unskilled labour and that it is permissible to ignore, as quantitatively negligible, skilled, 'higher' labour. The theory of wages would have been spared many errors had it been kept in mind what function the special treatment of labour in the theory of distribution is called upon to fulfil and at what point it becomes necessary to speak no longer simply of labour, but of labour of a definite quality that is offered or sought at a given time in a given place. It was still more difficult for the theory of capital to free itself of the idea of abstract capital, where the categorial difference between land, labour, and capital is no longer in question, but where the appraisement of definite capital goods, supplied or demanded in a definite place at a definite time, is to be considered. Likewise in the theory of distribution and in the theory of imputation, it was not easy to shake off the influence of the universalist view.

Our science deals with the forms and patterns of action under the various categories of its conditions. In pointing this out we are not drafting a plan for a future science. We do not maintain that the science of human action should be made aprioristic, but that it is so already. We do not want to discover a new method, but only to characterize correctly the method that is actually used. The theorems of economics are derived not from the observation of facts, but through deduction from the fundamental category of action, which has been expressed sometimes as the economic principle (i.e., the necessity to economize), sometimes as the value principle or as the cost principle. They are of aprioristic derivation and therefore lay claim to the apodictic certainty that belongs to basic principles so derived.

V

FROM SUBSTANTIVE TO PROCEDURAL RATIONALITY[1]

HERBERT A. SIMON

IN his paper on 'Situational Determinism in Economics',[2] Spiro J. Latsis has described two competitive research programmes dealing with the theory of the firm, one of which he calls 'situational determinism', the other, 'economic behaviouralism'. A basic contrast between these two programmes is that the latter does, but the former does not, require as an essential component a psychological theory of rational choice. Both situational determinism and economic behaviouralism postulate behaviour that is, in a certain sense,

From S. Latsis (ed.), *Method and Appraisal in Economics* (Cambridge: C.U.P., 1976).

[1] An earlier version of this paper was presented in the Autumn of 1973 at the University of Groningen, The Netherlands, on the occasion of the twenty-fifth anniversary of the faculty of economics there. The Nafplion Colloquium provided me with a welcome opportunity to revise it and make more explicit its relation to the competition among research programmes in economics that is discussed in the Colloquium papers of Messrs. Coats, Hutchison, and Latsis.

[2] Latsis (1972).

rational, but the meaning of the term 'rational' is quite different for the two programmes.

The conflict between situational determinism and economic behaviouralism has been most often discussed from the vantage point of the discipline of economics, and as though the discrepant views of rationality associated with the two programmes were both indigenous to economics. In point of fact, situational determinism is indigenous to economics, but economic behaviouralism is largely an import from psychology, brought into economics to handle certain problems that appeared not to be treated satisfactorily by the situational approach. Thus, the concept of rationality employed in the programme of economic behaviouralism is not merely an adaptation of the concept previously used by economists following the programme of situational determinism. It is a distinct concept that has its own independent origins within psychology. I shall use the phrase 'substantive rationality' to refer to the concept of rationality that grew up within economics, and 'procedural rationality' to refer to the concept that developed within psychology.

A person unfamiliar with the histories and contemporary research preoccupations of economics and cognitive psychology might imagine that there were close relations between them—a constant flow of theoretical concepts and empirical findings from the one to the other and back. Mr. Coats, in his chapter in this volume,* describes a whole series of earlier attempts, mostly unsuccessful, to bring the findings of psychology to bear upon economic theory. At the present time there is still little communication between the two fields. In the United States, at least, there seem to be no doctoral programmes in economics that require their students to master the psychological literature of rationality, and no psychology programmes that insist that their students become acquainted with economic theories of rationality. (I would be gratified to learn that such programmes exist, but if they do, they are inconspicuous in the extreme.) This state of mutual ignorance become understandable when we recognize that the two fields of economics and psychology are interested in answering rather different sets of research questions, and that each has adopted a view of rationality that is more or less appropriate to its own research concerns. As these concerns change, of course, so must the underlying concepts and the research programmes that imbed them.

In this paper, I will undertake, first, to explain the two terms 'substantive rationality' and 'procedural rationality'—the differences between them as well as their relations. I shall then try to document the growing interest,

---

* [A. W. Coats, 'Economics and Psychology: the Death and Resurrection of a Research Programme', pp. 43–64 of S. Latsis (ed.) (1976)—Eds.]

during the past twenty-five years, of economists in procedural rationality and in the associated programme of economic behaviouralism. Finally, I will set forth some reasons for thinking that procedural rationality will become an even more central concern of economics over the next twenty-five years. These changes, past and predicted, are a response to changes in the central research questions with which economics is occupied. The new research questions bring new empirical phenomena into the focus of attention, and the explanation of the new phenomena calls, in turn, for an understanding of the processes that underlie human rationality.

1. SUBSTANTIVE RATIONALITY

Behaviour is substantively rational when it is appropriate to the achievement of given goals within the limits imposed by given conditions and constraints.[3] Notice that, by this definition, the rationality of behaviour depends upon the actor in only a single respect—his goals. Given these goals, the rational behaviour is determined entirely by the characteristics of the environment in which it takes place.

Suppose, for example, that the problem is to minimize the cost of a nutritionally adequate diet, where nutritional adequacy is defined in terms of lower bounds on intakes of certain proteins, vitamins, and minerals, and upper and lower bounds on calories, and where the unit prices and compositions of the obtainable foods are specified. This diet problem can be (and has been) formulated as a straightforward linear-programming problem, and the correct solution found by applying the simplex algorithm or some other computational procedure. Given the goal of minimizing cost and the definition of 'nutritionally adequate', there are no two ways about it—there is only one substantively rational solution.

Classical economic analysis rests on two fundamental assumptions. The first assumption is that the economic actor has a particular goal, for example, utility maximization or profit maximization. The second assumption is that the economic actor is substantively rational. Given these two assumptions, and given a description of a particular economic environment, economic analysis (descriptive or normative) could usually be carried out using such standard tools as the differential calculus, linear programming, or dynamic programming.

Thus, the assumptions of utility or profit maximization, on the one hand, and the assumption of substantive rationality, on the other, freed economics from any dependence upon psychology. As long as these assumptions went unchallenged, there was no reason why an economist should acquaint

---

[3] Cf. the entry under 'rationality' in Gould & Kolb (1964), pp. 573–4.

himself with the psychological literature on human cognitive processes or human choice. There was absolutely no point at which the findings of psychological research could be injected into the process of economic analysis. The irrelevance of psychology to economics was complete.

2. PROCEDURAL RATIONALITY

Behaviour is procedurally rational when it is the outcome of appropriate deliberation. Its procedural rationality depends upon the process that generated it. When psychologists use the term 'rational', it is usually procedural rationality they have in mind. William James, for example, in his *Principles of Psychology*,[4] uses 'rationality' as synonymous with 'the peculiar thinking process called reasoning'. Conversely, behaviour tends to be described as 'irrational' in psychology when it represents impulsive response to affective mechanisms without an adequate intervention of thought.

Perhaps because 'rationality' resembles 'rationalism' too closely, and because psychology's primary concern is with process rather than outcome, psychologists tend to use phrases like 'cognitive processes' and 'intellective processes' when they write about rationality in behaviour. This shift in terminology may have contributed further to the mutual isolation of the concepts of substantive and procedural rationality.

(a) The study of cognitive processes

The process of rational calculation is only interesting when it is non-trivial—that is, when the substantively rational response to a situation is not instantly obvious. If you put a quarter and a dime before a subject and tell him that he may have either one, but not both, it is easy to predict which he will choose, but not easy to learn anything about his cognitive processes. Hence, procedural rationality is usually studied in problem situations—situations in which the subject must gather information of various kinds and process it in different ways in order to arrive at a reasonable course of action, a solution to the problem.

Historically, there have been three main categories of psychological research on cognitive processes: learning, problem solving, and concept attainment. Learning research is concerned with the ways in which information is extracted from one problem situation and stored in such a way as to facilitate the solving of similar problems subsequently. Problem-solving research (in this narrower sense) focuses especially upon the complementary roles of trial-and-error procedures and insight in reaching problem solutions.

[4] James (1890), chapter 22.

Concept attainment research is concerned with the ways in which rules or generalizations are extracted from a sequence of situations and used to predict subsequent situations. Only in recent years, particularly since the Second World War, has there been much unification of theory emerging from these three broad lines of research.

(b) Computational efficiency

Let us return for a moment to the optimal diet problem which we used to illustrate the concept of substantive rationality. From a procedural standpoint, our interest would lie not in the problem solution—the prescribed diet itself—but in the method used to discover it. At first blush, this appears to be more a problem in computational mathematics than in psychology. But that appearance is deceptive.

What is the task of computational mathematics? It is to discover the relative efficiencies of different computational processes for solving problems of various kinds. Underlying any question of computational efficiency is a set of assumptions about the capabilities of the computing system. For an omniscient being, there are no questions of computational efficiency, because the consequences of any tautology are known as soon as the premises are stated; and computation is simply the spinning out of such consequences.[5]

Nowadays, when we are concerned with computational efficiency, we are concerned with the computing time or effort that would be required to solve a problem by a system, basically serial in operation, requiring certain irreducible times to perform an addition, a multiplication, and a few other primitive operations. To compare the simplex method with some other method for solving linear programming problems, we seek to determine how much total computing time each method would need.

The search for computational efficiency is a search for procedural rationality, and computational mathematics is a normative theory of such rationality. In this normative theory, there is no point in prescribing a particular substantively rational solution if there exists no procedure for finding that solution with an acceptable amount of computing effort. So, for example, although there exist optimal (substantively rational) solutions for combinatorial problems of the travelling-salesman type, and although these solutions can be discovered by a finite enumeration of alternatives, actual computation of the optimum is infeasible for problems of any size and complexity. The combinatorial explosion of such problems simply outraces the capacities of computers, present and prospective.

---

[5] This statement is a little over-simple in ignoring the distinction between induction and deduction, but greater precision is not needed for our purposes.

Hence, a theory of rationality for problems like the travelling-salesman problem is not a theory of best solutions—of substantive rationality—but a theory of efficient computational procedures to find good solutions—a theory of procedural rationality. Notice that this change in viewpoint involves not only a shift from the substantive to the procedural, but a shift also from concern for optimal solutions to a concern for good solutions. I shall discuss this point later.

(c) Computation: risky decisions

But now it is time to return to psychology and its concern with computational efficiency. Man, viewed as a thinker, is a system for processing information. What are his procedures for rational choice?

One method of testing a theory of human rational choice is to study choice behaviour in relatively simple and well-structured laboratory situations where the theory makes specific predictions about how subjects will behave. This method has been used by a number of investigators—including W. Edwards, G. Pitts, A. Rapaport, and A. Tversky—to test whether human decisions in the face of uncertainty and risk can be explained by the normative concepts of statistical decision theory. This question is particularly interesting because these norms are closely allied, both historically and logically, to the notions of substantive rationality that have prevailed in economics, and make no concessions to computational difficulties—they never choose the computable second-best over the non-computable best.

Time does not permit me to review the extensive literature that this line of inquiry has produced. A recent review by Rapoport[6] covers experimental tests of SEU (subjective expected utility) maximization, of Bayesian strategies for sequential decisions, and of other models of rational choice under uncertainty. I think the evidence can be fairly summarized by the statements (i) that it is possible to construct gambles sufficiently simple and transparent that most subjects will respond to them in a manner consistent with SEU theory; but (ii) the smallest departures from this simplicity and transparency produce behaviour in many or most subjects that *cannot* be explained by SEU or Bayesian models. I will illustrate this statement by just three examples, which I hope are not atypical.

The first is the phenomenon of event matching.[7] Suppose that you present a subject with a random sequence of Xs and 0s, of which 70 per cent are Xs and 30 per cent 0s. You ask the subject to predict the next symbol, rewarding him for the number of correct predictions. 'Obviously' the rational behaviour

---

[6] Rapoport and Wallsten (1972).

[7] Feldman (1963).

is always to predict X. This is what subjects almost never do.[8] Instead, they act as though the sequence were patterned, not random, and guess by trying to extrapolate the pattern. This kind of guessing will lead X to be guessed in proportion to the frequency with which it occurs in the sequence. As a result, the sequence of guesses has about the same statistical properties as the original sequence, but the prediction accuracy is lower than if X had been predicted each time (58 per cent instead of 70 per cent).

In a recent study by Kahneman and Tversky,[9] a quite different phenomenon showed up. The rational procedure for combining new information with old is to apply Bayes's theorem. If a set of probabilities has been assigned to the possible outcomes of an uncertain event, and then new evidence is presented, Bayes's theorem provides an algorithm for revising the prior probabilities to take the new evidence into account. One obvious consequence of Bayes's theorem is that the more extensive and reliable the new evidence, the greater should be its influence on the new probabilities. Another consequence is that the new probabilities should not depend on the new evidence only, but upon the prior probabilities as well. In the experiments conducted by Kahneman and Tversky, the estimates of subjects were independent of the reliability of the new evidence, and did not appear to be influenced by the prior probabilities at all.

On the other hand, Ward Edwards[10] has reviewed a large body of experimental evidence describing quite conservative behaviour. In these experiments, subjects did not revise prior probability estimates nearly as much as would be called for by Bayes's theorem. It appears, then, that humans can either over-respond to new evidence or ignore it, depending upon the precise experimental circumstances. If these differences in behaviour manifest themselves even in laboratory situations so simple that it would be possible for subjects to carry out the actual Bayes calculations, we should be prepared to find variety at least as great when people are required to face the complexities of the real world.

(d) Man's computational efficiency

If these laboratory demonstrations of human failure to follow the canons of substantive rationality in choice under uncertainty caused any surprise to economists (and I do not know that they did), they certainly did not to experimental psychologists familiar with human information processing capabilities.

---

[8] The sole exceptions of which I am aware were two well-known and expert game theorists who served as subjects in this experiment at the RAND Corporation many years ago!

[9] Kahneman and Tversky (1973).

[10] Edwards (1968).

Like a modern digital computer's, Man's equipment for thinking is basically serial in organization. That is to say, one step in thought follows another, and solving a problem requires the execution of a large number of steps in sequence. The speed of his elementary processes, especially arithmetic processes, is much slower, of course, than those of a computer, but there is much reason to think that the basic repertoire of processes in the two systems is quite similar.[11] Man and computer can both recognize symbols (patterns), store symbols, copy symbols, compare symbols for identity, and output symbols. These processes seem to be the fundamental components of thinking as they are of computation.

For most problems that Man encounters in the real world, no procedure that he can carry out with his information processing equipment will enable him to discover the optimal solution, even when the notion of 'optimum' is well defined. There is no logical reason why this need be so; it is simply a rather obvious empirical fact about the world we live in—a fact about the relation between the enormous complexity of that world and the modest information-processing capabilities with which Man is endowed. One reason why computers have been so important to Man is that they enlarge a little bit the realm within which his computational powers can match the complexity of the problems. But as the example of the travelling-salesman problem shows, even with the help of the computer, Man soon finds himself outside the area of computable substantive rationality.

The problem space associated with the game of chess is very much smaller than the space associated with the game of life. Yut substantive rationality has so far proved unachievable, both for Man and computer, even in chess. Chess books are full of norms for rational play, but except for catalogues of opening moves, these are procedural rules: how to detect the significant features of a position, what computations to make on these features, how to select plausible moves for dynamic search, and so on.

The psychology of chess-playing now has a considerable literature. A pioneer in this research was Professor Adriaan de Groot, of the University of Amsterdam, whose book, *Het Denken van den Schaker*, has stimulated much work on this subject both in Amsterdam, and in our own laboratory at Carnegie-Mellon.[12] These studies have told us a great deal about the thought processes of an expert chessplayer. First, they have shown how he compensates for his limited computational capacity by searching very

[11] In my comparison of computer and Man, I am leaving out of account the greater sophistication of Man's input and output system, and the parallel processing capabilities of his senses and his limbs. I will be primarily concerned here with thinking, secondarily with perceiving, and not at all with sensing or acting.

[12] Newell and Simon (1972); Chase and Simon (1973*a*).

selectively through the immense tree of move possibilities, seldom considering as many as 100 branches before making a move. Second, they have shown how he stores in long-term memory a large collection of common patterns of pieces, together with procedures for exploiting the relations that appear in these patterns. The expert chessplayer's heuristics for selective search and his encyclopedic knowledge of significant patterns are at the core of his procedural rationality in selecting a chess move. Third, the studies have shown how a player forms and modifies his aspirations for a position, so that he can decide when a particular move is 'good enough' (satisfices), and can end his search.

Chess is not an isolated example. There is now a large body of data describing human behaviour in other problem situations of comparable complexity. All of the data point in the same direction, and provide essentially the same descriptions of the procedures men use to deal with situations where they are not able to compute an optimum. In all these situations, they use selective heuristics and means–end analysis to explore a small number of promising alternatives. They draw heavily upon past experience to detect the important features of the situation before them, features which are associated in memory with possibly relevant actions. They depend upon aspiration-like mechanisms to terminate search when a satisfactory alternative has been found.

To a moderate extent, this description of choice has been tested outside the laboratory, in even more complex 'real-life' situations; and where it has been tested, has held up well. I will only mention as examples Clarkson's well-known microscopic study of the choices of an investment trust officer,[13] and Peer Soelberg's study of the job search and job choice of graduating management students.[14] I cannot supply you with a large number of more recent examples, possibly because they do not exist, or possibly because my own research has taken me away from the area of field studies in recent years.

Contrast this picture of thought processes with the notion of rationality in the classical theory of the firm in its simplest form. The theory assumes that there is given, in addition to the goal of profit maximization, a demand schedule and a cost curve. The theory then consists of a characterization of the substantively rational production decision: for example, that the production quantity is set at the level where marginal cost, calculated from the cost curve, equals marginal revenue, calculated from the demand schedule. The question of whether data are obtainable for estimating these quantities or the demand and cost functions on which they are based is

[13] Clarkson (1963).

[14] Soelberg (1967).

outside the purview of the theory. If the actual demand and cost curves are given, the actual calculation of the optimum is trivial. This portion of economic theory certainly has nothing to do with procedural rationality.

3. ECONOMICS' CONCERN WITH PROCEDURAL RATIONALITY

In my introductory remarks, I said that while economics has traditionally concerned itself with substantive rationality, there has been a noticeable trend, since the Second World War, toward concern also with procedural rationality. This trend has been brought about by a number of more or less independent developments.

(a) The real world of business and public policy

The first of these developments, which predated the war to some extent, was increasing contact of academic economists with real-world business environments. An early and important product was the 1939 Hall–Hitch paper 'Price Theory and Business Behaviour',[15] which advanced the heretical proposition that prices are often determined by applying a fixed mark-up to average direct cost rather than by equating them with marginal cost.

I am not concerned here to determine whether Hitch and Hall, or others who have made similar observations, were right or wrong. My point is that first-hand contact with business operations leads to observation of the procedures that are used in reaching decisions, and not simply the final outcomes. Independently of whether the decision processes have any importance for the questions to which classical economics has addressed itself, the phenomena of problem solving and decision-making cannot help but excite the interest of anyone with intellectual curiosity who encounters them. They represent a fascinating and important domain of human behaviour, which any scientist will wish to describe and explain.

In the United States, in the decade immediately after the Second World War, a number of large corporations invited small groups of academic economists to spend periods of a month or more as 'interns' and observers in their corporate offices. Many young economists had their first opportunity, in this way, to try their hands at applying the tools of economic theory to the decisions of a factory departments, or a regional sales office.

They found that businessmen did not need to be advised to 'set marginal cost equal to marginal revenue'. Substantive norms of profit maximization helped real decisions only to the extent that appropriate problem-solving procedures could be devised to implement them. What businessmen needed—from anyone who could supply it—was help in inventing and

[15] Hall and Hitch (1939).

constructing such procedures, including the means for generating the necessary data. How could the marginal productivity of R & D expenditures be measured? Or of advertising expenditures? And if they could not be, what would be reasonable procedures for fixing these quantities? These—and not abstract questions of profit maximization in a simplified model of the firm— were the questions businessmen wrestled with in their decisions.

Matters were no different with the economists who were increasingly called upon by governments to advise on national fiscal and monetary policy, or on economic development plans. We have the notable example in The Netherlands of Tinbergen's schemes for target planning[16]—a pioneering example of 'satisficing', if I may speak anachronistically. In the face of difficult problems of formulating models, designing appropriate and implementable instruments of measurement, taking account of multidimensional criteria and side conditions, questions of optimization generally faded into the background. The rationality of planning and development models was predominately a procedural rationality.

(b) Operations research

With the end of the war also, businessmen and government departments began to exhibit an interest in the tools of operations research that had been developed for military application during the war. At the same time, operations analysts began to cast about for peacetime problems to which their skills might be applicable. Since the rapid burgeoning of operations research and management science in industry, and the even more rapid development of powerful analytic tools during the first decade after the war is familiar to all of you, it does not need recounting.

The coincidence of the introduction of the digital computer at the same time undoubtedly accelerated these developments. In fact, it is quite unclear whether operations research would have made any considerable impact on practical affairs if the desk calculator had been its only tool.

Operations research and management science did not alter the economic theory of substantive rationality in any fundamental way. With linear programming and activity analysis it did provide a way of handling the old problems and their solutions without the differential calculus, and the classical theorems of marginalism were soon restated in terms of the new formalism.[17]

What was genuinely new for economics in operations research was the concern for procedural rationality—finding efficient procedures for computing actual solutions to concrete decision problems. Let me expand on the

[16] Tinbergen (1952).

[17] Dorfman, Samuelson, and Solow (1958).

specific example with which I am most intimately familiar: decision rules for inventory and work-force smoothing.[18] Here the problem was to devise a decision rule for determining periodically the production level at which a factory should operate. Since the decision for one period was linked to the decisions for the following periods by the inventories carried over, the problem fell in the domain of dynamic programming.

The nub of the problem was to devise a dynamic programming scheme that could actually be carried out using only data that could be obtained in the actual situation. Dynamic programming, in its general formulations, is notoriously extravagant of computational resources. A general algorithm for solving dynamic programming problems would be a non-solution to the real-world decision problem.

The scheme we offered was an algorithm, requiring only a small amount of computing effort, for solving a very special class of dynamic programming problems. The algorithm required the costs to be represented by a quadratic function. This did not mean that we thought real-world cost functions were quadratic; it meant that we thought that many cost functions could be reasonably approximated by a quadratic, and that the deviations from the actual function would not lead to seriously non-optimal decisions. This assumption must, of course, be justified in each individual case, before an application can safely be made. Not only did the quadratic function provide good computational efficiency, but it also greatly reduced the data requirements, because it could be proved that, with this function, only the expected values of predicted variables, and not their higher moments, affected the optimal decision.[19]

This is only part of what was involved in devising a procedurally rational method for making these inventory and production decisions. The problems had also to be solved of translating an aggregate 'production level' into specific production schedules for individual products. I will not, however, go into these other aspects of the matter.

Observe of our solution that we constructed a quite classical model for profit maximization, but we did not have the illusion that the model reflected accurately all the details of the real-world situation. All that was expected of the solution was that the *optimal* decision in the world of the model be a *good* decision in the real world. There was no claim that the solution was

[18] Holt, Modigliani, Muth, and Simon (1960).

[19] It is interesting that this same dynamic programming procedure for quadratic cost functions was invented independently and simultaneously by Henri Theil of the Rotterdam School of Economics. See Theil (1958). The Rotterdam group was also concerned with concrete applications—in this case to national economic planning in The Netherlands—and hence gave a high priority to the demands of procedural rationality in the solutions it developed.

substantively optimal, but rather that formal optimization in the dynamic programming model was an effective procedural technique for making acceptable decisions (i.e., decisions better than those that would be made without this formal apparatus).

Some operations research methods take the other horn of this dilemma: they retain more of the real-world detail in the model, but then give up, for reasons of computational feasibility, the goal of searching for an optimum, and seek a satisfactory solution instead.[20]

Thus, the demands of computability led to two kinds of deviation from classical optimization: simplification of the model to make computation of an 'optimum' feasible, or, alternatively, searching for satisfactory, rather than optimal choices. I am inclined to regard both of these solutions as instances of satisficing behaviour rather than optimization. To be sure, we can *formally* view these as optimizing procedures by introducing, for example, a cost of computation and a marginal return from computation, and using these quantities to compute the optimal stopping-point for the computation. But the important difference between the new procedures and the classical ones remain. The problem has been shifted from one of characterizing the substantively optimal solution to one of devising practical computation procedures for making reasonable choices.

(c) *Imperfect competition*

More than a century ago, Cournot identified a problem that has become the permanent and ineradicable scandal of economic theory. He observed that where a market is supplied by only a few producers, the notion of profit-maximization is ill-defined. The choice that would be substantively rational for each actor depends on the choices made by the other actors; none can choose without making assumptions about how others will choose.

Cournot proposed a particular solution for the problem, which amounted to an assumption about the *procedure* each actor would follow: each would observe the quantities being produced by his competitors, and would assume these quantities to be fixed in his own calculations. The Cournot solution has often been challenged, and many alternative solutions have been proposed—conjectural variations, the kinky demand curve, market leadership, and others. All of them rest on postulates about the decision process, in particular, about the information each decision-maker will take into account, and the assumptions he will make about the reactions of the others to his behaviour.

[20] I have already mentioned the pioneering work of Jan Tinbergen in The Netherlands who employed national planning models that aimed at target values of key variables instead of an optimum.

I have referred to the theory of imperfect competition as a 'scandal' because it has been treated as such in economics, and because it is generally conceded that no defensible formulation of the theory stays within the framework of profit maximization and substantive rationality. Game theory, initially hailed as a possible way out, provided only a rigorous demonstration of how fundamental the difficulties really are.

If perfect competition were the rule in the markets of our modern economy, and imperfect competition and oligopoly rare exceptions, the scandal might be ignored. Every family, after all, has some distant relative it would prefer to forget. But imperfect competition is not a 'distant relative', it is the characteristic form of market structure in a large part of the industries in our economy.

In the literature on oligopoly and imperfect competition one can trace a gradual movement toward more and more explicit concern with the processes used to reach decisions, even to the point—unusual in most other areas of economics—of trying to obtain empirical data about these processes. There remains, however, a lingering reluctance to acknowledge the impossibility of discovering at last 'The Rule' of substantively rational behaviour for the oligopolist. Only when the hope of that discovery has been finally extinguished will it be admitted that understanding imperfect competition means understanding procedural rationality.[21]

This change in viewpoint will have large effects on many areas of economic research. There has been a great burgeoning, for example, of 'neoclassical' theories of investment—theories that undertake to deduce the rates of investment of business firms from the assumptions of profit-maximization and substantive rationality. Central to such theories is the concept of 'desired capital'—that is, the volume of capital that would maximize profits. Jorgenson, for example, typically derives 'desired capital' by an argument that assumes a fixed price for the firm's products and a production function of the Cobb–Douglas type, all in the absence of uncertainty.[22] Under these assumptions, he shows that the optimal level of capital is proportional to output.

Since the data which Jorgenson and others use to test these theories of investment derive mostly from oligopolistic industries, their definitions of rationality are infected with precisely the difficulties we have been discussing.

[21] My colleagues Richard Cyert and Morris de Groot have recently developed some interesting dynamic decision rules for oligopolists, which illustrate further the wide range of alternative formulations of what 'rationality' means in this situation. See Cyert and de Groot (1973).

[22] Jorgenson (1963). For a thorough critique of Jorgenson's approach, see Kornai (1971). Kornai's book also develops other arguments about the nature of economic rationality that are much in the spirit of this essay.

Can we speak of the capital desired by General Motors or the American Can Company without considering their expectations for size and share of market or the interactions of these expectations with price policies and with the responses of competitors?[23] Under conditions of imperfect competition, one can perhaps speak of the procedural rationality of an investment strategy, but surely not of its substantive rationality. At most, the statistical studies of investment behaviour show that some business firms relate their investments to output; they do not show that such behaviour is predictable from an objective theory of profit maximization. (And if that is what is being demonstrated, what is the advantage of doing it by means of elaborate statistical studies of public data, rather than by making inquiries or observations of the actual decision processes in the firms themselves?)

(d) Expectations and uncertainty

Making guesses about the behaviour of a competitor in an oligopolistic industry is simply a special case of forming expectations in order to make decisions under uncertainty. As economics has moved from statics to dynamics—to business cycle theory, growth theory, dynamic investment theory, theory of innovation and technological change—it has become more and more explicit in its treatment of uncertainty.

Uncertainty, however, exists not in the outside world, but in the eye and mind of the beholder. We need not enter into philosophical arguments as to whether quantum-mechanical uncertainty lies at the very core of nature, for we are not concerned with events at the level of the atom. We are concerned with how men behave rationally in a world where they are often unable to predict the relevant future with accuracy. In such a world, their ignorance of the future prevents them from behaving in a substantively rational manner; they can only adopt a rational choice procedure, including a rational procedure for forecasting or otherwise adapting to the future.

In a well-known paper, my former colleague, John F. Muth,[24] proposed to objectify the treatment of uncertainty in economics by removing it from the decision-maker to nature. His hypothesis is 'that expectations of firms (or, more generally, the subjective probability distribution of outcomes) tend to be distributed, for the same information set, about the prediction of the theory (or the "objective" probability distributions of outcomes)'. In application this hypothesis involves setting the expected value (in the statistical sense) of a future economic variable equal to its predicted value.

---

[23] Cyert, Feigenbaum, and March (1959).

[24] Muth (1961).

Muth's proposal is ingenious and important. Let us see exactly what it means. Suppose that a producer has an accurate knowledge of the consumer demand function and the aggregate supply function of producers in his industry. Then he can estimate the equilibrium price—the price at which the quantities that producers will be induced to offer will just balance demand. Muth proposes essentially that each producer takes this equilibrium price as his price forecast. If random shocks with zero expected value are now introduced into the supply equation, and if producers continue to act on price forecasts made in the manner just described, then the forecast price will equal the expected value of the actual price.

Notice that the substantively rational behaviour for the producer would be to produce the quantity that would be optimal for the price that is *actually* realized. The assumption of Muth's model that the random shocks are completely unpredictable makes this impossible. The producer then settles for a procedure that under the assumptions of the model will give him an unbiased prediction of the price. Nor, as Muth himself notes, will this procedure be optimal, even under uncertainty, unless the loss function is quadratic.

Uncertainty plays the same innocuous role in the optimal linear production smoothing rule I described earlier,[25] which is closely related to Muth's analysis. Here the explicit assumption of a quadratic cost function makes it possible to prove that only the expected values and not the higher moments of predicted variables are relevant to decision. This does not mean that action based on unbiased estimates is substantively rational, independently of the variances of those estimates. On the contrary, performance can always be improved if estimation errors can be reduced.

Even if it turns out to be empirically true that the forecasts of business firms and other economic actors are unbiased forecasts of future events, this finding will have modest implications for the nature of human rationality. Unbiased estimation can be a component of all sorts of rational and irrational behaviour rules.

In an earlier section I commented on the psychological evidence as to human choice in the face of uncertainty. Only in the very simplest situations does behaviour conform reasonably closely to the predictions of classical models of rationality. But even this evidence exaggerates the significance of those classical models for human affairs; for all of the experiments are limited to situations where the alternatives of choice are fixed in advance, and where information is available only from precisely specified sources.

Once we become interested in the procedures—the rational processes—

---

[25] See footnote 19 above.

that economic actors use to cope with uncertainty, we must broaden our horizons further. Uncertainty not only calls forth forecasting procedures; it also calls forth a whole range of actions to reduce uncertainty, or at least to make outcomes less dependent upon it. These actions are of at least four kinds:

(i) intelligence actions to improve the data on which forecasts are based, to obtain new data, and to improve the forecasting models;

(ii) actions to buffer the effects of forecast errors: holding inventories, insuring, and hedging, for example;

(iii) actions to reduce the sensitivity of outcomes to the behaviour of competitors: steps to increase product and market differentiation, for example;

(iv) actions to enlarge the range of alternatives whenever the perceived alternatives involve high risk.

A theory of rational choice in the face of uncertainty will have to encompass not only the topic of forecasting, but these other topics as well. Moreover, it will have to say something about the circumstances under which people will (or should) pursue one or the other of these lines of action.

Confronting a list of contingencies of this sort fills many economists with malaise. How can a unique answer be found to the problem of choice if all of these considerations enter it? How much more attractive is classical economics, in allowing strong conclusions to be drawn from a few *a priori* assumptions, with little need for empirical observation!

Alas, we must take the world as it is. As economics becomes more concerned with procedural rationality, it will necessarily have to borrow from psychology or build for itself a far more complete theory of human cognitive processes than it has had in the past. Even if our interest lies in normative rather than descriptive economics, we will need such a theory. There are still many areas of decision—particularly those that are illstructured—where human cognitive processes are more effective than the best available optimization techniques or artificial intelligence methods. Every Class A chessplayer plays a far better game than any existing chess-playing computer program. A great deal can still be learned about effective decision procedures by studying how humans make choices.

The human mind is programmable: it can acquire an enormous variety of different skills, behaviour patterns, problem-solving repertoires, and perceptual habits. Which of these it will acquire in any particular case is a function of what it has been taught and what it has experienced. We can expect substantive rationality only in situations that are sufficiently simple as to be transparent to this mind. In all other situations, we must expect that the mind will use such imperfect information as it has, will simplify and represent the situation as it can, and will make such calculations as are within its powers. We cannot expect to predict what it will do in such situations unless we know what information it has, what forms of representation it prefers, and what algorithms are available to it.

There seems to be no escape. If economics is to deal with uncertainty, it will have to understand how human beings in fact behave in the face of uncertainty, and by what limits of information and computability they are bound.

4. THE EMPIRICAL STUDY OF DECISION-MAKING

Since may own recent research has removed me from the study of decision-making in organization settings, I am not in a position to comment on the current state of our empirical knowledge of organizational decision-making. In trying to understand procedural rationality as it relates to economics, we do not have to limit ourselves, however, to organizational studies. I have already commented upon the understanding we have gained, during the past 20 years, of human problem-solving processes—mostly by study in the laboratory, using puzzle-like tasks. Most of these studies have used naïve subjects performing tasks with which they had little or no previous experience. In one case, however—the research on chess-playing—an intensive investigation has been made of highly skilled, professional performance, and a body of theory constructed to explain that performance.

Chess may seem a rather esoteric domain, but perhaps business is no less esoteric to those who do not practise it. There is no reason to believe that the basic human faculties that a chess professional of 20 years' experience brings to bear upon his decisions are fundamentally different from the faculties used by an experienced professional businessman. In fact, to the extent that comparable studies of business decision-making have been carried out, they give us positive reasons to believe in the basic similarity of those faculties.

On the basis of the research on chessplayers, what appears to distinguish expert from novice is not only that the former has a great quantity and variety of information, but that his perceptual experience enables him to detect familiar patterns in the situations that confront him, and by recognizaing these patterns, to retrieve speedily a considerable amount of relevant information from long-term memory.[26] It is this perceptual experience that permits the chessmaster to play, and usually win, many simultaneous games against weaker opponents, taking only a few seconds for each move. It is very likely similar perceptual experience about the world of business that enables

---

[26] de Groot (1965); Chase and Simon (1973b).

the executive to react 'intuitively', without much awareness of his own cognitive processes, to business situations as they arise.

There is no reason to suppose that the theory of cognitive processes that will emerge from the empirical study of the chessmaster's or businessman's decision processes will be 'neat' or 'elegant', in the sense that the Laws of Motion or the axioms of classical utility theory are neat and elegant. If we are to drawn an analogy with the natural sciences, we might expect the theory of procedural rationality to resemble molecular biology, with its rich taxonomy of mechanisms, more closely than either classical mechanics or classical economics. But as I suggested earlier, an empirical science cannot remake the world to its fancy: it can only describe and explain the world as it is.

A major source of complication in theories of professional decision-making is the dependence of decisions upon large quantities of stored information and previously learned decision procedures. This is true not only at an individual psychological level, but also at a social and historical level. The play of two chessplayers differs as a result of differences in what they know about chess: no less do the decisions of two businessmen differ as a result of differences in what they know about business. Moreover, Bobby Fischer, in 1972, played chess differently from Paul Morphy, in 1861. Much of that latter difference was the result of the knowledge of the game that had cumulated over the century through the collective experience of the whole society of professional chessplayers.

Economics, like chess, is inevitably culture-bound and history-bound. A business firm equipped with the tools of operations research does not make the same decisions as it did before it possessed those tools. The substantial secular decline over recent years of inventories held by American firms is probably due in considerable part to this enhancement of rationality by new theory and new computational tools.

Economics is one of the sciences of the artificial.[27] It is a description and explanation of human institutions, whose theory is no more likely to remain invariant over time than the theory of bridge design. Decision processes, like all other aspects of economic institutions, exist inside human heads. They are subject to change with every change in what human beings know, and with every change in their means of calculation. For this reason the attempt to predict and prescribe human economic behaviour by deductive inference from a small set of unchallengeable premises must fail and has failed.

Economics will progress as we deepen our understanding of human thought processes; and economics will change as human individuals and human societies use progressively sharpened tools of thought in making their

[27] Simon (1969).

decisions and designing their institutions. A body of theory for procedural rationality is consistent with a world in which human beings continue to think and continue to invent; a theory of substantive rationality is not.

5. CONCLUSION

In this paper I have contrasted the concept of substantive rationality, which has dominated classical economics and provided it with its programme of structural determinism, with the concept of procedural rationality, which has prevailed in psychology. I have described also some of the concerns of economics that have forced that discipline to begin to concern itself with procedural rationality—with the actual processes of cognition, and with the limits on the human organism that give those processes their peculiar character.

One can conceive of at least two alternative scenarios for the continuation into the future of this gradual change in the programme of economics. One involves the direct 'psychologizing' of economics, the explicit adoption of the programme of economic behaviouralism.[28] The second scenario pictures economists as borrowing the notions of optimal search and computational efficiency from operations research and statistical decision theory, and introducing a wider and wider range of computational considerations into the models of rationality. Since these computational constraints can be viewed (at least formally) as located in the external world rather than in the mind of the decision-maker, they give the appearance of avoiding the need for psychologizing. Of course that need is in fact only postponed, not avoided permanently. It is illusory to describe a decision as 'situationally determined' when a part of the situation that determines it is the mind of the decision-maker. Choosing between alternative models of the situation then calls for determining empirically the processes used by the person or organization making the decisions. Hence, our second scenario leads as inevitably, if not as directly, as does the first to economic behaviouralism.

The shift from theories of substantive rationality to theories of procedural rationality requires a basic shift in scientific style, from an emphasis on deductive reasoning within a tight system of axioms to an emphasis on detailed empirical exploration of complex algorithms of thought. Undoubtedly the uncongeniality of the latter style to economists has slowed the transition, and accounts in part for the very limited success of economic behaviouralism in the past. For this reason, the second scenario appears

[28] This path has already been followed for some distance, for example, in Part IV of my own *Models of Man* (1957), in Cyert and March (1963), and in Katona's *Psychological Analysis of Economic Behavior* (1951).

more promising than the first, and, indeed, appears to be unfolding visibly at the present time.

In other chapters in this volume, Messrs. Coats and Latsis have described the largely successful resistance of economics to earlier attempts at injecting behavioural premises into its body of theory. The present situation is different from the earlier ones because economics is now focusing on new research questions whose answers require explicit attention to procedural rationality. As economics becomes more and more involved in the study of uncertainty, more and more concerned with the complex actuality of business decision-making, the shift in programme will become inevitable. Wider and wider areas of economics will replace the over-simplified assumptions of the situationally constrained omniscient decision-maker with a realistic (and psychological) characterization of the limits on Man's rationality, and the consequences of those limits for his economic behaviour.

REFERENCES

CHASE, W. G. and SIMON, H. A. (1973*a*): 'Skill in Chess', *American Scientist*, **61**, pp. 394–403.

CHASE, W. G. and SIMON, H. A. (1973*b*): 'Perception in Chess', *Cognitive Psychology*, **4**, pp. 55–81.

CLARKSON, G. P. E. (1963): 'A Model of the Trust Investment Process', in E. A. Feigenbaum and J. Feldman (eds.): *Computers and Thought*, pp. 347–71.

CYERT, R. M., FEIGENBAUM, E. A. and MARCH, J. G. (1959): 'Models in a Behavioral Theory of the Firm', *Behavioral Science*, **4**, pp. 81–95.

CYERT, R. M. and MARCH, J. G. (1963): *Behavioral Theory of the Firm.*

CYERT, R. M. and DE GROOT, M. H. (1973): 'An Analysis of Cooperation and Learning in a Duopoly Context', *American Economic Review*, **63**, pp. 24–37.

DORFMAN, R., SAMUELSON, P. A. and SOLOW, R. M. (1958): *Linear Programming and Economic Analysis.*

EDWARDS, W. (1968): 'Conservatism in Human Information Processing', in B. Kleinmuntz (ed.): *Formal Representation of Human Judgment*, pp. 17–52.

FELDMAN, J. (1963): 'Simulation of Behaviour in the Binary Choice Experiment', in E. A. Feigenbaum and J. Feldman (eds.): *Computers and Thought*, pp. 329–46.

GOULD, J. and KOLB, W. L. (eds.) (1964): *The Dictionary of the Social Sciences.*

GROOT, A. D. DE (1965): *Thought and Choice in Chess.*

HALL, R. L. and HITCH, C. H. (1939): 'Price Theory and Business Behaviour', *Oxford Economic Papers*, **2**, pp. 12–45.

HOLT, H. G., MODIGLIANI, F., MUTH, J. F. and SIMON, H. A. (1960): *Planning Production, Inventories and Work Force*.

JAMES, W. (1890): *Principles of Psychology*.

JORGENSON, D. W. (1963): 'Capital Theory and Investment Behavior', *American Economic Review Proceedings*, **53**, pp. 247–59.

KAHNEMAN, D. and TVERSKY, A. (1973): 'On the Psychology of Prediction', *Psychological Review*, **80**, pp. 237–51.

KATONA, G. (1951): *Psychological Analysis of Economic Behavior*.

KORNAI, J. (1971): *Anti-Equilibrium*.

LATSIS, S. J. (1972): 'Situational Determinism in Economics', *The British Journal for the Philosophy of Science*, **23**, pp. 207–45.

MUTH, J. F. (1961): 'Rational Expectations and the Theory of Price Movements', *Econometrica*, **29**, pp. 315–35.

NEWELL, A. and SIMON, H. A. (1972): *Human Problem Solving*.

RAPOPORT, A. and WALLSTEN, T. S. (1972): 'Individual Decision Behavior', *Annual Review of Psychology*, **23**, pp. 131–76.

SIMON, H. A. (1957): *Models of Man*.

SIMON, H. A. (1969): *The Sciences of the Artificial*.

SOELBERG, P. (1967): 'A Study of Decision Making: Job Choice'. Unpublished Ph.D. dissertation, Carnegie-Mellon University.

THEIL, H. (1958): *Economic Forecasts and Policy*.

TINBERGEN, J. (1952): *On the Theory of Economic Policy*.

VI

RATIONAL FOOLS: A CRITIQUE OF THE BEHAVIOURAL FOUNDATIONS OF ECONOMIC THEORY*

AMARTYA K. SEN

I

In his *Mathematical Psychics*, published in 1881, Edgeworth asserted that 'the first principle of Economics is that every agent is actuated only by self interest'.[1] This view of man has been a persistent one in economic models, and the nature of economic theory seems to have been much influenced by this basic premiss. In this essay I would like to examine some of the problems that have arisen from this conception of human beings.

I should mention that Edgeworth himself was quite aware that this so-called first principle of Economics was not a particularly realistic one. Indeed, he felt that 'the concrete nineteenth century man is for the most part an impure egoist, a mixed utilitarian'.[2] This raises the interesting question as to why Edgeworth spent so much of his time and talent in developing a line of inquiry the first principle of which he believed to be false. The issue is not why abstractions should be employed in pursuing general economic questions— the nature of the inquiry makes this inevitable—but why would one choose

From *Philosophy and Public Affairs*, 6, 1976–7, pp. 317–44.

* This Herbert Spencer Lecture, delivered at Oxford University in October 1976, will appear in *Scientific Models and Man*, ed. H. Harris (forthcoming 1978) and is printed here by kind permission of Oxford University Press. For helpful comments on an earlier version, I am grateful to the Editors of this journal, and to Åke Andersson, Isaiah Berlin, Frank Hahn, Martin Hollis, Janos Kornai, Derek Parfit, Christopher Peacocke, and Tibor Scitovsky.

[1] F. Y. Edgeworth, *Mathematical Psychics: An Essay on the Application of Mathematics to the Moral Sciences* (London, 1881), p. 16.

[2] Edgeworth, p. 104. In fact, he went on to make some interesting remarks on the results of 'impure' egoism, admitting an element of sympathy for each other. The remarks have been investigated and analyzed by David Collard, 'Edgeworth's Propositions on Altruism', *Economic Journal*, 85 (1975).

an assumption which he himself believed to be not merely inaccurate in detail but fundamentally mistaken? As we shall see, this question is of continuing interest to modern economics as well.

Part of the answer, as far as Edgeworth was concerned, undoubtedly lay in the fact that he did not think the assumption to be fundamentally mistaken in the *particular* types of activities to which he applied what he called 'economical calculus'; (i) war and (ii) contract. 'Admitting that there exists in the higher parts of human nature a tendency towards and feeling after utilitarian institutions', he asked the rhetorical question: 'could we seriously suppose that these moral considerations were relevant to war and trade; could eradicate the controlless core of human selfishness, or exercise an appreciable force in comparison with the impulse of self-interest'.[3] He interpreted Sidgwick to have dispelled the 'illusion' that 'the interest of all is the interest of each', noting that Sidgwick found the 'two supreme principles—Egoism and Utilitarianism' to be 'irreconcilable, unless indeed by religion'. 'It is far from the spirit of the philosophy of pleasure to deprecate the importance of religion', wrote Edgeworth, 'but in the present inquiry, and dealing with the lower elements of human nature, we should have to seek a more obvious transition, a more earthy passage, from the principle of self-interest to the principle, or at least the practice, of utilitarianism'.[4]

Notice that the context of the debate is important to this argument. Edgeworth felt that he had established the acceptability of 'egoism' as the fundamental behavioural assumption for his particular inquiry by demolishing the acceptability of 'utilitarianism' as a description of actual behaviour. Utilitarianism is, of course, far from being the only non-egoistic approach. Furthermore, between the claims of oneself and the claims of all lie the claims of a variety of groups—for example, families, friends, local communities, peer groups, and economic and social classes. The concepts of family responsibility, business ethics, class consciousness, and so on, relate to these intermediate areas of concern, and the dismissal of utilitarianism as a descriptive theory of behaviour does not leave us with egoism as the only alternative. The relevance of some of these considerations to the economics of negotiations and contracts would be difficult to deny.

It must be noted that Edgeworth's query about the outcome of economic contact between purely self-seeking individuals had the merit of being immediately relevant to an abstract enquiry that had gone on for more than a hundred years already, and which was much discussed in debates involving Herbert Spencer, Henry Sidgwick, and other leading thinkers of the period.

---

[3] Edgeworth, p. 52.

[4] Ibid., pp. 52–3.

Two years before Edgeworth's *Mathematical Psychics* appeared, Herbert Spencer had published his elaborate analysis of the relation between egoism and altruism in *The Data of Ethics*. He had arrived at the comforting—if somewhat unclear—conclusion that 'general happiness is to be achieved mainly through the adequate pursuit of their own happinesses by individuals; while, reciprocally, the happiness of individuals are to be achieved in part by their pursuit of the general happiness'.[5] In the context of this relatively abstract enquiry, Edgeworth's tight economic analysis, based on a well-defined model of contracts between two self-seeking individuals, or between two types of (identical) self-seeking individuals, gave a clear answer to an old hypothetical question.

It appeared that in Edgeworth's model, based on egoistic behaviour, there was a remarkable correspondence between exchange equilibria in competitive markets and what in modern economic terms is called 'the core' of the economy. An outcome is said to be in 'the core' of the economy if and only if it fulfils a set of conditions of unimprovability. These conditions, roughly speaking, are that not only is it the case that no one could be made better off without making somebody else worse off (the situation is what is called a 'Pareto optimum'), but also that no one is worse off than he would be without trade, and that no coalition of individuals, by altering the trade among themselves, could on their own improve their own lot. Edgeworth showed that given certain general assumptions, any equilibrium that can emerge in a competitive market must satisfy these conditions and be in 'the core'. Thus, in Edgeworth's model the competitive market equilibria are, in this sense, undominated by any feasible alternative arrangement, given the initial distribution of endowments. More surprising in some ways was the converse result that if the number of individuals of each type were increased without limit, the core (representing such undominated outcomes) would shrink towards the set of competitive equilibria; that is, the core would not be much more extensive than the set of competitive equilibria. This pair of results has been much elaborated and extended in the recent literature on general equilibrium with similar models and with essentially the same behavioural assumptions.[6]

Being in the core, however, is not as such a momentous achievement from the point of view of social welfare. A person who starts off ill-endowed may stay poor and deprived even after the transactions, and if being in the core is all that competition offers, the propertyless person may be forgiven for not

[5] H. Spencer, *The Data of Ethics* (London, 1879; extended edition, 1887), p. 238.

[6] See, especially, K. J. Arrow and F. H. Hahn, *General Competitive Analysis* (San Francisco, 1971).

regarding this achievement as a 'big deal'. Edgeworth took some note of this by considering the problem of choice between different competitive equilibria. He observed that for the utilitarian good society, 'competition requires to be supplemented by arbitration, and the basis of arbitration between self-interested contractors is the greatest possible sum-total utility'.[7] Into the institutional aspects of such arbitration and the far-reaching implications of it for the distribution of property ownership, Edgeworth did not really enter, despite superficial appearance to the contrary. On the basis of the achievement of competition, however limited, Edgeworth felt entitled to be 'biassed to a more conservative caution in reform'. In calculating 'the utility of pre-utilitarian institutions', Edgeworth felt impressed 'with a view of Nature, not, as in the picture left by Mill, all bad, but a first approximation to the best'.[8]

I am not concerned in this essay with examining whether the approximation is a rather remote one. (This I do believe to be the case even within the structure of assumptions used by Edgeworth, but it is not central to the subject of this paper.) I am concerned here with the view of man which forms part of Edgeworth's analysis and survives more or less intact in much of modern economic theory. The view is, of course, a stylized one and geared specifically to tackling a relatively abstract dispute with which Spencer, Sidgwick, and several other leading contemporary thinkers were much concerned—namely, in what sense and to what extent would egoistic behaviour achieve general good? Whether or not egoistic behaviour is an accurate assumption in reality does not, of course, have any bearing on the accuracy of Edgeworth's answer to the question posed. Within the structure of a limited economic model it provided a clear-cut response to the abstract query about egoism and general good.

This particular debate has gone on for a long time and continues to provide motivation for many recent exercises in economic theory today. The limited nature of the query has had a decisive influence on the choice of economic models and the conception of human beings in them. In their distinguished text on general equilibrium theory, Arrow and Hahn state (pp. vi–vii):

There is by now a long and fairly imposing line of economists from Adam Smith to the present who have sought to show that a decentralized economy motivated by self-interest and guided by price signals would be compatible with a coherent disposition of economic resources that could be regarded, in a well-defined sense, as superior to a large class of possible alternative dispositions. Moreover, the price signals would operate in a way to establish this degree of coherence. It is important to understand

---

[7] Edgeworth, p. 56.

[8] Ibid., p. 82.

how surprising this claim must be to anyone not exposed to the tradition. The immediate 'common sense' answer to the question 'What will an economy motivated by individual greed and controlled by a very large number of different agents look like?' is probably: There will be chaos. That quite a different answer has long been claimed true and has indeed permeated the economic thinking of a large number of people who are in no way economists is itself sufficient ground for investigating it seriously. The proposition having been put forward and very seriously entertained, it is important to know not only whether it *is* true, but whether it *could* be true. A good deal of what follows is concerned with this last question, which seems to us to have considerable claims on the attention of economists.

The primary concern here is not with the relation of postulated models to the real economic world, but with the accuracy of answers to well-defined questions posed with preselected assumptions which severely constrain the nature of the models that can be admitted into the analysis. A specific concept of man is ingrained in the question itself, and there is no freedom to depart from this conception so long as one is engaged in answering this question. The nature of man in these current economic models continues, then, to reflect the particular formulation of certain general philosophical questions posed in the past. The realism of the chosen conception of man is simply not a part of this inquiry.

II

There is another nonempirical—and possibly simpler—reason why the conception of man in economic models tends to be that of a self-seeking egoist. It is possible to define a person's interests in such a way that no matter what he does he can be seen to be furthering his own interests in every isolated act of choice.[9] While formalized relatively recently in the context of the theory of revealed preference, this approach is of respectable antiquity, and Joseph Butler was already arguing against it in the Rolls Chapel two-and-a-half centuries ago.[10] The reduction of man to a self-seeking animal depends in this approach on careful definition. If you are observed to choose x rejecting y, you are declared to have 'revealed' a preference for x over y. Your personal utility is then defined as simply a numerical representation of this

---

[9] If a person's actions today affect his well-being in the future, then under this approach his future interests must be defined in terms of the way they are *assessed today*. In general, there is no reason to presume that the future interests as assessed today will coincide with those interests as assessed in the future. This adds an additional dimension to the problem, and I am grateful to Derek Parfit for convincing me of the conceptual importance of this question.

[10] J. Butler, *Fifteen Sermons Preached at the Rolls Chapel* (London, 1726); see also T. Nagel, *The Possibility of Altruism* (Oxford, 1970), p. 81.

'preference', assigning a higher utility to a 'preferred' alternative. With this set of definitions you can hardly escape maximizing your own utility, except through inconsistency. Of course, if you choose x and reject y on one occasion and then promptly proceed to do the exact opposite, you can prevent the revealed preference theorist from assigning a preference ordering to you, thereby restraining him from stamping a utility function on you which you must be seen to be maximizing. He will then have to conclude that either you are inconsistent or your preferences are changing. You can frustrate the revealed-preference theorist through more sophisticated inconsistencies as well.[11] But if you are consistent, then no matter whether you are a single-minded egoist or a raving altruist or a class conscious militant, you will appear to be maximizing your own utility in this enchanted world of definitions. Borrowing from the terminology used in connection with taxation, if the Arrow–Hahn justification of the assumption of egoism amounts to an *avoidance* of the issue, the revealed preference approach looks more like a robust piece of *evasion*.

This approach of definitional egoism sometimes goes under the name of rational choice, and it involves nothing other than internal consistency. A person's choices are considered 'rational' in this approach if and only if these choices can *all* be explained in terms of some preference relation consistent with the revealed preference definition, that is, if all his choices can be explained as the choosing of 'most preferred' alternatives with respect to a postulated preference relation.[12] The rationale of this approach seems to be based on the idea that the only way of understanding a person's real preference is to examine his actual choices, and there is no choice-independent way of understanding someone's attitude towards alternatives. (This view, by the way, is not confined to economists only. When, many years ago, I had to take my qualifying examination in English Literature at Calcutta University, one of the questions we had to answer concerning *A Midsummer Night's Dream* was: Compare the characters of Hermia and Helena. Whom would you choose?)

I have tried to demonstrate elsewhere that once we eschew the curious definitions of preference and welfare, this approach presumes both too little and too much: too little because there are non-choice sources of information on preference and welfare as these terms are usually understood, and too

---

[11] See H. S. Houthakker, 'Revealed Preference and the Utility Function', *Economica* 17 (1950); P. A. Samuelson, 'The Problem of Integrability in Utility Theory', *Economica* 17 (1950).

[12] For the main analytical results, see M. K. Richter, 'Rational Choice', *Preference, Utility and Demand Theory*, ed. J. S. Chipman *et al.* (New York, 1971).

much because choice may reflect a compromise among a variety of considerations of which personal welfare may be just one.[13]

The complex psychological issues underlying choice have recently been forcefully brought out by a number of penetrating studies dealing with consumer decisions[14] and production activities.[15] It is very much an open question as to whether these behavioural characteristics can be at all captured within the formal limits of consistent choice on which the welfare-maximization approach depends.[16]

III

Paul Samuelson has noted that many economists would 'separate economics from sociology upon the basis of rational or irrational behavior, where these terms are defined in the penumbra of utility theory'.[17] This view might well be resented, for good reasons, by sociologists, but the cross that economists have to bear in this view of the dichotomy can be seen if we note that the approach of 'rational behaviour', as it is typically interpreted, leads to a remarkably mute theory. Behaviour, it appears, is to be 'explained in terms of preferences, which are in turn defined only by behaviour'. Not surprisingly,

---

[13] A. K. Sen, 'Behaviour and the Concept of Preference', *Economica* 40 (1973). See also S. Körner's important recent study, *Experience and Conduct* (Cambridge, 1971). Also T. Schwartz, 'Von Wright's Theory of Human Welfare: A Critique', forthcoming in P. A. Schlipp (ed.), *The Philosophy of Georg Henrik von Wright*; T. Majumdar, 'The Concept of Man in Political Economy and Economics', mimeographed (Jawaharlal Nehru University, New Delhi, 1976); and F. Schick, 'Rationality and Sociality', mimeographed (Rutgers University, Philosophy of Science Association, 1976).

[14] See T. Scitovsky, *The Joyless Economy: An Inquiry into Human Satisfaction and Consumer Dissatisfaction* (London and New York, 1976). See also the general critique of the assumption of 'rational' consumer behaviour by J. Kornai, *Anti-Equilibrium* (Amsterdam and London, 1971), chap. 11; and the literature on 'psychological choice models', in particular, D. McFadden, 'Economic Applications of Psychological Choice Models' (presented at the Third World Econometric Congress, August 1975).

[15] See H. Liebenstein, 'Allocative Efficiency vs. x-Efficiency', *American Economic Review* 56 (1966). Also critiques of the traditional assumption of profit maximization in *business* behaviour, particularly W. J. Baumol, *Business Behavior, Value and Growth* (New York, 1959); R. Marris, *The Economic Theory of Managerial Capitalism* (London, 1964); O. Williamson, *The Economics of Discretionary Behavior* (Chicago, 1967); and A. Silberston, 'Price Behaviour of Firms', *Economic Journal* 80 (1970), reprinted in Royal Economic Society, *Surveys of Applied Economics*, vol. 1 (London, 1973).

[16] On the required conditions of consistency for viewing choice in terms of a binary relation, see my 'Choice Functions and Revealed Preference', *Review of Economic Studies* 38 (1971); H. G. Herzberger, 'Ordinal Preference and Rational Choice', *Econometrica* 41 (1973); K. Suzumura, 'Rational Choice and Revealed Preference', *Review of Economic Studies* 43 (1976); S. Kanger, 'Choice Based on Preference', mimeographed (Uppsala University, 1976).

[17] P. A. Samuelson, *The Foundation of Economics* (Cambridge, Mass., 1955), p. 90.

excursions into circularities have been frequent. Nevertheless, Samuelson is undoubtedly right in asserting that the theory 'is not in a technical sense *meaningless*'.[18] The reason is quite simple. As we have already discussed, the approach does impose the requirement of internal consistency of observed choice, and this might well be refuted by actual observations, making the theory 'meaningful' in the sense in which Samuelson's statement is intended.

The requirement of consistency does have surprising cutting power. Various general characteristics of demand relations can be derived from it. But in the present context, the main issue is the possibility of using the consistency requirement for actual *testing*. Samuelson specifies the need for 'ideal observational conditions' for the implications of the approach to be 'refuted or verified'. This is not, however, easy to satisfy since, on the one hand, our love of variety makes it illegitimate to consider individual acts of choice as the proper units (rather than *sequences* of choices) while, on the other hand, lapse of time makes it difficult to distinguish between inconsistencies and changing tastes. There have, in fact, been very few systematic attempts at testing the consistency of people's day-to-day behaviour, even though there have been interesting and useful contrived experiments on people's reactions to uncertainty under laboratory conditions. What counts as admissible evidence remains unsettled. If today you were to poll economists of different schools, you would almost certainly find the coexistence of beliefs (i) that the rational behaviour theory is unfalsifiable, (ii) that it is falsifiable and so far unfalsified, and (iii) that it is falsifiable and indeed patently false.[19]

However, for my purposes here this is not the central issue. Even if the required consistency were seen to obtain, it would still leave the question of egoism unresolved except in the purely definitional sense, as I have already noted. A consistent chooser can have any degree of egoism that we care to specify. It is, of course, true that in the special case of pure consumer choice over private goods, the revealed preference theorist tries to relate the person's 'preference' or 'utility' to his *own* bundle of commodities. This restriction arises, however, not from any guarantee that he is concerned only with his own interests, but from the fact that his own consumption bundle—or that of his family—is the only bundle over which he has direct *control* in his acts of choice. The question of egoism remains completely open.

---

[18] Ibid., p. 91.

[19] The recent philosophical critiques of rational behaviour theory include, among others, M. Hollis and E. J. Nell, *Rational Economic Man* (Cambridge, 1975); S. Wong, 'On the Consistency and Completeness of Paul Samuelson's Programme in the Theory of Consumer Behaviour' (Ph.D. thesis, Cambridge University, 1975, forthcoming). See also the pragmatic criticisms of Kornai, *Anti-Equilibrium*, chap. 11.

I believe the question also requires a clearer formulation than it tends to receive, and to this question I shall now turn.

IV

As we consider departures from 'unsympathetic isolation abstractly assumed in Economics', to use Edgeworth's words, we must distinguish between two separate concepts: (i) sympathy and (ii) commitment. The former corresponds to the case in which the concern for others directly affects one's own welfare. If the knowledge of torture of others makes you sick, it is a case of sympathy; if it does not make you feel personally worse off, but you think it is wrong and you are ready to do something to stop it, it is a case of commitment. I do not wish to claim that the words chosen have any very great merit, but the distinction is, I think, important. It can be argued that behaviour based on sympathy is in an important sense egoistic, for one is oneself pleased at others' pleasure and pained at others' pain, and the pursuit of one's own utility may thus be helped by sympathetic action. It is action based on commitment rather than sympathy which would be non-egoistic in this sense. (Note, however, that the *existence* of sympathy does not imply that the action helpful to others must be *based on* sympathy in the sense that the action would not take place had one got less or no comfort from others' welfare. This question of *causation* is to be taken up presently).

Sympathy is, in some ways, an easier concept to analyze than commitment. When a person's sense of well-being is psychologically dependent on someone else's welfare, it is a case of sympathy; other things given, the awareness of the increase in the welfare of the other person then makes this person directly better off. (Of course, when the influence is negative, the relation is better named 'antipathy', but we can economize on terminology and stick to the term 'sympathy', just noting that the relation can be positive or negative.) While sympathy relates similar things to each other—namely, welfares of different persons—commitment relates choice to anticipated levels of welfare. One way of defining commitment is in terms of a person choosing an act that he believes will yield a lower level of personal welfare to him than an alternative that is also available to him. Notice that the comparison is between *anticipated* welfare levels, and therefore this definition of commitment excludes acts that go against self-interest resulting purely from a failure to foresee consequences.

A more difficult question arises when a person's choice happens to coincide with the maximization of his anticipated personal welfare, but that is not the *reason* for his choice. If we wish to make room for this, we can expand the definition of commitment to include cases in which the person's choice, while maximizing anticipated personal welfare, would be unaffected under at least one counterfactual condition in which the act chosen would cease to maximize personal welfare. Commitment in this more inclusive sense may be difficult to ascertain not only in the context of others' choices but also in that of one's own, since it is not always clear what one would have done had the circumstances been different. This broader sense may have particular relevance when one acts on the basis of a concern for duty which, if violated, could cause remorse, but the action is really chosen out of the sense of duty rather than just to avoid the illfare resulting from the remorse that would occur if one were to act otherwise. (Of course, even the narrower sense of commitment will cover the case in which the illfare resulting from the remorse, if any, is *outweighed* by the gain in welfare.)

I have not yet referred to uncertainty concerning anticipated welfare. When this is introduced, the concept of sympathy is unaffected, but commitment will require reformulation. The necessary modifications will depend on the person's reaction to uncertainty. The simplest case is probably the one in which the person's idea of what a 'lottery' offers to him in terms of personal gain is captured by the 'expected utility' of personal welfare (that is, adding personal welfares from different outcomes weighted by the probability of occurrence of each outcome). In this case, the entire discussion is reformulated simply replacing personal welfare by *expected* personal welfare; commitment then involves choosing an action that yields a lower expected welfare than an alternative available action. (The broader sense can also be correspondingly modified.)

In the terminology of modern economic theory, sympathy is a case of 'externality'. Many models rule out externalities, for example, the standard model to establish that each competitive equilibrium is a Pareto optimum and belongs to the core of the economy. If the existence of sympathy were to be permitted in these models, some of these standard results would be upset, though by no means all of them.[20] But this would not require a serious revision of the basic structure of these models. On the other hand, commitment does involve, in a very real sense, counterpreferential choice, destroying the crucial assumption that a chosen alternative must be better than (or at least as good as) the others for the person choosing it, and this would certainly require that models be formulated in an essentially different way.

The contrast between sympathy and commitment may be illustrated with

---

[20] See A. K. Sen, 'Labour Allocation in a Co-operative Enterprise', *Review of Economic Studies* 33 (1966); S. G. Winter, Jr., 'A Simple Remark on the Second Optimality Theorem of Welfare Economics', *Journal of Economic Theory* 1 (1969); Collard, 'Edgeworth's Propositions'; G. C. Archibald and D. Donaldson, 'Non-paternalism and Basic Theorems of Welfare Economics', *Canadian Journal of Economics* 9 (1976).

the story of two boys who find two apples, one large, one small. Boy *A* tells boy *B*, 'You choose'. *B* immediately picks the larger apple. *A* is upset and permits himself the remark that this was grossly unfair. 'Why?' asks *B*. 'Which one would *you* have chosen, if you were to choose rather than me?' 'The smaller one, of course', *A* replies. *B* is now triumphant: 'Then what are you complaining about? That's the one you've got!' *B* certainly wins this round of the argument, but in fact *A* would have lost nothing from *B*'s choice had his own hypothetical choice of the smaller apple been based on sympathy as opposed to commitment. *A*'s anger indicates that this was probably not the case.

Commitment is, of course, closely connected with one's morals. But moral this question is in a very broad sense, covering a variety of influences from religious to political, from the ill-understood to the well-argued. When, in Bernard Shaw's *The Devil's Disciple*, Judith Anderson interprets Richard Dudgeon's willingness to be hanged in place of her husband as arising from sympathy for him or love for her, Richard is adamant in his denial: 'What I did last night, I did in cold blood, caring not half so much for your husband, or for you as I do for myself. I had no motive and no interest: all I can tell you is that when it came to the point whether I would take my neck out of the noose and put another man's into it, I could not do it'.[21]

The characteristic of commitment with which I am most concerned here is the fact that it drives a wedge between personal choice and personal welfare, and much of traditional economic theory relies on the identity of the two. This identity is sometimes obscured by the ambiguity of the term 'preference', since the normal use of the word permits the identification of preference with the concept of being better off, and at the same time it is not quite unnatural to define 'preferred' as 'chosen'. I have no strong views on the 'correct' use of the word 'preference', and I would be satisfied as long as both uses are not *simultaneously* made, attempting an empirical assertion by virtue of two definitions.[22] The basic link between choice behaviour and welfare achievements in the traditional models is severed as soon as commitment is admitted as an ingredient of choice.

V

'Fine', you might say, 'but how relevant is all this to the kind of choices with which economists are concerned? Economics does not have much to do with Richard Dudgeon's march to the gallows'. I think one should immediately agree that for many types of behaviour, commitment is unlikely to be an

[21] G. B. Shaw, *Three Plays for Puritans*(Harmondsworth, 1966), p. 94.

[22] See my 'Behaviour and the Concept of Preference', *Economica* 40 (1973); and Schick, 'Rationality and Sociality'.

important ingredient. In the private purchase of many consumer goods, the scope for the exercise of commitment may indeed be limited and may show up rather rarely in such exotic acts as the boycotting of South African avocados or the eschewing of Spanish holidays. Therefore, for many studies of consumer behaviour and interpretations thereof, commitment may pose no great problem. Even sympathy may not be extremely important, the sources of interpersonal interdependence lying elsewhere, for example, in the desire to keep up with the Joneses or in being influenced by other people's habits.[23]

But economics is not concerned only with consumer behaviour; nor is consumption confined to 'private goods'. One area in which the question of commitment is most important is that of the so-called public goods. These have to be contrasted with 'private goods' which have the characteristic that they cannot be used by more than one person: if you ate a piece of apple pie, I wouldn't consider devouring it too. Not so with 'public goods', for example, a road or a public park, which you and I may both be able to use. In many economic models private goods are the only ones around, and this is typically the case when the 'invisible hand' is given the task of doing visible good. But, in fact, public goods are important in most economies and cover a wide range of services from roads and street lighting to defence. There is much evidence that the share of public goods in national consumption has grown rather dramatically in most countries in the world.

The problem of optimal allocation of public goods has also been much discussed, especially in the recent economic literature.[24] A lot of attention, in particular, has been devoted to the problem of correct revelation of preferences. This arises most obviously in the case of subscription schemes where a person is charged according to benefits received. The main problem centres on the fact that it is in everybody's interest to understate the benefit he expects, but this understatement may lead to the rejection of a public project which would have been justified if true benefits were known. Analysis of this difficulty, sometimes referred to as the 'free rider' problem, has recently led to some extremely ingenious proposals for circumventing this inefficiency

[23] See J. S. Duesenberry, *Income, Saving and the Theory of Consumer Behavior* (Cambridge, Mass., 1949); S. J. Prais and H. S. Houthakker, *The Analysis of Family Budgets* (Cambridge, 1955); W. Gaertner, 'A Dynamic Model of Interdependent Consumer Behaviour', mimeographed (Bielefeld University, 1973); R. A. Pollak, 'Interdependent Preferences', *American Economic Review* 66 (1976).

[24] See E. Lindahl, *Die Gerechtigkeit der Besteuerung* (Lund, 1919), translated in R. A. Musgrave and A. Peacock, *Classics in the Theory of Public Finance* (London, 1967); P. A. Samuelson, 'The Pure Theory of Public Expenditure', *Review of Economic Studies* 21 (1954); R. Musgrave, *The Theory of Public Finance* (New York, 1959); L. Johansen, *Public Economics* (Amsterdam, 1966); D. K. Foley, 'Lindahl's Solution and the Core of an Economy with Public Goods', *Econometrica* 38 (1970); E. Malinvaud, 'Prices for Individual Consumption, Quantity Indicators for Collective Consumption', *Review of Economic Studies* 39 (1972).

within the framework of egoistic action.[25] The reward mechanism is set up with such ungodly cunning that people have an incentive to reveal exactly their true willingness to pay for the public good in question. One difficulty in this solution arises from an assumed limitation of strategic possibilities open to the individual, the removal of which leads to an impossibility result.[26] Another difficulty concerns the fact that in giving people the incentive to reveal the truth, money is handed out and the income distribution shifts in a way unguided by distributional considerations. This effect can, of course, be undone by a redistribution of initial endowments and profit shares,[27] but that action obviously raises difficulties of its own.

Central to this problem is the assumption that when asked a question, the individual gives that answer which will maximize his personal gain. How good is this assumption? I doubt that in general it is very good. ('Where is the railway station?' he asks me. 'There', I say, pointing at the post office, 'and would you please post this letter for me on the way?' 'Yes', he says, determined to open the envelope and check whether it contains something valuable.) Even in the particular context of revelation of preferences for public goods the gains-maximizing behaviour may not be the best assumption. Leif Johansen, one of the major contributors to public economics, is, I think, right to question the assumption in this context:

Economic theory in this, as well as in some other fields, tends to suggest that people are honest only to the extent that they have economic incentives for being so. This is a homo oeconomicus assumption which is far from being obviously true, and which needs confrontation with observed realities. In fact, a simple line of thought suggests that the assumption can hardly be true in its most extreme form. No society would be viable without some norms and rules of conduct. Such norms and rules are necessary for viability exactly in fields where strictly economic incentives are absent and cannot be created.[28]

[25] T. Groves and J. Ledyard, 'Optimal Allocation of Public Goods: A Solution to the "Free Rider Problem"', Discussion Paper No. 144 (Center for Mathematical Studies in Economics and Management Science, Northwestern University, 1975); J. Green and J. J. Laffont, 'On the Revelation of Preference for Public Goods', Technical Report No. 140 (Institute for Mathematical Studies in the Social Sciences, Stanford University, 1974). See also J. Dreze and D. de la Vallee Poussin, 'A Tatonnement Process for Public Goods', Review of Economic Studies 38 (1971); E. Malinvaud, 'A Planning Approach to the Public Goods Problem', Swedish Journal of Economics 73 (1971); V. L. Smith, 'Incentive Compatible Experimental Processes for the Provision of Public Goods', mimeographed (Econometric Society Summer Meeting, Madison, 1976).

[26] See J. Ledyard and D. J. Roberts, 'On the Incentive Problem for Public Goods', Discussion Paper No. 116 (CMSEMS, Northwestern University, 1974). See also L. Hurwicz, 'On Informationally Decentralized Systems', in R. Radner and B. McGuire, Decisions and Organizations (Amsterdam, 1972).

[27] See Theorem 4.2 in Groves and Ledyard, 'Optimal Allocation of Public Goods'.

[28] L. Johansen, 'The Theory of Public Goods: Misplaced Emphasis' (Institute of Economics, University of Oslo, 1976). See also J. J. Laffont, 'Macroeconomic Constraints, Economic Efficiency and Ethics', mimeographed (Harvard University, 1974); P. Bohm, 'Estimating Demand for Public Goods: An Experiment', European Economic Review 3 (1972).

What is at issue is not whether people invariably give an honest answer to every question, but whether they always give a gains-maximizing answer, or at any rate, whether they give gains-maximizing answers often enough to make that the appropriate general assumption for economic theory. The presence of non-gains-maximizing answers, including truthful ones, immediately brings in commitment as a part of behaviour.

The question is relevant also to the recent literature on strategic voting. A number of beautiful analytical results have recently been established showing the impossibility of any voting procedure satisfying certain elementary requirements and making honest voting the gains-maximizing strategy for everyone.[29] The correctness of these results is not in dispute, but is it appropriate to assume that people always do try to maximize personal gains in their voting behaviour? Indeed, in large elections, it is difficult to show that any voter has any real prospect of affecting the outcome by his vote, and if voting involves some cost, the expected net gain from voting may typically be negative. Nevertheless, the proportion of turnout in large elections may still be quite high, and I have tried to argue elsewhere that in such elections people may often be 'guided not so much by maximization of expected utility, but something much simpler, viz, just a desire to record one's true preference'.[30] If this desire reflects a sense of commitment, then the behaviour in question would be at variance with the view of man in traditional economic theory.

VI

The question of commitment is important in a number of other economic contexts.[31] It is central to the problem of work motivation, the importance of which for production performance can hardly be ignored.

It is certainly costly and may be impossible to devise a system of

[29] A. Gibbard, 'Manipulation of Voting Schemes: A General Result', *Econometrica* 41 (1973); M. A. Satterthwaite, 'Strategy-proofness and Arrow's Conditions', *Journal of Economic Theory* 10 (1975); D. Schmeidler and H. Sonnenschein, 'The Possibility of Non-manipulable Social Choice Functions' (CMSEMS, Northwestern University, 1974); B. Dutta and P. K. Pattanaik, 'On Nicely Consistent Voting Systems' (Delhi School of Economics, 1975); P. K. Pattanaik, 'Strategic Voting without Collusion under Binary and Democratic Group Decision Rules', *Review of Economic Studies* 42 (1975); B. Peleg, 'Consistent Voting Systems' (Institute of Mathematics, Hebrew University, Jerusalem, 1976); A. Gibbard, 'Social Decision, Strategic Behavior, and Best Outcomes: An Impossibility Result', Discussion Paper No. 224 (CMSEMS, Northwestern University, 1976).

[30] See A. K. Sen, *Collective Choice and Social Welfare* (Edinburgh and San Francisco, 1970), p. 195.

[31] See Ragnar Frisch's discussion of the need for 'a realistic theoretical foundation for social policy' in his 'Samarbeid mellom Politikere og Økonometrikere om Formuleringen av Politiske Preferenser' (Socialøkonomen, 1971). (I am grateful to Leif Johansen for translating the relevant portions of the paper for me.) See also J. A. Mirrlees, 'The Economics of Charitable Contributions', Econometric Society European meeting (Oslo, 1973).

supervision with rewards and punishment such that everyone has the incentive to exert himself. Every economic system has, therefore, tended to rely on the existence of attitudes toward work which supersedes the calculation of net gain from each unit of exertion. Social conditioning plays an extremely important part here.[32] I am persuaded that Britain's present economic difficulties have a great deal to do with work-motivation problems that lie outside the economics of rewards and punishments, and one reason why economists seem to have so little to contribute in this area is the neglect in traditional economic theory of this whole issue of commitment and the social relations surrounding it.[33]

These questions are connected, of course, with ethics, since moral reasoning influences one's actions, but in a broader sense these are matters of culture, of which morality is one part. Indeed, to take an extreme case, in the Chinese 'cultural revolution' one of the primary aims was the increase of the sense of commitment with an eye on economic results: 'the aim of the Great Proletarian Cultural Revolution is to revolutionize people's ideology and as a consequence to achieve greater, faster, better and more economical results in all fields of work'.[34] Of course, China was experimenting with reducing dramatically the role of material incentives in production, which would certainly have increased the part that commitment was meant to play, but even within the traditional systems of payments, much reliance is usually placed on rules of conduct and modes of behaviour that go beyond strictly economic incentives.[35] To run an organization *entirely* on incentives to personal gain is pretty much a hopeless task.

I will have a bit more to say presently on what might lie behind the sense of commitment, but I would like to emphasize at this stage that the morality or

[32] See A. Fox, *Beyond Contract: Work, Power and Trust Relations* (London, 1974); H. G. Nutzinger, 'The Firm as a Social Institution: The Failure of a Contractarian Viewpoint', Working Paper No. 52 (Alfred Weber Institute, University of Heidelberg, 1976).

[33] Cf. 'Nor . . . should we forget the extent to which conventional theory ignores how and why work is organized within the firm and establishment in the way it is, what may be called the "social relations" of the production process', R. A. Gordon, 'Rigor and Relevance in a Changing Institutional Setting', Presidential Address, *American Economic Review* 66 (1976). See also R. Dahrendorf, *Class and Class Conflict in Industrial Society* (Stanford, 1959); O. E. Williamson, 'The Evolution of Hierarchy: An Essay on the Organization of Work', Fels Discussion Paper No. 91 (University of Pennsylvania, 1976); and S. A. Marglin, 'What Do Bosses Do? The Origins and Functions of Hierarchy in Capitalist Production', *Review of Radical Political Economics* 6 (1974).

[34] 'The Decision of the Central Committee of the Chinese Communist Party Concerning the Great Proletarian Cultural Revolution', adopted on 8 August 1966, reproduced in Joan Robinson, *The Cultural Revolution in China* (Harmondsworth, 1969). See also A. K. Sen, *On Economic Inequality* (Oxford, 1973); and C. Riskin, 'Maoism and Motivation: A Discussion of Work Motivation in China', *Bulletin of Concerned Asian Scholars*, 1973.

[35] See Williamson, 'The Evolution of Hierarchy', for a critical analysis of the recent literature in this area.

culture underlying it may well be of a limited kind—far removed from the grandeur of approaches such ad utilitarianism. The 'implicit collusions' that have been observed in business behaviour in oligopolies seem to work on the basis of a system of mutual trust and sense of responsibility which has well-defined limits, and attempts at 'universalization' of the same kind of behaviour in other spheres of action may not go with it at all. There it is strictly a question of business ethics which is taken to apply within a fairly limited domain.

Similarly, in wage negotiations and in collective bargaining the sense of solidarity on either side may have well-defined limits, and may not fit in at all with an approach such as that of general utilitarianism. Edgeworth's implicit assumption, on which I commented earlier, that egoism and utilitarianism exhaust the possible alternative motivations, will be especially unhelpful in this context. While the field of commitment may be large, that of commitment based on utilitarianism and other universalized moral systems may well form a relatively small part of it.

VII

The economic theory of utility, which relates to the theory of rational behaviour, is sometimes criticized for having too much structure; human beings are alleged to be 'simpler' in reality. If our argument so far has been correct, precisely the opposite seems to be the case: traditional theory has *too little* structure. A person is given *one* preference ordering, and as and when the need arises this is supposed to reflect his interests, represent his welfare, summarize his idea of what should be done, and describe his actual choices and behaviour. Can one preference ordering do all these things? A person thus described may be 'rational' in the limited sense of revealing no inconsistencies in his choice behaviour, but if he has no use for these distinctions between quite different concepts, he must be a bit of a fool. The *purely* economic man is indeed close to being a social moron. Economic theory has been much preoccupied with this rational fool decked in the glory of his *one* all-purpose preference ordering. To make room for the different concepts related to his behaviour we need a more elaborate structure.

What kind of a structure do we need? A bit more room up top is provided by John Harsanyi's important distinction between a person's 'ethical' preferences and his 'subjective' preferences: 'the former must express what this individual prefers (or, rather, would prefer), on the basis of impersonal social considerations alone, and the latter must express what he actually prefers, whether on the basis of his personal interests or on any other basis'.[36]

[36] J. Harsanyi, 'Cardinal Welfare, Individualistic Ethics, and Interpersonal Comparisons of Utility', *Journal of Political Economy* 63 (1955), p. 315.

This dual structure permits us to distinguish between what a person thinks is good from the social point of view and what he regards as good from his own personal point of view. Presumably sympathy enters directly into the so-called subjective preference, but the role of commitment is left somewhat unclear. In so far as a person's 'subjective' preferences are taken to 'define his utility function', the intention seems to be to exclude commitment from it, but an ambiguity arises from the fact that these are defined to 'express his preferences in the full sense of the word as they actually are'. Is this in the sense of choice, or in the sense of his conception of his own welfare? Perhaps Harsanyi intended the latter, since 'ethical' preferences are by contrast given the role of expressing 'what he prefers only in those possibly rare moments when he forces a special impartial and impersonal attitude on himself'.[37] But what if he departs from his personal welfare maximization (including any sympathy), not through an impartial concern for all,[38] but through a sense of commitment to some particular group, say to the neighbourhood or to the social class to which he belongs? The fact is we are still short of structure.

Even in expressing moral judgements from an impersonal point of view, a *dual* structure is deficient. Surely a preference ordering can be *more* ethical than another but *less* so than a third. We need more structure in this respect also. I have proposed elsewhere—at the 1972 Bristol conference on 'practical reason'—that we need to consider *rankings of preference rankings* to express our moral judgements.[39] I would like to discuss this structure a bit more. A particular morality can be viewed, not just in terms of the 'most moral' ranking of the set of alternative actions, but as a moral ranking of the rankings of actions (going well beyond the identification merely of the 'most moral' ranking of actions). Let X be the set of alternative and mutually exclusive combinations of actions under consideration, and let Y be the set of rankings of the elements of X. A ranking of the set Y (consisting of action-rankings) will be called a meta-ranking of action-set X. It is my claim that a particular ranking of the action-set X is not articulate enough to express much about a given morality, and a more robust format is provided by

[37] Ibid., pp. 315–16.

[38] Note that for Harsanyi 'an individual's preferences satisfy this requirement of impersonality if they indicate what social situation he would choose if he did not know what his general position would be in the new situation chosen (and in any of its alternatives) but rather had an equal chance of obtaining any of the social positions existing in this situation, from the highest down to the lowest' (p. 316).

[39] A. K. Sen, 'Choice, Orderings and Morality', in S. Körner (ed.), *Practical Reason* (Oxford, 1974). See also J. Watkins's rejoinder and my reply in the same volume, and R. C. Jeffrey, 'Preferences among Preferences', *Journal of Philosophy* 71 (1974); K. Binmore, 'An Example in Group Preference', *Journal of Economic Theory* 10 (1975); and B. A. Weisbrod, 'Toward a State-Preference Model of Utility Function Preferences: A Conceptual Note', mimeographed (University of Wisconsin, 1976).

choosing a meta-ranking of actions (that is, a ranking of Y rather than of X). Of course, such a meta-ranking may include *inter alia* the specification of a particular action-ranking as the 'most moral', but in so far as actual behaviour may be based on a compromise between claims of morality and the pursuit of various other objectives (including self-interest), one has to look also at the relative moral standings of those action-rankings that are *not* 'most moral'.

To illustrate, consider a set X of alternative action combinations and the following three rankings of this action-set X: ranking A representing my personal welfare ordering (thus, in some sense, representing my personal interests), ranking B reflecting my 'isolated' personal interests ignoring sympathy (when such a separation is possible, which is not always so),[40] and ranking C in terms of which actual choices are made by me (when such choices are representable by a ranking, which again is not always so).[41] The 'most moral' ranking M can, conceivably, be any of these rankings A, B, or C. Or else it can be some other ranking quite distinct from all three. (This will be the case if the actual choices of actions are not the 'most moral' in terms of the moral system in question, and if, furthermore, the moral system requires sacrifice of some self-interest and also of 'isolated' self-interest.) But even when some ranking M distinct from A, B, and C is identified as being at the top of the moral table, that still leaves open the question as to how A, B, and C may be ordered *vis-à-vis* each other. If, to take a particular example, it so happens that the pursuit of self-interest, including pleasure and pain from sympathy, is put morally above the pursuit of 'isolated' self-interest (thereby leading to a partial coincidence of self-interest with morality), and the actual choices reflect a morally superior position to the pursuit of self-interest (perhaps due to a compromise in the moral direction), then the morality in question precipitates the meta-ranking M, C, A, B, in descending order. This, of course, goes well beyond specifying that M is 'morally best'.

The technique of meta-ranking permits a varying extent of moral articulation. It is not being claimed that a moral meta-ranking must be a *complete* ordering of the set Y, that is, must completely order all rankings of X. It can be a *partial* ordering, and I expect it often will be incomplete, but I should think that in most cases there will be no problem in going well beyond the limited expression permitted by the twofold specification of 'ethical' and 'subjective' preferences.

The rankings of action can, of course, be ordered also on grounds other

---

[40] This presupposes some 'independence' among the different elements influencing the level of over-all welfare, implying some 'separability'. See W. M. Gorman, 'Tricks with Utility Functions', in M. Artis and A. R. Nobay (eds), *Essays in Economic Analysis* (Cambridge, 1975).

[41] See fn. 16 above.

than a particular system of morality: meta-ranking is a general technique usable under alternative interpretations of the meta-ranking relation. It can be used to describe a particular ideology or a set of political priorities or a system of class interests. In quite a different context, it can provide the format for expressing what preferences one would have preferred to have ('I wish I liked vegetarian foods more', or 'I wish I didn't enjoy smoking so much'). Or it can be used to analyze the conflicts involved in addiction ('Given my current tastes, I am better off with heroin, but having heroin leads me to addiction, and I would have preferred not to have these tastes'). The tool of meta-rankings can be used in many different ways in distinct contexts.

This is clearly not the occasion to go into a detailed analysis of how this broader structure permits a better understanding of preference and be-haviour. A structure is not, of course, a theory, and alternative theories can be formulated using this structure. I should mention, however, that the structure demands much more information than is yielded by the observation of people's actual choices, which would at most reveal only the ranking C. It gives a role to introspection and to communication. To illustrate one use of the apparatus, I may refer to some technical results. Suppose I am trying to investigate your conception of your own welfare. You first specify the ranking A which represents your welfare ordering. But I want to go further and get an idea of your *cardinal* utility function, that is, roughly speaking, not only which ranking gives you more welfare but also by how much. I now ask you to order the different rankings in terms of their 'closeness' to your actual welfare ranking A, much as a policeman uses the technique of photofit: is this more like him, or is that? If your answers reflect the fact that reversing a stronger preference makes the result more distant then reversing a weaker intensity of preference, your replies will satisfy certain consistency properties, and the order of rankings will permit us to compare your welfare *differences* between pairs. In fact, by considering higher and higher order rankings, we can determine your cardinal welfare function as closely as you care to specify.[42] I am not saying that this type of dialogue is the best way of discovering your welfare function, but it does illustrate that once we give up the assumption that observing choices is the only source of data on welfare, a whole new world opens up, liberating us from the informational shackles of the traditional approach.

This broader structure has many other uses, for example, permitting a clearer analysis of *akrasia*—the weakness of will—and clarifying some conflicting considerations in the theory of liberty, which I have tried to

---

[42] This result and some related ones emerged in discussions with Ken Binmore in 1975, but a projected joint paper reporting them is still, alas, unwritten. More work on this is currently being done also by R. Nader-Ispahani.

discuss elsewhere.[43] It also helps in analyzing the development of behaviour involving commitment in situations characterized by games such as the Prisoners' Dilemma.[44] This game is often treated, with some justice, as the classic case of failure of individualistic rationality. There are two players and each has two strategies, which we may call selfish and unselfish to make it easy to remember without my having to go into too much detail. Each player is better off personally by playing the selfish strategy *no* matter what the other does, but both are better off if both choose the unselfish rather than the selfish strategy. It is individually optimal to do the selfish thing: one can only affect one's own action and not that of the other, and given the other's strategy—no matter what—each player is better off being selfish. But this combination of selfish strategies, which results from self-seeking by both, produces an outcome that is worse for both than the result of both choosing the unselfish strategy. It can be shown that this conflict can exist even if the game is repeated many times.

Some people find it puzzling that individual self-seeking by each should produce an inferior outcome for all, but this, of course, is a well-known conflict, and has been discussed in general terms for a very long time. Indeed, it was the basis of Rousseau's famous distinction between the 'general will' and the 'will of all'.[45] But the puzzle from the point of view of rational behaviour lies in the fact that in actual situations people often do not follow the selfish strategy. Real life examples of this type of behaviour in complex circumstances are well known, but even in controlled experiments in laboratory conditions people playing the Prisoners' Dilemma frequently do the unselfish thing.[46]

In interpreting these experimental results, the game theorist is tempted to put it down to the lack of intelligence of the players: 'Evidently the run-of-

---

[43] See Sen, 'Choice, Orderings and Morality'; and also Sen, 'Liberty, Unanimity and Rights', *Economica* 43 (1976). Note also the relevance of this structure in analyzing the incompleteness of the conception of liberty in terms of the ability to do what one *actually wishes*. Cf. 'If I find that I am able to do little or nothing of what I wish, I need only contract or extinguish my wishes, and I am made free. If the tyrant (or "hidden persuader") manages to condition his subjects (or customers) into losing their original wishes and embrace ("internalize") the form of life he has invented for them, he will, on this definition, have succeeded in liberating them'. I. Berlin, 'Two Concepts of Liberty', in *Four Essays on Liberty* (Oxford, 1969), pp. 139–40).

[44] See R. D. Luce and H. Raiffa, *Games and Decisions* (New York, 1958); A. Rapoport and A. M. Chammah, *Prisoners' Dilemma: A Study in Conflict and Cooperation* (Ann Arbor, 1965); W. G. Runciman and A. K. Sen, 'Games, Justice and the General Will', *Mind*, 74 (1965); N. Howard, *Paradoxes of Rationality* (Cambridge, Mass., 1971).

[45] See Runciman and Sen.

[46] See, for example, L. B. Lave, 'An Empirical Approach to the Prisoner's Dilemma Game', *Quarterly Journal of Economics* 76 (1962), and Rapoport and Chammah, *Prisoners' Dilemma*.

the-mill players are not strategically sophisticated enough to have figured out that strategy DD [the selfish strategy] is the only rationally defensible strategy, and this intellectual short-coming saves them from closing'.[47] A more fruitful approach may lie in permitting the possibility that the person is *more* sophisticated than the theory allows and that he has asked himself what type of preference he would like the other player to have, and on somewhat Kantian grounds has considered the case for himself having those preferences, or behaving *as if* he had them. This line of reasoning requires him to consider the modifications of the game that would be brought about by acting through commitment (in terms of 'revealed preferences', this would look *as if* he had different preferences from the ones he actually had), and he has to assess alternative behaviour norms in that light. I have discussed these issues elsewhere;[48] thus I shall simply note here that the apparatus of *ranking of rankings* assists the reasoning which involves considering the merits of having different types of preferences (or of acting as if one had them).

VIII

Admitting behaviour based on commitment would, of course, have far-reaching consequences on the nature of many economic models. I have tried to show why this change is necessary and why the consequences may well be serious. Many issues remain unresolved, including the empirical importance of commitment as a part of behaviour, which would vary, as I have argued, from field to field. I have also indicated why the empirical evidence for this cannot be sought in the mere observation of actual choices, and must involve other sources of information, including introspection and discussion.

There remains, however, the issue as to whether this view of man amounts to seeing him as an irrational creature. Much depends on the concept of rationality used, and many alternative characterizations exist. In the sense of *consistency* of choice, there is no reason to think that admitting commitment must imply any departure from rationality. This is, however, a weak sense of rationality.

The other concept of rationality prevalent in economics identifies it with the possibility of justifying each act in terms of self-interest: when act x is chosen by person i and act y rejected, this implies that i's personal interests are expected by i to be better served by x than by y. There are, it seems to me, three distinct elements in this approach. First, it is a consequentialist view:

[47] Rapoport and Chammah, p. 29.

[48] Sen, 'Choice, Orderings and Morality'. See also K. Baier, 'Rationality and Morality', and A. K. Sen, 'Rationality and Morality: A Reply', both forthcoming in *Erkenntnis*; K. Baier, *The Moral Point of View* (Ithaca, 1958); and Fred Schick's analysis, 'Rationality and Sociality'.

judging acts by consequences only.[49] Second, it is an approach of *act* evaluation rather than *rule* evaluation. And third, the only consequences considered in evaluating acts are those on one's own interests, everything else being at best an intermediate product. It is clearly possible to dispute the claims of each of these elements to being a necessary part of the conception of rationality in the dictionary sense of 'the power of being able to exercise one's reason'. Moreover, arguments for rejecting the straightjacket of each of these three principles are not hard to find. The case for actions based on commitment can arise from the violation of any of these three principles. Commitment sometimes relates to a sense of obligation going beyond the consequences. Sometimes the lack of personal gain in particular *acts* is accepted by considering the value of *rules* of behaviour. But even within a consequentialist act-evaluation framework, the exclusion of any consideration other than self-interest seems to impose a wholly arbitrary limitation on the notion of rationality.

Henry Sidgwick noted the arbitrary nature of the assumption of egoism:

> If the Utilitarian has to answer the question, 'Why should I sacrifice my own happiness for the greater hapiness of another?' it must surely be admissible to ask the Egoist, 'Why should I sacrifice a present pleasure for one in the future? Why should I concern myself about my own future feelings any more than about the feelings of other persons?' It undoubtedly seems to Common Sense paradoxical to ask for a reason why one should seek one's own happiness on the whole; but I do not see how the demand can be repudiated as absurd by those who adopt views of the extreme empirical school of psychologists, although those views are commonly supposed to have a close affinity with Egoistic Hedonism. Grant that the Ego is merely a system of coherent phenomena, that the permanent identical 'I' is not a fact but a fiction, as Hume and his followers maintain; why, then, should one part of the series of feelings into which the Ego is resolved be concerned with another part of the same series, any more than with any other series?[50]

The view of rationality that identifies it with consequentialist act-evaluation using self-interest can be questioned from any of these three angles. Admitting commitment as a part of behaviour implies no denial of reasoned assessment as a basis for action.

There is not much merit in spending a lot of effort in debating the 'proper' definition of rationality. The term is used in many different senses, and none of the criticisms of the behavioural foundations of economic theory

[49] On the nature of 'consequentialism' and problems engendered by it, see B. Williams, 'A Critique of Utilitarianism', in J. J. C. Smart and B. Williams, *Utilitarianism: For and Against*(Cambridge, 1973).

[50] H. Sidgwick, *The Method of Ethics* (London, 1874; 7th edn., 1907), pp. 418–19. See also Nagel's forceful exposition of the thesis that 'altruism itself depends on a recognition of the reality of other persons, and on the equivalent capacity to regard oneself as merely one individual among many', *The Possibility of Altruism*, p. 1.

presented here stands or falls on the definition chosen. The main issue is the acceptability of the assumption of the invariable pursuit of self-interest in each act. Calling that type of behaviour rational, or departures from it irrational, does not change the relevance of these criticisms, though it does produce an arbitrarily narrow definition of rationality. This paper has not been concerned with the question as to whether human behaviour is better described as rational or irrational. The main thesis has been the need to accommodate commitment as a part of behaviour. Commitment does not presuppose reasoning, but it does not exclude it; in fact, in so far as consequences on others have to be more clearly understood and assessed in terms of one's values and instincts, the scope for reasoning may well expand. I have tried to analyze the structural extensions in the conception of preference made necessary by behaviour based on reasoned assessment of commitment. Preferences as rankings have to be replaced by a richer structure involving meta-rankings and related concepts.

I have also argued against viewing behaviour in terms of the traditional dichotomy between egoism and universalized moral systems (such as utilitarianism). Groups intermediate between oneself and all, such as class and community, provide the focus of many actions involving commitment. The rejection of egoism as description of motivation does not, therefore, imply the acceptance of some universalized morality as the basis of actual behaviour. Nor does it make human beings excessively noble.

Nor, of course, does the use of reasoning imply remarkable wisdom.

> It is as true as Caesar's name was Kaiser,
> That no economist was ever wiser,

said Robert Frost in playful praise of the contemporary economist. Perhaps a similarly dubious tribute can be paid to the economic man in our modified conception. If he shines at all, he shines in comparison—in contrast—with the dominant image of the rational fool.

VII

VALUES AND COLLECTIVE DECISION-MAKING[1]

KENNETH J. ARROW

1. VALUES OF A SINGLE INDIVIDUAL

As an exercise in clarifying terminology, let us consider what can be said about the values of an imaginary, completely isolated individual. His personal skills and qualities and the physical world available to him jointly delimit a range of *actions* possible to him. To be precise, I shall so define the concept of action that alternative actions are mutually exclusive. An action, then, means a complete description of all the activities that an individual carries on, and two alternative actions are any two descriptions which differ in any relevant way. For example, an individual may describe his activities by indicating the amount of time he spends on each of the alternative modalities of performance available to him; thus, three hours at farming, three hours at hunting, four hours at violin playing, etc. A change in any one of these time allocations would represent a change in action. This particular definition is truly a formal choice of language, and does not by itself change the nature of the problem. It simply brings out formally that the basic question of the individual is a choice of actions.

I *Values, Tastes, and Hypothetical Imperatives*

To an economist, and I suppose to most philosophers, a value system would, in these terms, be simply the rule an individual uses to choose which of the mutually exclusive actions he will undertake. If an individual is facing a given set of alternative actions, he will choose one, and there seems to be little

From P. Laslett and W. G. Runciman (eds.), *Philosophy, Politics and Society*, Third Series (Blackwell, 1967).

[1] This paper is a slightly revised version of 'Public and Private Values', presented at a symposium on *Human Values and Economic Policy* at the New York University Institute of Philosophy in 1966.

interesting to talk about. However, the problem, at least to the economist, is put in slightly different form. Consider an individual who does not yet know which actions will be available and which will not. Let us term the set of available actions the *environment*. One might ask him what action he *would choose* if offered some particular environment. By repeating this question for many alternative environments we have obtained a description of his value system in the sense of a rule giving his hypothetical choice for many or all possible environments.[2]

One might want to reserve the term 'values' for a specially elevated or noble set of choices. Perhaps choices in general might be referred to as 'tastes'. We do not ordinarily think of the preference for additional bread over additional beer as being a value worthy of philosophic inquiry. I believe, though, that the distinction cannot be made logically, and certainly not in dealing with the single isolated individual. If there is any distinction between values and tastes it must lie in the realm of interpersonal relations.

II *The Assumptions of Ordering*

The description of a value system as a correlation between possible environments and the hypothetical choices to be made from them is not by itself a very informative procedure. Economists have been accustomed to adding considerable strength (empirical restrictiveness) by specifying that the value system shall have a particular structure—namely, being derivable from an *ordering*. To define this concept let us first consider environments consisting of just two alternative actions. For such two-member environments we can find the one chosen, in accordance with the individual's value system, and we will speak of it as having been *preferred* to the other action in the environment. We may have to admit that the individual is equally willing to choose neither of the two actions, in which case we speak of the two actions as being *indifferent*. The assumption of an ordering means that certain consistency assumptions are postulated about the relations of preference and indifference, and it is further assumed that choices from any environment can be described in terms of the ordering, which relates to choices in two-member environments.

The first assumption is that of *connexity* (or connectedness, or completeness, or comparability). It is assumed that for each pair of alternatives, either one is preferred to the other or the two are indifferent. The second

---

[2] For technical mathematical reasons one must admit that sometimes more than one action should be regarded as chosen in a given environment, by which is meant the individual does not care which of the chosen actions is in fact adopted in a particular set of circumstances. We must also allow for the fact that there may be no chosen action; for an example of the latter, consider an individual with a normal desire for money who can choose any amount of gold less than (but not equal to) one ounce.

assumption is that of *transitivity*. Consider three alternatives, to be designated by x, y, and z. Then if x is preferred to y, and y is preferred to z, we assume that x is preferred to z. We can and must also include in the definition cases where some of the choices are indifferent: for example, if x is indifferent to y, and y is indifferent to z, then x is indifferent to z.

For later use we introduce some symbolic notation to express these ordering relations. Specifically, we denote alternatives by x, y, ... Then

xPy means 'x is preferred to y',

xIy means 'x is indifferent to y',

xRy means 'x is preferred or indifferent to y'.

If we start with the relation R (that is, only knowing for which ordered pairs of alternatives, x, y, the statement xRy holds), then we can define the relations P and I in terms of R:

xIy is defined to be xRy and yRx;

xPy is defined to be xRy and not yRx.

The assumption of connexity can be stated:

For all x and y, xRy or yRx.

(Here, and below, 'or' does not exclude 'and'.) The assumption of transitivity can be stated:

For all x, y, and z, if xRy and yRz, then xRz.

Finally, and perhaps most important, it is assumed that the choice from any environment is determined by the ordering in the sense that if there is an alternative which is preferred to every other alternative in the environment, then it is the chosen element. This is an additional assumption not logically implied by the existence of an ordering itself.

In symbols, let S be any environment (set of alternatives), $C(S)$ the alternative (or alternatives) chosen from S. Then

$C(S)$ is the set of alternatives x in S for which xRy for all y in S.

It is easy to see that if x^1 and x^2 are both in $C(S)$ (both chosen alternatives in S), then x^1Ix^2.

Obviously, the assumption of ordering is by no means unreasonable. The notion of connexity carries the idea that choices have to be made whether we will or no. The idea of transitivity clearly corresponds to some strong feeling of the meaning of consistency in our choice. Economists have typically identified the concept of rationality with the notion of choices derivable from an ordering.

It may be worthwhile dwelling on the meaning of these two assumptions a little more, in view of their importance. It is not at all uncommon to find denials of the connexity assumption. Sufficiently remote alternatives are held to be incomparable. But I must say I do not find this line of argument at all convincing. If a choice has to be made, it has to be made. In most practical choice situations there is some *null* alternative, which will be chosen in the absence of what might be termed a positive decision. Thus, if there is dispute about the nature of new legislation, the pre-existing legislation remains in force. But this does not mean that no choice is made; it means rather that the system produces as its choice the null alternative. I think what those who emphasize incomparability have in mind is rather that if one is forced to make a choice between alternatives which are difficult to compare, then the choice is not apt to satisfy the assumption of transitivity.

The possibility of regarding inaction as an always available alternative is part of the broader question of whether social choices should be historically conditioned. It is here that the importance of transitivity becomes clear. Transitivity implies that the final choice made from any given environment is independent of the path by which it has been derived. From any environment there will be a given chosen alternative, and in the absence of a deadlock no place for the historically given alternatives to be chosen by default.

III *Independence of Irrelevant Alternatives*

Since the chosen element from any environment is completely defined by knowledge of the preferences as between it and any other alternative in the environment, it follows that the choice depends only on the ordering of the elements of that environment. In particular, the choice made does not depend on preferences as between alternatives which are not in fact available in the given environment, nor—and this is probably more important—on preferences as between elements in the environment and those not in the environment. It is never necessary to compare available alternatives with those which are not available at a given moment in order to arrive at a decision. It is this point which is being made when it is argued that only ordinal measures of utility or preference are relevant to decisions. Any cardinal measure, any attempt to give a numerical representation of utility, depends basically on comparisons involving alternative actions which are not, or at least may not be, available, given the environment prevailing at the moment.

IV *Omitted Considerations*

For the sake of economy of discussion we pass by many interesting issues. Most important, probably, is the relation between hypothetical choices and real ones. It is implied in the above discussion and below that a preference will in fact be translated into a choice if the opportunity ever comes. But the question may be raised how we can possibly know about hypothetical choices if they are not actually made. This is not merely a problem of finding

out about somebody else's values; we may not know our own values until put
to the crucial test.

Even the actual preferences may not be regarded as in some sense true
values. An observer looking from the outside on our isolated individual may
say that his decision was wrong either in the sense that there is some other
standard of values to which it does not conform or in the sense that it was
made on the grounds of insufficient information or improper calculation.
The latter possibility is a real and important one, but I will simply state that I
am abstracting from it in the course of the present discussion. The former
interpretation I am rejecting here. For the single isolated individual there can
be no other standard than his own values. He might indeed wish to change
them under criticism, but this, I take it, means basically that he has not fully
thought through or calculated the consequences of his actions and upon
more consideration wishes to modify them.

2. PUBLIC VALUES

I *Interpersonal Nature of Social Action*

The fundamental fact which causes the need for discussing public values at all
is that all significant actions involve joint participation of many individuals.
Even the apparently simplest act of individual decision involves the
participation of a whole society.

It is important to note that this observation tells us all non-trivial actions
are essentially the property of society as a whole, not of individuals. It is quite
customary to think of each individual as being able to undertake actions on
his own (e.g., decisions of consumption, production, and exchange, moving
from place to place, forming and dissolving families). Formally, a social
action is then taken to be the resultant of all individual actions. In other
words, any social action is thought of as being factored into a sequence of
individual actions.

I certainly do not wish to deny that such factoring takes place, but I do
wish to emphasize that the partition of a social action into individual
components, and the corresponding assignment of individual responsibility,
is *not* a datum. Rather, the particular factoring in any given context is itself
the result of a social policy and therefore already the outcome of earlier and
logically more primitive social values.

In economic transactions the point is clearest when we consider what we
call property. Property is clearly a creation of society through its legal
structure. The actions of buying and selling through offers of property are
only at a superficial level the actions of an individual. They reflect a whole
series of social institutions, and with different institutions different people
would be having control over any given piece of property. Furthermore, the

very notion of control over one's 'own' property, as is apparent upon the most casual inspection, itself acquires its meaning through the regulations of society.

These are no idle or excessively nice distinctions. When it comes to racial discrimination, notions of liability and responsibility for injury to others, or the whole concept of a corporation and its special and complex relations to the world as a whole, economic and social, we know that social values have altered considerably the terms on which property can be used in the market-place or transmitted to others. Needless to say, the taxation system constitutes one of the strongest examples in which the state, as one aspect of society, makes clear the relative nature of ownership. Nor, in this context, should it be forgotten that the claims of society, as modifying the concept of ownership, are by no means confined to the state. Our particular culture has tended to minimize non-coercive obligations relative to the predominant role they have played elsewhere, but they are far from absent even today. There is certainly a whole complex of obligations implied in the concept of a 'good neighbour'. The use of one's real property is limited by more than legal conditions. As everyone knows—sometimes painfully—there are obligations of generosity and organized giving appropriate to an individual's income status and social position. In short, we argue that the facts of social life show clearly that there is no universally acceptable division of actions with regard to property into mine and thine.

To be sure, there is another category of actions, those which involve the person himself as opposed to his property. We have a stronger feeling here that there is a natural meaning to speaking of one's own actions as opposed to others. Presumably there is a meaningful sense in which we say that *I* am writing this paper—not anyone else. But of course even here the action is full of social interconnections. I am here in a conference arranged by others, using words which are a common part of the culture, expressing ideas which draw upon a wide range of concepts of others, and which embody my education.

To be sure, I am using my own capacities at some point in this process. But how logically do we distinguish between the capacities which somehow define the person, and those which are the result of external actions of a society? I may see well because my vision is intrinsically good or because I have glasses. Is the vision more peculiarly *mine* in one case than in the other? One may concede that there is more of an intrinsic idea of property here in certain personal actions, but I think this whole matter needs deeper exploration than it has received thus far. In any case, there are obviously very strong social obligations on personal behaviour and the use of one's personal capacities, just as there are on the use of property.

To conclude, then, we must in a general theory take as our unit a social action, that is, an action involving a large proportion or the entire domain of society. At the most basic axiomatic level, individual actions play little role. The need for a system of public values then becomes evident; actions being collective or interpersonal in nature, so must the choice among them. A public or social value system is essentially a logical necessity.

The point is obvious enough in the contexts that we tend to regard as specifically political. The individuals in a country cannot have separate foreign policies or separate legal systems. Among economists the matter has been somewhat confused because economic analysis has supplied us with a model of factorization of social actions, that achieved through the price system. The system itself is certainly one of the most remarkable of social institutions and the analysis of its working is, in my judgement, one of the more significant intellectual achievements of mankind. But the factorization implied is a particular one made in a particular way. It is one that has turned out to be highly convenient, particularly from the point of view of economizing on the flow of information in the economic system. But at the fundamental level of discourse we are now engaged in we cannot regard the price system as a datum. On the contrary, it is to be thought of as one of the instrumentalities, possibly the major one, by which whatever social value system there may be is realized.

II *Individual Preferences for Social Actions*

The individual plays a central role in social choice as the judge of alternative social actions according to his own standards. We presume that each individual has some way of ranking social actions according to his preferences for their consequences. These preferences constitute his value system. They are assumed to reflect already in full measure altruistic or egoistic motivations, as the case may be.

Following the discussion in Part I, we assume that the values are expressed in the form of an ordering. Thus, in effect, individuals are taken to be rational in their attitudes toward social actions.

In symbols, we now let $x, y, \ldots$, represent alternative social actions. Then the ith individual has an ordering among these actions which, as in 1.II, can be represented by a relation, to be denoted by R_i:

$x R_i y$ means 'x is preferred or indifferent to y in the view of individual i'. As before, we can define P_i (preference in the view of individual i) and I_i (indifference in the view of individual i) in terms of R_i:

$x P_i y$ is defined to be $x R_i y$ and not $y R_i x$;

$x I_i y$ is defined to be $x R_i y$ and $y R_i x$.

We are face to face with an extremely difficult point. A standard liberal point of view in political philosophy, which also has dominated formal welfare economics, asserts that an individual's preferences are or ought to be (a distinction not usually made clear) concerned only with the effects of social actions on him. But there is no logical way to distinguish a particular class of consequences which pertain to a given individual. If I feel that my satisfaction is reduced by somebody else's poverty (or, for that matter, by somebody else's wealth), then I am injured in precisely the same sense as if my purchasing power were reduced. To parallel the observations of the preceding section, I am in effect arguing here that just as we cannot factor social actions so as to make each component pertain to a given individual, so we cannot factor the consequences of social actions in any meaningful way into separable consequences to individual members of the society. That is, let me make it clear, we cannot do it as a matter of fact. The interdependence of mankind is after all not a novel ethical doctrine. The man who questioned whether he was his brother's keeper was, according to an ancient source, not highly approved of. The general conclusion here is not one that I find myself entirely comfortable with. I do share the general liberal view that every individual should have the opportunity to find his own way to personal development and satisfaction. The question of interference with the actions of others has been raised most acutely in recent years in legal rather than economic contexts, specifically in the English discussion on laws regulating deviant sexual behaviour. Homosexual behaviour between consenting adults is probably a classic example of an action affecting no one else, and therefore should be exempt from social control. Yet many find themselves shocked and outraged. They would strongly prefer, let us say, the situation to be different. Similarly, I may be disturbed that the Negro is discriminated against and judge accordingly social actions which lead to this result.

One could of course say that the general principle of restraint in judging the affairs of others is an empirical assumption that people in fact do not care about (or strictly have no preferences concerning) matters which would in the usual terminology be regarded as none of their business. But of course empirically we know that this is quite false. The very fact that restrictive legislation is passed or even proposed shows clearly that people are willing to sacrifice effort and time because of the satisfactions to be received from seeing others' patterns of life altered.

The only rational defence of what may be termed a liberal position, or perhaps more precisely a principle of limited social preference, is that it is itself a value judgement. In other words, an individual may have as part of his value structure precisely that he does not think it proper to influence consequences outside a limited realm. This is a perfectly coherent position, but I find it difficult to insist that this judgement is of such overriding importance that it outweighs all other considerations. Personally, my values are such that I am willing to go very far indeed in the direction of respect for the means by which others choose to derive their satisfactions.

At this stage I want to emphasize the value judgements in favour of limited social preference, just as other value judgements emphasizing social solidarity, must be counted as part of the value systems which individuals use in the judgement of alternative social actions.

3. WELFARE JUDGEMENTS AND THE AGGREGATION OF PREFERENCES

The problem of social choice is the aggregation of the multiplicity of individual preference scales about alternative social actions.

1 *Welfare Judgements and Constitutions*

Classical utilitarianism specifies that alternative social actions be judged in terms of their consequences for people. In the present terminology I take this to mean that they are to be judged in terms of the individual preference scales. This by itself does not supply a sufficient basis for action in view of the multiplicity and divergence of individual preference scales. It is therefore at least implicit in classical utilitarianism that there is a second level at which the individual judgements are themselves evaluated, and this point has been given explicit recognition in a classic paper of Abram Bergson.[3] Let us call this second-order evaluation a *welfare judgement*; it is an evaluation of the consequences to all individuals based on their evaluations. If in each individual evaluation two social actions are indifferent, then the welfare judgement as between the two must also be one of indifference.

The process of formation of welfare judgements is logically equivalent to a social decision process or *constitution*. Specifically, a constitution is a rule which associates to each possible set of individual orderings a social choice function, i.e., a rule for selecting a preferred action out of every possible environment. That a welfare judgement is a constitution indeed follows immediately from the assumption that welfare judgement can be formed given any set of individual preference systems for social actions. The classification of welfare judgements as constitutions is at this stage a tautology, but what makes it more than that is a specification of reasonable

[3] 'A Reformulation of Certain Aspects of Welfare Economics', *Quarterly Journal of Economics*, 52 (1938), 310–34; reprinted in A. Bergson, *Essays in Normative Economics* (Cambridge, Mass.: Harvard University Press, 1966), 1–49.

conditions to be imposed on constitutions, and it is here that any dispute must lie.

11 Social Decision Processes and the Notion of Social Welfare

While I have just argued that a welfare judgement is necessarily a constitution or process of social decision, the converse need not be true, at least not without further clarification of the meaning of 'welfare judgement'. A welfare judgement requires that some one person is judge; a rule for arriving at social decisions may be agreed upon for reasons of convenience and necessity without its outcomes being treated as evaluations by anyone in particular.[4] Indeed, I would go further and argue that the appropriate standpoint for analysing social decision processes is precisely that they not be welfare judgements of any particular individuals. This seems contrary to Bergson's point of view.[5] In my view, the location of welfare judgements in any individual, while logically possible, does not appear to be very interesting. 'Social welfare' is related to social policy in any sensible interpretation; the welfare judgements of any single individual are unconnected with action and therefore sterile. In a more recent paper Bergson has recognized that there may be this alternative interpretation of the concept of social welfare; I quote the passage at length since it displays the issue so well: 'I have been assuming that the concern of welfare economics is to counsel individual citizens generally. If a public official is counselled, it is on the same basis as any other citizen. In every instance reference is made to some ethical values which are appropriate for the counselling of the individual in question. In all this I believe I am only expressing the intent of welfare writings generally; or if this is not the intent, I think it should be. But some may be inclined nevertheless to a different conception, which allows still another interpretation of Arrow's theorem. *According to this view, the problem is to counsel not citizens generally but public officials.* [Emphasis added.] Furthermore, the values to be taken as data are not those which would guide the official if he were a private citizen. The official is envisaged instead as more or less neutral ethically. His one aim in life is to implement the values of other citizens as given by some rule of collective decision making'.[6] My interpretation of the social choice problem agrees fully with that given by Bergson beginning with the italicized statement, though, as can be seen, this is not the view that he himself endorses.

[4] This point has been well stressed by I. M. D. Little, 'Social Choice and Individual Values', *Journal of Political Economy*, 60 (1952), 422–32.

[5] A. Bergson, 'On the Concept of Social Welfare', *Quarterly Journal of Economics*, 68 (1954), 233–52, reprinted in *Essays in Normative Economics*, op. cit., 27–49, esp. pp. 35–6.

[6] A. Bergson, 'On the Concept of Social Welfare', op. cit., p. 242; *Essays*, op. cit., pp. 37–8.

4. SOME CONDITIONS FOR A SOCIAL DECISION PROCESS AND THE IMPOSSIBILITY THEOREM

The fundamental problem of public value formation, then, is the construction of constitutions. In general, of course, there is no difficulty in constructing a rule if one is content with arbitrary ones. The problem becomes meaningful if reasonable conditions are suggested, which every constitution should obey.[7]

I Some Conditions on Constitutions

I suggest here four conditions which seem very reasonable to impose on any constitution. More can undoubtedly be suggested but unfortunately, as we shall see in Section II below, these four more than suffice.

Recall that a constitution is a rule which assigns to any set of individual preference orderings a rule for making society's choices among alternative social actions in any possible environment. Thus, for a given set of individual orderings the result of the process is a particular value system in the sense of Part 1; that is, a rule for making selections out of all possible environments. The first condition may be termed that of: COLLECTIVE RATIONALITY: For any given set of orderings, the social choice function is derivable from an ordering.

In other words, the social choice system has the same structure as that which we have already assumed for individual value systems. The next condition is one that has been little disputed and is advanced by almost every writer in the economic literature:

PARETO PRINCIPLE: If alternative x is preferred to alternative y by every single individual according to his ordering, then the social ordering also ranks x above y.

Notice that we can use the term 'social ordering' in view of the previous condition of Collective Rationality. The next condition is perhaps the most important as well as the most controversial. For my own part, I am less tempted to regard it as ultimately satisfactory than I formerly did, but it has strong pragmatic justification:

INDEPENDENCE OF IRRELEVANT ALTERNATIVES: The social choice made from any environment depends only on the orderings of individuals with respect to the alternatives in that environment.

To take an extreme case, suppose that individuals are informed that there are a certain number of social actions available. They are not even aware that there are other conceivable social actions. They develop their own preference

---

[7] The analysis that follows is based on my book *Social Choice and Individual Values* (New York, London, and Sydney: Wiley, 1st edn. 1951; 2nd edn. 1963).

systems for the alternatives contained in this particular environment, and then the constitution generates a choice. Later they are told that in fact there were alternatives which were logically possible but were not in fact available. For example, a city is taking a poll of individual preferences on alternative methods of transportation (rapid transit, automobile, bus, etc.). Someone suggests that in evaluating these preferences they also ought to ask individual preferences for instantaneous transportation by dissolving the individual into molecules in a ray gun and reforming him elsewhere in the city as desired. There is no pretence that this method is in any way an available alternative. The assumption of Independence of Irrelevant Alternatives is that such preferences have no bearing on the choice to be made.

It is of course obvious that orindary political decision-making methods satisfy this condition. When choosing among candidates for an elected office, all that is asked are the preferences among the actual candidates, not also preferences among other individuals who are not candidates and who are not available for office.

Finally, we enunciate probably the least controversial of all the conditions: NON-DICTATORSHIP: There is no individual whose preferences are automatically society's preferences independent of the preferences of all other individuals.

There is a difference between the first two conditions and the last two which is worth noting. The assumptions of Collective Rationality and the Pareto Principle are statements which apply to any fixed set of individual orderings. They do not involve comparisons between social orderings based on different sets of individual orderings. On the contrary, the condition of Independence of Irrelevant Alternatives and of Non-Dictatorship are assertions about the responsiveness of the social ordering to variations in individual orderings.

II Impossibility Theorem

The conditions of Collective Rationality and of the Independence of Irrelevant Alternatives taken together imply that in a generalized sense all methods of social choice are of the type of voting. If we consider environments composed of two alternatives alone, then the condition of Independence of Irrelevant Alternatives tells us that the choice is determined solely by the preferences of the members of the community as between those two alternatives, and no other preferences are involved. Define a set of individuals to be *decisive* for alternative x over alternative y if the constitution prescribes that x is chosen over y whenever all individuals in the set prefer x to y and all others prefer y to x. Then the rule for choosing from any two-member environment has the form of specifying which sets of individuals are decisive for x over y and which for y over x. The majority voting principle, for example, states simply that any set containing a majority of the voters is decisive for any alternative over any other.

Then, if the social value system is generated by a social ordering, all social preferences are determined by the choices made for two-member environments, and hence by pairwise votes (thus systems like plurality voting are excluded).

Now it has been known for a long time that the system of majority voting can give rise to paradoxical consequences. Consider the following example. There are three alternatives, x, y, and z, among which choice is to be made. One-third of the voters prefer x to y and y to z, one-third prefer y to z and z to x, and one-third prefer z to x and x to y. Then x will be preferred to y by a majority, y to z by a majority, and z to x by a majority.[8]

One might be tempted to suppose that the paradox of voting is an imperfection in the particular system of majority voting, and more ingenious methods could avoid it. But unfortunately this is not so. The following general theorem may be stated:

There ean be no constitution simultaneously satisfying the conditions of Collective Rationality, the Pareto Principle, the Independence of Irrelevant Alternatives, and Non-Dictatorship.

The proof is given in the following Section III.

This conclusion is quite embarrassing, and it forces us to examine the conditions which have been stated as reasonable. It is hard to imagine anyone quarrelling either with the Pareto Principle or the condition of Non-Dictatorship. The principle of Collective Rationality may indeed be questioned. One might be prepared to allow that the choice from a given environment be dependent on the history of previous choices made in earlier environments, but I think many would find that situation unsatisfactory. There remains, therefore, only the Independence of Irrelevant Alternatives, which will be examined in greater detail in Section IV below.

III *Proof of the Impossibility Theorem*

We assume the existence of a social choice mechanism satisfying the conditions of Collective Rationality, the Pareto Principle, the Independence

---

[8] This paradox seems to have been first observed by the Marquis de Condorcet, *Essai sur l'application de l'analyse à la probabilité des décisions rendues à la pluralité des voix* (Paris, 1785). That a rational voting scheme requires knowledge of all preferences among the candidates and not only the first choice was already argued even earlier by Jean-Charles de Borda, 'Mémoire sur les élections au scrutin', *Mémoires de l'Académie Royale des Sciences* (1781), 657–65. For a modern analysis of Condorcet's work on voting, see G.-G. Granger, *La Mathématique Social du Marquis de Condorcet* (Paris: Presses Universitaires de France, 1956), esp. pp. 94–129. For an English translation of Borda's work see A. de Grazia, 'Mathematical Derivation of an Election System', *Isis*, 44 (1953), 42–51. For a general history of the theory of social choice, see D. Black, *The Theory of Committees and Elections* (Cambridge, U.K.: Cambridge University Press, 1958), Part II.

of Irrelevant Alternatives, and Non-Dictatorship, and show that the assumption leads to a contradiction. Since the condition of Collective Rationality requires that social choice be derivable from an ordering, we can speak of social preference and social indifference. In particular, as defined in the last section, a set of individuals V is *decisive* for x against y if x is socially preferred to y whenever all individuals in V prefer x to y and all others prefer y to x.[9]

The proof falls into two parts. It is first shown that if an individual is decisive for some pair of alternatives, then he is a dictator, contrary to the condition of Non-Dictatorship. Hence, no individual is decisive for any pair of alternatives, and the Impossibility Theorem itself then follows easily with the aid of the Pareto Principle.

We first distinguish one individual, called I, and introduce the following notations for statements about the constitution:

(1) $x\overline{D}y$ mean that x is socially preferred to y whenever individual I prefers x to y, regardless of the orderings of other individuals;

(2) xDy means that x is socially preferred to y if individual I prefers x to y and all other individuals prefer y to x.

Notice that this notation is legitimate only because of the assumption of Independence of Irrelevant Alternatives. Note too that the statement, $x\overline{D}y$, implies xDy and that xDy is the same as the assertion that I is a decisive set for x against y.

Suppose then that xDy holds for some x and y. We will first suppose that there are only three alternatives altogether. Let the third alternative be z. Suppose I orders the alternatives, x, y, z, in descending order, whereas all other individuals prefer y to both x and z, but may have any preferences as between the last two. Then I prefers x to y, whereas all others prefer y to x; from (2) this means that xPy. All individuals prefer y to z; by the Pareto principle, yPz. Then by transitivity, xPz; but then this holds whenever xP_iz, regardless of the orderings of other individuals as between x and z. In symbols,

(3) $$xDy \text{ implies } x\overline{D}z.$$

Again suppose xDy, but now suppose that I orders the alternatives, z, x, y, whereas all other individuals prefer both z and y to x. By a similar argument, xPy and zPx, so that zPy.

(4) $$xDy \text{ implies } z\overline{D}y.$$

[9] The following proof is quoted, with minor alterations, from Arrow, op. cit., pp. 98–100.

Interchanging y and z in (4) yields

(5) xDz implies $y\bar{D}z$.

Replacing x by y, y by z, and z by x in (3) yields

(6) yDz implies $y\bar{D}x$.

Since $x\bar{D}z$ implies xDz, and $y\bar{D}z$ implies yDz, we can, by chaining the implications (3), (5), and (6), deduce

(7) xDy implies $y\bar{D}x$.

If we interchange x and y in (3), (4), and (7), we arrive at the respective implications

$$yDx \text{ implies } y\bar{D}z,$$
$$yDx \text{ implies } z\bar{D}x,$$
$$yDx \text{ implies } x\bar{D}y,$$

and these can each be chained with the implication (7) to yield

(8) xDy implies $y\bar{D}z$, $z\bar{D}x$, and $x\bar{D}y$.

Implications (3), (4), (7), and (8) together can be summarized as saying

(9) If xDy, then $u\bar{D}v$ are for every ordered pair u, v from the three alternatives x, y, and z;

i.e., individual I is a dictator for the three alternatives.

We can extend this result to any number of alternatives by an argument due to Blau.[10] Suppose aDb holds, and let x and y be any pair of alternatives. If x and y are the same as a and b, either in the same or in the reverse order, we add a third alternative c to a and b; then we can apply (9) to the triple a, b, c and deduce $x\bar{D}y$ by letting $u = x$, $v = y$. If exactly one of x and y is distinct from a and b, add it to a and b to form a triple to which again (9) is applicable. Finally, if both x and y are distinct from a and b, two steps are needed. First, add x to a and b, and deduce from (9) that $a\bar{D}x$ and therefore aDx. Then, again applying (9) to the triple a, x, y, we find that $x\bar{D}y$. Thus, aDb for some a and b implies that $x\bar{D}y$ for all x and y, i.e., individual I is a dictator. From the Condition of Non-Dictatorship it can be concluded that

(10) xDy cannot hold for any individual I and any pair x, y.

The remainder of the proof is now an appropriate adaptation of the paradox of voting. By the Pareto Principle, there is at least one decisive set for

---

[10] J. H. Blau, 'The Existence of Social Welfare Functions', *Econometrica*, 25 (1957), 310.

any ordered pair, x, y, namely, the set of all individuals. Among all sets of individuals which are decisive for some pairwise choice, pick one such that no other is smaller; by (10) it must contain at least two individuals. Let V be the chosen set, and let the ordered pair for which it is decisive be x, y. Divide V into two parts, V_1, which contains only a single individual, and V_2, which contains all the rest. Let V_3 be the set of individuals not in V.

Consider now the case where the preference order of V_1 is x, y, z, that of all members of V_2 is z, x, y, and that of all members of V_3 is y, z, x. Since V is decisive for x against y, and all members of V prefer x to y while all others have the opposite preference xPy. On the other hand, it is impossible that society prefers z to y since that would require that V_2 be decisive on this issue; this is impossible since V_2 has fewer members than V, which, by construction, has as few members as a decisive set can have. Hence, yRz, and, since xPy, society must prefer x to z. But then the single member of V_1 would be decisive, and we have shown that to be impossible.

Thus the contradiction is established.

IV The Independence of Irrelevant Alternatives and Interpersonal Comparisons of Intensity

Modern economic theory has insisted on the ordinal concept of utility; that is, only orderings can be observed, and therefore no measurement of utility independent of these orderings has any significance. In the field of consumer's demand theory the ordinalist position turned out to create no problems; cardinal utility had no explanatory power above and beyond ordinal. Leibniz's Principle of the Identity of Indiscernibles demanded then the excision of cardinal utility from our thought patterns. Bergson's formulation of the social welfare function carried out the same principle in the analysis of social welfare. Social choices were to depend only on individual orderings; hence, welfare judgements were based only on interpersonally observable behaviour.

The condition of Independence of Irrelevant Alternatives extends the requirement of observability one step further. Given the set of alternatives available for society to choose among, it could be expected that ideally one could observe all preferences among the available alternatives, but there would be no way to observe preferences among alternatives not feasible for society.

I now feel, however, that the austerity imposed by this condition is stricter than desirable. In many situations we do have information on preferences for non-feasible alternatives. It can certainly be argued that when available this information should be used in social choice. Unfortunately, it is clear, as I have already suggested, that social decision processes which are independent of irrelevant alternatives have strong practical advantages, and it remains to be seen whether a satisfactory social decision procedure can really be based on other information.

The potential usefulness of irrelevant alternatives is that they may permit empirically meaningful interpersonal comparisons. The information which might enable us to assert that one individual prefers alternative x to alternative y more strongly than a second individual prefers y to x must be based on comparisons by the two individuals of the two alternatives, not only with respect to each other but also to other alternatives.

Let me conclude by suggesting one type of use of irrelevant alternatives, which may be termed 'extended sympathy'. We do seem prepared to make comparisons of the form: Action x is better (or worse) for me than action y is for you. This is probably in fact the standard way in which people make judgements about appropriate income distributions; if I am richer than you, I may find it easy to make the judgement that it is better for you to have the marginal dollar than for me.

How is this consistent with our general point of view that all value judgements are at least hypothetical choices among alternative actions? Interpersonal comparisons of the extended sympathy type can be put in operational form. The judgement takes the form: It is better (in my judgement) to be myself under action x than to be you under action y.

In this form the characteristics that define an individual are included in the comparison. In effect, these characteristics are put on a par with the items usually regarded as constituting an individual's wealth. The possession of tools is ordinarily regarded as part of the social state which is being evaluated; why not the possession of the skills to use those tools, and the intelligence which lies behind those skills? Individuals, in appraising each other's states of well-being, not only consider material possessions but also find themselves 'desiring this man's scope and that man's art'.[11] The principle of extended sympathy as a basis for interpersonal comparisons seems basic to many of the welfare judgements made in ordinary practice. It remains to be seen whether an adequate theory of social choice can be derived from this and other acceptable principles.

---

[11] The moral implications of the position that many attributes of the individual are similar in nature to external possessions have been discussed by V. C. Walsh, *Scarcity and Evil* (Englewood Cliffs, N.J.: Prentice-Hall, 1961).

VIII

THE IMPOSSIBILITY OF A PARETIAN LIBERAL*

1. INTRODUCTION

THE purpose of this paper is to present an impossibility result that seems to have some disturbing consequences for principles of social choice. A common objection to the method of majority decision is that it is illiberal. The argument takes the following form: Given other things in the society, if you prefer to have pink walls rather than white, then society should permit you to have this, even if a majority of the community would like to see your walls white. Similarly, whether you should sleep on your back or on your belly is a matter in which the society should permit you absolute freedom, even if a majority of the community is nosey enough to feel that you must sleep on your back. We formalize this concept of individual liberty in an extremely weak form and examine its consequences.

2. THE THEOREM

Let R_i be the ordering of the ith individual over the set X of all possible social states, each social state being a complete description of society including every individual's position in it. There are n individuals. Let R be the social preference relation that is to be determined.

From the *Journal of Political Economy*, vol. 78 (1970), pp. 152–7. For references to discussion arising from this paper, see A. K. Sen, 'Liberty, Unanimity and Rights', *Economica*, 43 (1976), pp. 217–45, where the topic is resumed.

*For comments and criticisms I am grateful to Kenneth Arrow, Peter Diamond, Milton Friedman, Tapas Majumdar, Stephen Marglin, and Thomas Schelling.

DEFINITION 1: *A collective choice rule* is a functional relationship that specifies one and only one social preference relation R for any set of n individual orderings (one ordering for each individual).

A special case of a collective choice rule is one that Arrow (1951) calls a social welfare function, namely, a rule such that R must be an ordering.

DEFINITION 2: *A social welfare function* is a collective choice rule, the range of which is restricted to orderings.

A weaker requirement is that each R should generate a 'choice function', that is, in every subset of alternatives there must be a 'best' alternative, or, in other words, there must be some (but not necessarily only one) alternative that is at least as good as all the other alternatives in that subset. This may be called a 'social decision function'.

DEFINITION 3: *A social decision function* is a collective choice rule, the range of which is restricted to social preference relations that generate a choice function.

It was shown in Sen (1969) that the conditions that were proven to be inconsistent by Arrow (1951, 1963) in his justly famous 'impossibility theorem' in the context of a social welfare function are in fact perfectly consistent if imposed on a social decision function. The impossibility theorem to be presented here holds, however, for social decision functions as well.

Arrow's condition of collective rationality (Condition 1') can be seen to be merely a requirement that the domain of the collective choice rule should not be arbitrarily restricted.

CONDITION U (Unrestricted Domain): Every logically possible set of individual orderings is included in the domain of the collective choice rule.

Arrow used a weak version of the Pareto principle.

CONDITION P: If every individual prefers any alternative x to another alternative y, then society must prefer x to y.

Finally, we introduce the condition of individual liberty in a very weak form.

CONDITION L (Liberalism): For each individual i, there is at least one pair of alternatives, say (x, y), such that if this individual prefers x to y, then society should prefer x to y, and if this individual prefers y to x, then society should prefer y to x.[1]

---

[1] The term 'liberalism' is elusive and is open to alternative interpretations. Some uses of the term may not embrace the condition defined here, while many uses will. I do not wish to engage in a debate on the right use of the term. What is relevant is that Condition L represents a value involving individual liberty that many people would subscribe to. Whether such people are best described as liberals is a question that is not crucial to the point of this paper.

The intention is to permit each individual the freedom to determine at least one social choice, for example, having his own walls pink rather than white, other things remaining the same for him and the rest of the society.[2]

The following impossibility theorem holds.

THEOREM I: There is no social decision function that can simultaneously satisfy Conditions U, P, and L.

In fact, we can weaken the condition of liberalism further. Such freedom may not be given at all, but to a proper subset of individuals. However, to make sense the subset must have more than one member, since if it includes only one then we might have a dictatorship. Hence, we demand such freedom for at least two individuals.

CONDITION L^* (Minimal Liberalism): There are at least two individuals such that for each of them there is at least one pair of alternatives over which he is decisive, that is, there is a pair of x, y, such that if he prefers x (respectively y) to y (respectively x), then society should prefer x (respectively y) to y (respectively x).

The following theorem is stronger than Theorem I and subsumes it.

THEOREM II: There is no social decision function that can simultaneously satisfy Conditions U, P, and L^*.

PROOF: Let the two individuals referred to in Condition L^* be 1 and 2, respectively, and the two pairs of alternatives referred to be (x, y) and (z, w), respectively. If (x, y) and (z, w) are the same pair of alternatives, then there is a contradiction. They have, therefore, at most one alternative in common, say $x = z$. Assume now that person 1 prefers x to y, and person 2 prefers w to $z (= x)$. And let everyone in the community including 1 and 2 prefer y to w. There is in this no inconsistency for anyone, not even for 1 and 2, and their respective orderings are: 1 prefers x to y and y to w, while 2 prefers y to w and w to x. By Condition U this should be in the domain of the social decision mechanism. But by Condition L^*, x must be preferred to y, and w must be preferred to $x (= z)$, while by the Pareto principle, y must be preferred to w. Thus, there is no best element in the set $(x = z, y, w)$ in terms of social preference, and every alternative is worse than some other. A choice function for the society does not therefore exist.

---

[2] Even this informal statement, which sounds mild, is much more demanding than Condition L. If the individual's preference over a personal choice (like choosing the colour of his wall) is to be accepted by the society, other things remaining the same, then this gives the individual rights not only over one pair, which is all that is required by Condition L, but over many pairs (possibly an infinite number of pairs) varying with the 'other things'. If it is socially all right for me to have my walls either pink or white as I like in a social state where you smoke cigars, it should be socially all right for me to do the same where you indulge yourself in ways other than smoking cigars. Even this is not required by Condition L, which seems to demand very little.

Next, let x, y, z, and w, be all distinct. Let 1 prefer x to y, and 2 prefer z to w. And let everyone in the community including 1 and 2 prefer w to x and y to z. There is no contradiction for 1 or 2, for 1 simply prefers w to x, x to y, and y to z, while 2 prefers y to z, z to w, and w to x. By Condition U this configuration of individual preferences must yield a social choice function. But by Condition L^* society should prefer x to y and z to w, while by the Pareto principle society must prefer w to x, and y to z. This means that there is no best alternative for this set, and a choice function does not exist for any set that includes these four alternatives. Thus, there is no social decision function satisfying Conditions U, P, and L^*, and the proof is complete.[3]

3. AN EXAMPLE

We give now a simple example of the type of impossibility that is involved in Theorem II by taking a special case of two individuals and three alternatives. There is one copy of a certain book, say *Lady Chatterley's Lover*, which is viewed differently by 1 and 2. The three alternatives are: that individual 1 reads it (x), that individual 2 reads it (y), and that no one reads it (z). Person 1, who is a prude, prefers most that no one reads it, but given the choice between either of the two reading it, he would prefer that he read it himself rather than exposing gullible Mr. 2 to the influences of Lawrence. (Prudes, I am told, tend to prefer to be censors rather than being censored.) In decreasing order of preference, his ranking is z, x, y. Person 2, however, prefers that either of them should read it rather than neither. Furthermore, he takes delight in the thought that prudish Mr. 1 may have to read Lawrence, and his first preference is that person 1 should read it, next best that he himself should read it, and worst that neither should. His ranking is, therefore, x, y, z.

Now if the choice is precisely between the pair (x, z), i.e., between person 1 reading the book and no one reading it, someone with liberal values may argue that it is person 1's preference that should count; since the prude would not like to read it, he should not be forced to. Thus, the society should prefer z to x. Similarly, in the choice exactly between person 2 reading the book (y) and no one reading it (z), liberal values require that person 2's preference should be decisive, and since he is clearly anxious to read the book he should

[3] We can strengthen this theorem further by weakening Condition L^* by demanding only that 1 be decisive for x against y, but not vice versa, and 2 be decisive for z against w, but not vice versa, and require that $x \neq z$, and $y \neq w$. This condition, too, can be shown to be inconsistent with Condition U and P, but the logical gain involved in this extension does not, alas, seem to be associated with any significant increase of relevance that I can think of.

be permitted to do this. Hence y should be judged socially better than z. Thus, in terms of liberal values it is better that no one reads it rather than person 1 being forced to read it, and it is still better that person 2 is permitted to read the book rather than no one reading it. That is, the society should prefer y to z, and z to x. This discourse could end happily with the book being handed over to person 2 but for the fact that it is a Pareto inferior alternative, being worse than person 1 reading it, in the view of both persons, i.e., x is Pareto superior to y.

Every solution that we can think of is bettered by some other solution, given the Pareto principle and the principle of liberalism, and we seem to have an inconsistency of choice. This is an example of the type of problem that is involved in Theorems I and II.

4. RELEVANCE

The dilemma posed here may appear to be somewhat disturbing. It is, of course, not necessarily disturbing for every conceivable society, since the conflict arises with only particular configurations of individual preferences. The ultimate guarantee for individual liberty may rest not on rules for social choice but on developing individual values that respect each other's personal choices. The conflict posed here is concerned with societies where such a condition does not hold and where pairwise choice based on liberal values may conflict with those based on the Pareto principle. Like Arrow's 'General Possibility Thoerem', here also the Condition of Unrestricted Domain is used.

However, unlike in the theorem of Arrow, we have not required transitivity of social preference. We have required neither transitivity of strict preference, nor transitivity of social preference. We have required neither transitivity of strict preference, nor transitivity of indifference, but merely the existence of a best alternative in each choice situation.[4] Suppose society prefers x to y, and y to z, and is indifferent between z and x. Arrow would rule this out, since there is an intransitivity; but we do not, for here alternative x is

---

[4] It may appear that one way of solving this dilemma is to dispense with the social choice function based on a binary relation, that is, to relax not merely transitivity but also *acyclicity*. A choice function that need not correspond to any binary relation has undoubtedly a wider scope. But then Condition P and Condition L would have to be redefined, for example, (1) x should not be chosen when y is available, if everyone prefers y to x, and (2) for each individual there is a pair (x_i, y_i) such that if he prefers x_i (respectively y_i) to y_i (respectively x_i), then y_i (respectively x_i) should not be chosen if x_i (respectively y_i) is available. Thus redefined, the choice set for the set of alternatives may be rendered empty even without bringing in acyclicity, and the contradiction will reappear. This and other possible 'ways out' are discussed more fully in my forthcoming book (Sen, 1970, chap. 6).

'best' in the sense of being at least as good as both the other alternatives. Our requirements are, in this respect, very mild, and we still have an impossibility.

Second, we have not imposed Arrow's much debated condition of 'the independence of irrelevant alternatives'.[5] Many people find the relaxation of this condition to be an appealing way of escaping the Arrow dilemma. This way out is not open here, for the theorem holds without imposing this condition.

The Pareto principle is used here in a very weak version, as in Arrow. We do not necessarily require that if someone prefers x to y and everyone regards x to be at least as good as y, then x is socially better. We permit the possibility of having collective choice rules that will violate this provided everyone strictly preferring x to y must make x socially better than y.

Nevertheless it turns out that a principle reflecting liberal values even in a very mild form cannot possibly be combined with the weak Pareto principle, given an unrestricted domain. If we do believe in these other conditions, then the society cannot permit even minimal liberalism. Society cannot then let more than one individual be free to read what they like, sleep the way they prefer, dress as they care to, etc., *irrespective* of the preferences of others in the community.

What is the moral? It is that in a very basic sense liberal values conflict with the Pareto principle. If someone takes the Pareto principle seriously, as economists seem to do, then he has to face problems of consistency in cherishing liberal values, even very mild ones.[6] Or, to look at it in another way, if someone does have certain liberal values, then he may have to eschew his adherence to Pareto optimality. While the Pareto criterion has been thought to be an expression of individual liberty, it appears that in choices involving more than two alternatives it can have consequences that are, in fact, deeply illiberal.

---

[5] Using the condition of the independence of irrelevant alternatives, A. Gibbard, in an unpublished paper, has recently proved the following important theorem: Any social decision function that must generate social preferences that are all transitive in the strict relation (quasi-transitive) and which must satisfy Conditions U, P, non-dictatorship, and the independence of irrelevant alternatives, must be an oligarchy in the sense that there is a unique group of individuals each of whom, by preferring x to y, can make the society regard x to be at least as good as y, and by all preferring x to y can make the society prefer x to y, irrespective of the preferences of those who are not in this group. Gibbard's Theorem is disturbing, for the conditions look appealing but the resultant oligarchy seems revolting, and it is a major extension of the problem posed by Arrow (1951, 1963). Gibbard argues against the simultaneous insistence on a binary relation of social preference generating a choice function and on the condition of the independence of irrelevant alternatives. We have no imposed the latter.

[6] The difficulties of *achieving* Pareto optimality in the presence of externalities are well known. What is at issue here is the *acceptability* of Pareto optimality as an objective in the context of liberal values, given certain types of externalities.

REFERENCES

ARROW, K. J., *Individual Values and Social Choice* (New York: Wiley, 1951; 2nd edn., 1963).

SEN, A. K., 'Quasi-transitivity, Rational Choice and Collective Decisions', Discussion paper no. 45, Harvard Institute of Economic Research 1968. *Rev. Econ. Studies*, 36, no. 3 (July 1969): 381–93.

——, *Collective Choice and Social Welfare* (San Francisco: Holden-Day; and Edinburgh: Oliver & Boyd, 1970).

IX

DISTRIBUTIVE JUSTICE, WELFARE ECONOMICS, AND THE THEORY OF FAIRNESS*

HAL R. VARIAN

ROBERT NOZICK'S recent article 'Distributive Justice' contains a pro-
vocative discussion of the meaning of justice.[1] A central point is his
distinction between 'historical' and 'end-state' principles, the idea being that
certain approaches to distributive justice, such as Rawls's approach and the
approach of welfare economics (what Arrow calls ordinal utilitarianism),
have concentrated on evaluating only 'current time-slices' of a distribution
and have not focused on the procedural aspects of distributive justice.

Nozick has done us a great service by describing an alternative to these
'end-state' theories of justice; for certainly *some* of our moral intuitions
about justice depend not only on the current description of a distribution but
also on how the distribution came to be. Thus discussions of the issues of
procedural justice should certainly spread some light on the questions of
distributive justice. Indeed they do; Nozick's article has—at least for me—
clarified some of the important interrelationships among the concepts of
justice, individual rights, liberty, and so on. Nevertheless, I do not entirely
agree with his analysis.

My objective here is threefold: (1) to question some of Nozick's arguments
and assumptions; (2) to clarify some of the results of welfare economics to
which Nozick refers; and (3) to present yet another theory of distributive
justice, which I believe is novel, interesting, and distinct from previous
theories.

From *Philosophy and Public Affairs*, vol. 4 (1974–5), pp. 223–47.

* I would like to acknowledge the helpful comments made on this paper by Lester Thurow,
Robert Nozick, and Susan Foster. I also wish to thank the editors of *Philosophy & Public Affairs* for
aid in clarifying the exposition of the economic issues and for valuable editorial assistance.

[1] *Philosophy & Public Affairs* 3, no. 1 (Fall 1973): 45–126.

THE ENTITLEMENT THEORY

Nozick's meta-ethical remarks imply that a valid theory of justice must include three parts: a description of how people legitimately acquire holdings, a description of how people legitimately transfer holdings, and a description of how past injustices should be rectified (pp. 46–9). He makes the following specification: 'A distribution is just if it arises from another (just) distribution by legitimate means' (p. 47). Nozick's theory is a procedural theory; the justice of a distribution is entirely dependent on the path used to reach it: 'Justice in holdings is historical; it depends on what actually has happened' (p. 48). Most of Nozick's article is devoted to justifying this *form* of a theory of justice; he sees this form in opposition to that of welfare economics and Rawls's theory, which, he argues, are basically ahistorical in that they examine only a current time-slice of a distribution.

Nozick hesitates to describe a specific theory:

To turn these general outlines into a specific theory we would have to specify the details of each of the three principles of justice in holdings: the principle of acquisition of holdings, the principle of transfer of holdings, and the principle of rectification of violations of the first two principles. I shall not attempt that task here (p. 49).

But despite this disclaimer, Nozick *does* attempt the task of describing what he believes are reasonable principles of acquisition, transfer, and rectification, as indeed he must. For we can always put any end-state principle into Nozick's form: we determine the desired distribution according to an end-state criterion and then rule that agents can only acquire or transfer holdings if doing so leads to the desired distribution. But Nozick rightly rejects this trick (p. 53). He devotes a considerable amount of space to examples of what he believes would be acceptable rules of acquisition, transfer, and rectification. The primary principle he uses in choosing acceptable rules is that the chosen rules should not violate agents' rights. Nozick's theory of rights is discussed at length elsewhere.[2]

Let us begin with rectification. How *are* we to rectify an unjust distribution? Nozick's answer goes something like this: if an injustice has occurred, we must determine what the expected outcome would be if that injustice had not occurred; in case of ties we can then perhaps use end-state principles to resolve which of these expected outcomes to choose.

As an example, consider Table 1. Let us suppose that some injustice occurred in the past and that if the injustice had not occurred, the three listed allocations had the various listed probabilities of occurring today. (All other allocations have zero probability of occurring.) But because of the effect of the injustice, the actual distribution today is something else. Nozick suggests

[2] Robert Nozick, *Anarchy, State, and Utopia* (New York, 1974).

that we rectify the past injustice by redistributing today's allocation according to a weighted average of the allocations in the other possible states. This distribution is also listed in Table 1; it is constructed by multiplying each possible allocation by the probability of its occurrence and then adding all these numbers together.

TABLE 1

| | Possible allocations | | | |
| | 1 | 2 | 3 | Weighted average |
Probability	$p = 0.2$	$p = 0.3$	$p = 0.5$	
Agent 1	5	1	6	4.3
Agent 2	0	3	0	0.9
Agent 3	5	6	4	4.8

I find the idea of this weighted average somewhat at odds with Nozick's explicitly historical theory. If the justice of an end-state is really so dependent on the historical process used to reach it, isn't a more reasonable choice the distribution that has the greatest probability of actually having occurred? In the example described above, the weighted-average distribution actually has zero probability of having arisen from some historical process, while distribution three is likely to have actually arisen. In any probability distribution where extreme distributions of wealth or income are likely, the weighted average will often be very different from the most likely allocation.[3] One can well argue that the private ownership, *laissez-faire* society Nozick describes does indeed tend to generate extreme distributions of wealth; thus the problem of choosing the most likely allocation or the weighted-average allocation in rectification becomes rather serious.

It seems to me that the weighted-average allocation *really is* a more reasonable way to rectify, the primary reason being that it takes into account the whole range of possible outcomes in a way that the most likely allocation does not. The expected value—i.e. the weighted average—is after all a measure of central tendency. The case depicted in Table 1 has two rather extreme allocations as possible outcomes, and the expected value tends to choose an intermediate allocation. But it also seems that the most likely

[3] Only in the case of a symmetric, unimodal probability distribution will the expected value and the mode (maximum probability point) coincide.

allocation is more consistent with the historical approach Nozick describes. If the justice of a particular allocation depends on what actually happened, then one allocation should be more just than another if it is more likely to occur. One cannot say this is a logical inconsistency in Nozick's theory. After all, the principles of rectification are presumably independent of the other principles. But if the historical process is so important to the justice of an end-state, it seems peculiar to have a rectification procedure that can pick a rectifying allocation which is actually unlikely to occur.

I think that Nozick is led to this position precisely because the extreme historical approach he advocates is incompatible with some of our moral intuitions of justice. Of course, how an allocation was reached has *something* to do with justice; but it is just not the whole story. This becomes clearer when we consider processes that include large random elements. Here we may start the process with an equal distribution and let legitimate transfers lead us to new allocations; but the large random component—acts of God, depressions, accumulation of fortunes that may be transferred to new generations—may very well move the society to an unequal final allocation. One might well argue that the role of the state in such a situation is to avoid such distortions. Nozick chides Rawls for worrying about the fact that natural assets are distributed randomly; however, he himself proposes no mechanism to correct for any kind of randomness. If a process can be radically affected by turns of fortune that are arbitrary from a moral point of view, it seems unreasonable to attach great moral significance to the outcome of such a process.

The impression one gets from reading Nozick is that the problem of rectification is somehow minor. It seems to me that the reverse is the case: the problem of rectification is central to the issue of justice. We are interested in the question of justice precisely because we live in an unjust world; injustices have occurred in the past and are occurring now. The question is what should we do about them. Proponents of end-state principles, such as Rawls, are attempting to answer this question: we decide what a perfectly just state is and then try to move toward it.

HISTORICAL PRINCIPLES AND END-STATE PRINCIPLES

As a justification for his consideration of historical facts in evaluating distributional equity, Nozick points out that

most persons do not accept current time-slice principles as constituting the whole story about distributive shares. They think it relevant in assessing the justice of a situation to consider not only the distribution it embodies, but also how that distribution came about.... We think it relevant to ask whether someone did something so that he ... deserved to have a lower share (p. 50).

Nozick is perfectly correct here; naïve theories of justice that provide for a fixed social product to be divided without regard for those who contributed to the formation of that product ignore the most difficult and important problem of formalizing our notions of justice.

At some points Nozick interprets 'how the distribution came about' in the explicit sense of how the patterns of production were arranged. Thus he criticizes Rawls's theory and welfare economics for ignoring the interaction of production and distribution:

> To think that the task of a theory of distributive justice is to fill the blank in 'to each according to his ——' is to be predisposed to search for a pattern; and the separate treatment of 'from each according to his ——' treats production and distribution as two separate and independent issues. On the entitlement view these are *not* two separate questions (p. 56).

This is a peculiar criticism; both Rawls and welfare economics devote very careful consideration to the interaction of production and distribution. The whole point of the difference principle in Rawls is to take account of production; welfare economics deals explicitly with production, as I will next discuss.

WELFARE ECONOMICS

Because several points I want to make subsequently depend on some of the basic concepts and results of welfare economics, a summary of a few of these ideas will be of use here. It also, I hope, will be of independent interest, since I believe these concepts and results to be crucial to any discussion of distributional issues.

Suppose that we have a set of economic agents—producers and consumers—and that the consumers have some *initial endowments* of goods. The definition of goods considered here is very broad—we can think of goods as being indexed by time, location, or state of the world, and in particular we can consider the consumer's original endowment of his own labour time as being one of his goods. Since one agent's labour is different from another's, we often think of each agent's labour as being a separate good. If we want to be very simple-minded about it, we can think instead that there is only one kind of 'labour power': 'able' agents are endowed with a lot of this labour power, and 'unable' agents with only a little. Given the possible models of production available, there will be some set of *feasible allocations*, that is, a set of descriptions of how much of each good each agent consumes, how much each agent works, and how much each producer produces. The set of feasible allocations is just the set of all *possible* allocations; this of course includes all possible redistributions of the intial endowments.

A simply story may clarify the concepts here. We consider a group of agents who each morning take to the town market their bundles of goods, which we can think of as farm produce—carrots, eggs, tomatoes, and so on. In particular, one element of each agent's bundle is his available labour time for that day. During the day agents may produce new goods and transfer these and the old goods among themselves in various ways, not necessarily voluntarily. For example, one agent could appropriate all of the other agents' goods, or the agents could vote on a way to divide up the goods, or whatever. However they decide to divide the goods, it must be a feasible way in that the total amount of each good must be equal to the total amount started with plus the amount produced minus the amount used up in production. The set of all such allocations—the set of all possible ways of dividing the goods—is called the set of *feasible allocations*. Thus a particular feasible allocation is simply a description of what each agent takes with him in the evening, when he returns home from the town market.

The basic problem of welfare economics—and of course the basic problem of distributive justice—is to determine at which feasible allocation the economy *should* operate, i.e. what bundles each agent should be allowed to take home. One very weak criterion that has been proposed is that of pareto efficiency: an allocation is defined as being pareto efficient if and only if there is no feasible allocation where *all* agents are at least as well off and some agents are strictly better off. (I will often abbreviate this clumsy condition and say '... where all agents are better off'.) An equivalent way of stating the definition is that at a pareto efficient allocation there is no way to make some one agent better off without making some other agent worse off.

As it stands, the criterion of pareto efficiency is certainly reasonable: if there is some way to make everyone better off, why not do it? Unfortunately, it is a weak criterion. For example, the allocation where one agent gets everything is pareto efficient. Why? Because the only way we can make one of the 'slaves' better off is to take something away from the 'privileged' agent—there is no way to make *everyone* better off.

Even though we may choose to limit ourselves to pareto efficient allocations, there is still a large set of allocations to choose from. The basic idea of welfare economics is to assume that there is a welfare function which evaluates the 'goodness' of the social states as a function of the utility evaluations of those states by the agents in the society. Thus every welfare function is of the form $W(u_1(x_1), u_2(x_2), \ldots, u_n(x_n))$, where u_i is the utility function of the ith agent and x_i is a description of the consumption–labour bundle of the ith agent. The important restriction is that W depends only on the utility evaluations of each individual's bundle and not directly on the bundle itself. Of course, we also require that a welfare function depends on these utilities in a positive way: if the utility of any agent increases and no agent's utility declines, we want the value of the welfare function to increase. The classic utilitarian welfare function, $\sum U_i(x_i)$ is of course a very special case of a function of this form. Nevertheless, for any function of this form, one can show that if we choose a feasible allocation of maximum welfare, it must necessarily be a pareto efficient allocation. Hence, the choice of a welfare function 'solves' the problem of choosing a best pareto efficient point. The proof is very simple. Suppose x is a feasible allocation that maximizes some *specific* welfare function $W(u_1(x_1)\ldots u_n(x_n))$. Suppose x were not pareto efficient; then by definition there is some feasible allocation y such that $u_i(y_i)$ is greater than $u_i(x_i)$ for all agents i. Since a welfare function is required to be increasing in all of its arguments, this implies $W(u_1(y_1)\ldots u_n(y_n))$ must be greater than $W(u_1(x_1)\ldots u_n(x_n))$, which is a contradiction.

There is a completely different way to choose an allocation at which the economy can operate; namely to use the market mechanism. That is, we assume that a market forms with well-defined prices and each agent takes these prices as being outside of his control and does the best he can under this constraint—that is, each consumer tries to purchase the best bundle he can afford given the value of his initial endowment, and each producer attempts to maximize profits at the going prices. If these prices are such that supply equals demand in all markets, this mechanism determines a well-defined allocation called a *market equilibrium*.[4]

The prices paid for the various goods are not arbitrary; one can show that the hypotheses presented above imply, loosely speaking, that the 'factors of production' will be paid their 'marginal product'. That is, the wage rate of one unit of a certain kind of labour will be equal to the difference between the value of the output produced using the total labour used by a profit-maximizing firm minus the value of output produced using one less unit of that kind of labour. Similarly, the owner of a particular plot of land or the owners of capital equipment will be paid according to the marginal contribution of their product to the production process. Hence, each factor will be paid according to its *marginal contribution* to the value of the output.

There are two important facts about this concept of marginal product that are often misunderstood. First, only the *price* of a factor of production is determined by its marginal product; the rewards reaped by an owner of this factor depend on how much of that factor he owns, i.e. on his *initial endowment* of that factor. An agent's *net* reward, his income, is the product of the price of the goods and labour he holds and the *amount* of his endowment of those goods and labour.

---

[4] Such a market-clearing price-system will generally exist; see K. Arrow and F. Hahn, *General Competitive Analysis* (San Francisco, 1972), chap. 2.

Second, the marginal product of a factor itself will in general depend on the level of output and on the initial distribution of endowments. Thus to think of the market mechanism as 'solving' the distribution problem by itself is unreasonable. The market distribution depends completely on the initial distribution of resources in the economy. How is *that* distribution to be determined?

Let us restate this crucial point in terms of the simple story we discussed earlier. We now imagine that the agents use a *particular* method of determining a final allocation; namely, the market mechanism described above. The prices of the items they sell on the market will depend in general on the available supplies and demands for the goods, and the value of each agent's final bundle of goods will depend, of course, on the value of his initial bundle of goods. The market mechanism will determine a *particular* allocation that depends very much on the pattern of initial endowments.

Thus when Nozick describes a *laissez-faire* world, in which each agent is paid his 'marginal product', and asks what is the role of a theory of justice here (pp. 82–3) we can well answer: in the determination of the initial endowment—*for the market equilibrium is completely indeterminate until it has been specified who owns what in the beginning.*

Now that the appropriate concepts have been defined I can present the two main results of welfare economics.[5]

Proposition A

The outcome of the market mechanism as previously described—the market equilibrium—will, under very general assumptions, be a pareto efficient allocation.

Thus the *laissez-faire* economy described above generally will operate in an efficient manner; however, there is no other ethical content to this result. If, for example, the initial endowment gives one agent everything, the market equilibrium from this endowment will also give this agent everything. There is nothing *just* about that.

Proposition B

Under somewhat more restrictive assumptions, one can show that every pareto efficient allocation is a market equilibrium for some initial endowment of goods.

Since the pareto efficient allocations are precisely those that maximize *some* welfare function of the form discussed earlier, we can restate this result as:

[5] For a detailed discussion, see A. Bergson, 'A Reformulation of Certain Aspects of Welfare Economics', *Readings in Welfare Economics*, ed. K. Arrow and T. Scitovsky (Homewood, Ill., 1969); A. Lerner, *Economics of Control* (New York, 1970); and Arrow and Hahn, *General Competitive Analysis*.

Proposition B'

If an allocation is a point of maximum welfare of some particular welfare function, it can be achieved by a suitable reallocation of endowments followed by trading to a market equilibrium.

This theorem is considerably deeper; the point is that the market mechanism can be used to support whatever efficient allocation society wishes. It can therefore serve as a 'self-correcting' distribution mechanism, once the initial endowments are determined. This result inspired the school of market socialists such as Lange and Lerner, who argued that the appropriate way for a socialist society to handle the immense task of allocating efficiently all goods to both consumption and production activities was to allow the *laissez-faire* market to do the allocation, while the government worried only about ensuring a just distribution of initial endowments (wealth). In this way the socialist state could be assured of efficient operation no matter what the desired distribution was.

When Nozick remarks that 'the socialist society would have to forbid capitalist acts between consenting adults' (p. 59), he is implicitly assuming that the socialist society must be operating in a pareto inefficient manner. For if the society were pareto efficient, no such trades would be possible because they would contradict the assumption of pareto efficiency. If the goal of the socialist society were pareto efficient use of resources, there would be no need to forbid agents to use the resources in any way they saw fit. As Lerner puts it: 'The fundamental aim of socialism is not the abolition of private property, but the extension of democracy' (p. 1).

At first glance this kind of market socialism seems quite feasible; however, some further thought shows some problems in the concept of redistribution of endowments. Recall that a description of an agent's endowment includes a description of how much labour he has; a reallocation of endowments may well involve giving some agent control over some other agent's labour—in a word, reallocation of endowments may well involve slavery. (Compare to Nozick: 'This process . . . makes them a *part owner* of you; it gives them a property right in you' (pp. 68–9).)

Now the situation is not quite as bad as all that; one could also reallocate money just as well, i.e. impose a lump-sum tax on initial endowments and redistribute the proceeds. After all, we are assuming that an agent's choice set is described by the set of bundles he can *afford*, the set of bundles whose value is less than or equal to the value of his endowment. We can change this choice set by changing *what* he has to sell, or merely by transferring money to begin with.

This lump-sum tax must be a tax on *endowments*—not a tax on what an agent actually sells. In particular, when we tax an agent's labour, we tax his whole endowment of labour. Thus agents may find a tax bill waiting for them before they even begin to trade; they will then be forced to work to get the money necessary to pay the bill. In the market equilibrium it matters not at all whether an agent works to pay his taxes, which are then transferred to another agent, or whether at the outset the other agent owns some part of the first agent's labour power.

Of course the lump-sum taxation scheme is almost as impractical as the slavery scheme. The main problem is one of information: different agents have different kinds of labour. To be rather one-dimensional: different agents have different abilities. Thus to determine the lump-sum tax, one needs to determine with how much labour power each agent is endowed. The lump-sum tax would therefore be based on *ability*, as opposed to the normal sort of tax based on value of labour sold, i.e. an income tax.

To determine an agent's ability may be difficult, so difficult that no one takes this lump-sum tax very seriously. The common practice of re-distribution via an income tax of course distorts relative prices and produces an inefficient outcome—by placing a tax on labour sold, one encourages people to sell less labour and thus to produce less total output. It should be emphasized that even though the result of an income tax may be *inefficient*— in that there is some way to make everyone better off—it still may be better in terms of general social welfare than no tax. Even though there may be some way that everyone can be made better off, the information is not available to determine how to do it.

Nevertheless, there is a large part of agents' endowments that is not labour but consts instead of physical wealth—primarily land and capital. After all, in a capitalist society, every factor of production is owned by someone and the payments to each factor contribute to the incomes of agents. Even if we allow only the reallocation of physical wealth, we could still achieve a sizeable number of different pareto efficient allocations. Such a scheme is discussed later under the name 'people's capitalism'; it could just as well be called 'market socialism'.

It should be emphasized that both of the propositions of welfare economics follow from a simple and unrealistic model of economic activity. If the assumptions of the model are violated, the propositions need not be true. In particular, if agents do not take prices as given, but instead take into account their influence on the market price—that is, act as monopolists—the resulting equilibrium need not be pareto efficient. In other words, there will be in general some way to make both the consumers of the monopolist's product *and* the monopolist better off. Thus when Nozick says, 'But an entitlement theorist would find acceptable whatever distribution resulted from the party's voluntary exchanges' (p. 84), he leaves himself open to the charge that without some restrictions on the way agents behave, i.e. through antitrust legislation or whatever, his system of voluntary exchanges may result in an allocation that is pareto *inefficient*.

The outcome of this discussion of welfare economics is as follows: yes, the market (if it works) leads to efficient allocations where each agent is paid his marginal product; however, each agent's total earnings depend crucially on his initial endowment of factors. Thus the resulting allocation need have no particular significance with respect to a measure of welfare. However, one can further assert that any welfare-maximizing (and thus pareto efficient) allocation can be supported by a market mechanism, after endowments have been suitably redistributed.

THE QUESTION OF ENDOWMENTS

The above discussion shows that the naïve notions of *laissez-faire* economics do not take us very far in determining what a just allocation of goods (and labour) should be. Thus when Nozick says: 'From each as they choose, to each as they are chosen', we might well reply: 'Fine, but how are the initial endowments of agents to be determined?'

As far as I can tell, Nozick's discussion of this issue is contained almost entirely in the sections entitled 'Locke's Theory of Acquisition' and 'The Proviso'. Our previous discussion of the workings of the free market and welfare economics indicates how crucial this question of acquiring initial endowments is. For the theorems of welfare economics show that a certain *end-state principle*—that of maximum social welfare—can be supported by a certain *procedure*—the use of the market mechanism. In this sense the 'historical' and the 'end-state' need not be in contradiction. The question that is left open, of course, is that of the original endowments of consumption goods and of the factors of production.

Nozick begins the discussion by considering Locke's view that one acquires property rights in an unowned object by 'mixing his labour with it'; however, he soon rejects this theory: 'No workable or coherent value-added property scheme has yet been devised, and any such scheme presumably would fall to objections . . .' (pp. 71–2). He then goes on to present his own view that nearly *any* appropriation is legitimate so long as it 'does not worsen the situation of others' in the sense that they can still use freely the same things that they previously could (p. 75).

Nozick then considers an immediate objection to this: eventually nearly all *valuable* things become owned (almost by definition) and the unfortunate people who are born at this late date have nothing left to appropriate while the descendants of the original appropriators live in unearned wealth. The system of appropriation of anything that is unowned seems rather vacuous when virtually nothing is unowned. When we couple this with the historical fact that little has been unowned for the last few hundred years (at least) and that most 'property rights' held today can trace their lineage back to forceful (presumably illegitimate) appropriation, one wonders again at the workability of Nozick's theory. Are we supposed to trace back ownership of American land to the Indians and then try to rectify the wrongful appropriation of it by the methods Nozick discusses?

Furthermore, Nozick's theory that the current distribution of wealth should depend on initial endowments of wealth randomly determined centuries ago seems totally unacceptable. For if the initial endowments really are random from the moral point of view, depending as they do on historical accidents, how can one base a theory of justice on such a foundation? (The similarity with my remarks on rectification should be apparent.) It is not enough even to distribute wealth equally in the first generation; for if we adopt a principle of equal distribution, why should we discriminate among generations? If we desire equality of endowments it seems that we should demand an equal distribution of wealth *each generation*.

Of course, Nozick does not necessarily want equality of endowments; his suggestions for a principle of acquisition allow virtually any kind of acquisition that 'does not worsen the situation of others'. The problem, as Nozick well realizes, lies in the choice of the baseline against which we make our comparison: 'Lockean appropriation makes people no worse off than they would be *how*?' (p. 74).

Am I worse off now because of the existence of private property? Does private property itself fall afoul of the Lockean proviso? 'Is the situation of persons who are unable to appropriate (there being no more accessible and useful unowned objects) worsened by a system allowing appropriation and permanent property?' (p. 73).

Nozick's answer to this question is a brief defence of the market mechanism: 'Here enter the various familiar social considerations favouring private property: it increases the social product by putting means of production in the hands of those who can use them most efficiently (profitably); experimentation is encouraged, because with separate persons controlling resources, there is no one person, or small group whom someone with a new idea must convince to try it out; . . '.

But what does this have to do with the question of *permanent* property? Suppose we considered a scheme of the type where the ownership of the factors of production was indeed private, but this ownership was non-transferable except through the market and reverted to the state upon death to be redistributed equally to new generations. This 'people's capitalism' still has the above desirable characteristics of encouraging efficiency and innovation, without any notion of *permanent*, inheritable, property.

'. . . Private property enables people to decide on the patterns and types of risks they wish to bear, leading to specialized types of risk bearing; . . '.

Arguments concerning risk bearing are often used to show that production should be centralized: by the virtue of the Law of Large Numbers, the larger an organization is, the better equipped it is to pool risks. Several economists have argued that, for example, government-owned electrical power plants are more innovative techologically than privately owned plants because mistakes made in one plant are outweighed by successes in another plant. A private firm can afford only one shot at success and therefore must be more conservative in its approach.

'. . . Private property protects future persons by leading some to hold back resources from current consumption for future markets; . . '.

Again, the reverse may often be the case: free-market capitalism may overuse resources, resulting in an inefficient social state. If a number of independent, competitive wildcatters are all drilling on the same pool of oil, they will tend to sink *too many* wells, because each producer views his actions as being independent from those of the rest and ignores the total effect of the feedback of his decisions. (Another good practical example is the situation of the many small fishing companies which, without co-operation, tend to overfish common waters.)

Private property 'provides alternate sources of employment for unpopular persons who don't have to convince any one person or small group to hire them, and so on'.

But 'people's capitalism' does the same. Nozick's arguments here are, as he says, familiar. One can quarrel with them in many respects—I have mentioned a few caveats above—but over all they do provide several good reasons for the use of the market mechanism as a means of allocating resources. *However, they are not arguments for the existence of permanent private property.*

Nozick himself brings up these reasons to show that private property does not violate the Lockean proviso, not as a utilitarian justification for property (p. 73). However, such reasons *are* often used by others to support arguments for permanent private property. It is important to realize that the market mechanism, which does have many desirable features, can work perfectly well without such a notion of property. The fundamental feature of the market mechanism is not private property but the price system. Within the market mechanism, prices serve two roles: an allocative role and a distributive role. The allocative function of prices is to indicate the scarcity value of goods and thereby reward efficient use of resources. This is quite distinct from the distributive function which simply provides one way of distributing wealth among agents—namely, via permanent private ownership of the factor payments to property. It is perfectly possible to use prices for *allocation*, while basing *distribution* on factors other than the blind-chance assignment of initial endowments.[6]

Some of Nozick's arguments for the market mechanism are clear, others are questionable. It is a technical question of economics—perhaps the *central* question of economics in a mixed economy such as ours—what should be done by the market and what should be done by the government. However, this issue in itself has very little to do with the question of whether society should have permanent property rights. Nozick presents arguments for the market as a process of allocating resources; but, of course, the description of the market must include a description of the *initial* allocation of endowments, and Nozick's (and Locke's) theories shed little light on how these are to be determined.

Nozick's meta-ethics imply that a correct theory of justice requires three parts: a description of how people legitimately acquire holdings, a description of how people legitimately transfer holdings, and a description of how past injustices should be rectified.

As we have seen, Nozick believes that a free-market economy is a reasonable way to achieve the second part and that the third part should be achieved by asking what would have happened if the injustice had not occurred. But he gives no acceptable analysis of how the initial endowments of the agents are to be determined. And yet, as we have seen, this question is absolutely crucial to the whole analysis. The description of a process is incomplete until a description of its starting position is given, and to determine the justice of a given starting position we must use end-state criteria.

The interesting result of welfare economics is that we can relate an end-state principle of justice—maximum 'social welfare'—to an allocative procedure—the market mechanism. Nozick's own theory is most deficient in failing to provide such a relationship: the first part—how agents come to

[6] See John Rawls, *A Theory of Justice* (Cambridge, Mass., 1971), section 42, p. 273.

acquire legitimate holdings—seems to require some sort of end-state principle and is crucial in determining the entire outcome.

Unfortunately, welfare economics is itself too arbitrary in that it leaves unanalysed the basic normative question of the choice of the social welfare function. In the next section I shall consider an alternative to classical welfare theory. This alternative leads to a more determinate answer to the distributional question as well as relating end-state criteria of justice to a procedure for achieving just allocations.

THE THEORY OF FAIRNESS

I now wish to discuss another theory of distributional justice, which, I believe, can serve as a viable alternative to the basically utilitarian theory of welfare economics, the contractual theory of Rawls, or the entitlement theory of Nozick. The theory of fairness, as I shall call it, is founded in the notion of 'extended sympathy'[7] and in the ideas of 'symmetry' in the treatment of agents.

Let us consider the simplest situation of distributive justice: a group of agents has some bundle of goods to be divided among them in a 'fair' way. No production is possible, and each agent's bundle consists only of goods; no labour is present. What criteria can we use to choose a fair division? First of all, our discussion of the issues of welfare economics leads us to limit ourselves to pareto efficient allocations—for if all agents are to be made better off, we might as well do it. But then which of the efficient allocations shall we choose? We notice that the division problem is a symmetric one—no agent is privileged over any other agent—hence we wish the solution to be symmetric. But symmetric in what sense? I submit that we want the solution to be symmetric in the sense that no agent wishes to hold any other agent's final bundle. I shall *define* an allocation that has this property as an *equitable* allocation. This is a formal definition of an abstract concept and is not necessarily meant to reflect ordinary usage. Of course, I hope to show that this definition is of interest in formalizing certain ordinary concepts of equity, for example, the concepts of equal distribution of wealth, equal distribution of income, and so on.

Thus to determine whether an allocation is equitable, we have only to present each agent with the consumption bundle held by each of the other agents to see whether any agent would wish to exchange his bundle for another agent's bundle. If not, the allocation is equitable. It is clear that equitable allocations exist; for example, the allocation where everyone gets the same bundle—the even-division allocation—is of course equitable.

[7] K. Arrow, *Social Choice and Individual Values* (New Haven, 1963), p. 114.

However, there is no reason for this allocation to be pareto efficient; in general it will not be.

The properties of equity and efficiency are both desirable. Is it possible to find an allocation that has both of these properties? Such an allocation will be called a *fair* allocation. Notice that the concept of fairness is quite operational; we have not postulated some hypothetical welfare function or some hypothetical original position. Instead we have given a simple criterion based on the preferences of the individual agents which can be used to determine a just solution to the problem of fair division. In effect, we are asking each agent to put himself in the position of each of the other agents to determine if that is a better or a worse position than the one he is now in.[8]

The first question is, do fair allocations exist? Is it always possible to find an allocation which is equitable and at the same time efficient? The answer is yes. We can demonstrate this in the following manner: first, make an equal division of the socially owned bundle. This is certainly equitable, but if the agents have different preferences it will generally not be efficient. Next, allow the agents to trade to a market equilibrium by the use of a price system. It is important to ensure that this particular method of trading is used. Now, by the basic theorems of welfare economics, the resulting allocation is efficient; the question is, is it still equitable? Let us suppose not and derive a contradiction.

Recall the definition of a market equilibrium: each agent has chosen the bundle he prefers most out of all the bundles he can afford at the current prices. Thus if some agent I envies some other agent J—that is, if agent I prefers the bundle of agent J to his own bundle—it must be that agent J's bundle costs more than the value of agent I's endowment. Otherwise I could have bought it himself. But agent J and agent I both had the *same* endowment since the original bundle was divided equally. Thus agent J is holding a bundle which costs more than the value of his initial endowment, a contradiction of the definition of market equilibrium.

This approach to the question of a just distribution has the very appealing feature that one can draw on the methods and techniques of economic analysis to *prove* that fair allocations will in general exist. Furthermore, the fairness approach is an improvement on the rather general approach of

[8] As far as I know, the original definition of equity is due to D. Foley, 'Resource Allocation and the Public Sector', *Yale Economic Essays* 7 (Spring 1967). The idea of combining the concepts of equity and efficiency into the concept of fairness is due to D. Schmeidler and M. Yaari. Others who have treated this and similar topics include S. C. Kolm, *Justice et Equité*, Éditions du Centre National de la Recherche Scientifique (Paris, 1972); D. Schmeidler and K. Vind, 'Fair Net Trades', *Econometrica* (1974); A. Feldman and A. Kirman, 'Fairness and Envy', *American Economic Review* (1974); and H. Varian, 'Equity, Envy, and Efficiency', *Journal of Economic Theory* (September 1974), pp. 63–91, in which all of the results I describe below are proved.

welfare economics in that it actually specifies the characteristics of the solution allocation rather than allowing everything to depend on an *unspecified* social welfare function. After all, economic welfare theory is really giving us much more than we have asked for. An economic welfare function gives us a complete *ordering* of social states, when all we are really after is an answer to the question, what is the best state? It may be possible to answer the second question without answering the first. This is both a strength and a weakness of the fairness approach—a strength in that the fairness criterion provides a reasonable specification of a desirable social state and a weakness in that it does not provide any clues about how to compare nonfair allocations.[9]

FAIRNESS AND PRODUCTION

There is, however, an important criticism of the fairness model as it has thus far been presented: namely, that it ignores the question of production. For, as Nozick cogently points out, the question of *who* has contributed to the formation of the social product is very important when we consider the question of how to divide that product. Indeed the problem of fair division when there is no asymmetry in the agents' contribution to the social product is in fact quite simple. The real issue in the question of distributive justice is how to discriminate with respect to different contributions.

A first approach in extending the concept of equity to the production case might go something like this: let us imagine now that an agent's bundle consists not only of his goods but also of his labour contribution. We describe a consumer's position not only by how much he consumes but also by how much he works. Given a description of the technology, we can then determine the set of all feasible allocations of goods and labour and identify those which are pareto efficient. The equity concept makes sense just as before: we can ask each agent if he prefers the consumption–labour bundle of any other agent. If all agents answer no, we call the resulting allocation *fair*.

So far, so good. The concept of fairness previously introduced can be extended in a natural way to the production context. As before, we would like a proof of existence. Here, unfortunately, we run into problems. If we try to apply the old method of 'divide and trade' we immediately run into a thorny conceptual issue: what do we mean by equal division when labour is present? Should we correct for ability? Should we give one agent some of the other agent's labour? Or what? Even if we resolve this dispute, the solution will be

---

[9] But see H. Varian, 'Two Problems in the Theory of Fairness', where I suggest a way to use the fairness idea to make second-best comparisons.

of no avail in determining the existence of a fair allocation in the production case, since it can be shown that in general a fair allocation will *not* exist in this case.[10]

The problem is that agents' abilities may not coincide with their tastes and, unfortunately, abilities cannot be transferred. However, it is possible to *partially* transfer ability: even if I cannot produce as much of a product as you can with the same amount of time or effort, I may be able to produce as much if I work longer or harder. There is some *degree* of substitution that can allow for a new extension of the concept of equity. Suppose we again ask each agent to compare his consumption–labour bundle with the consumption–labour bundles of the other agents. Only this time each agent evaluates each of the other agents' bundles not on the basis of how much time each actually worked to produce his bundle but rather on the basis of how much time each agent would have to work to produce what each other agent produced. Equivalently, each agent compares his consumption–*output* bundle to the consumption–*output* bundle of each other agent. If, then, one agent prefers another agent's position, he is saying that he prefers the *complete* position of the other agent: he would rather consume what he consumes *and* produce what he produces. Hence the first agent has a legitimate complaint about the distribution of the social products. (If one agent cannot possibly produce what another agent produces, then no complaint against him can be made. Of course, problems arise with handicapped agents, etc. This seems to me to be a secondary issue that can be handled in a variety of other ways—by insurance, for example.)

If an allocation is such that each agent prefers his consumption–output bundle to that of every other agent, I will say that allocation is wealth-equitable; if the allocation also happens to be efficient, I will say that the allocation is wealth-fair. Happily, this definition does allow us to prove a general existence theorem; the basic idea of the proof is as before. One equally divides the total bundle of consumption goods, excluding labour, and allows each agent to start from this position of 'equal wealth' and trade via the market mechanism to a market equilibrium. There is no correction for the different abilities of the agents; they simply buy and sell their labour at the market-wage rate. It is possible to show that the resulting market equilibrium is wealth-fair by an argument similar to the original argument.

This is the formalization of the concept of 'people's capitalism' I discussed earlier. Property—in particular, productive property—is privately owned.

---

[10] For explicit examples, see Varian, 'Equity, Envy, and Efficiency'; and E. Pazner and D. Schmeidler, 'A Difficulty in the Concept of Fairness', *Review of Economic Studies* (July 1974), pp. 441–3.

All of the incentives of capitalism are present, as are all of the liberties, with one exception—the liberty to transfer wealth to others. Nozick would no doubt object to this scheme on the grounds discussed on page 64 of his article: it ignores the *right* of agents to give gifts. But it seems that this may be a small price to pay for such a desirable allocation. Agents give up the right of transfer, but receive instead the right of equal opportunity in the economic domain.

It is interesting to note that a wealth-fair allocation is immune to arguments such as Nozick's Wilt Chamberlain example (p. 57). The liberty to trade does not upset the pattern of the wealth-fair allocation. When Wilt Chamberlain reaches maturity, he owns some share of society's wealth as well as his own labour power. He can sell that labour power to other agents or keep it for himself; either way is wealth-fair. The state does not interfere with such decisions; the state need only interfere with an agent's transfers when they take place outside of the market: for example, when an agent gives gifts or bequests that upset the initial endowment of goods.

Another approach to the question of fair allocation in this production context has been suggested by Pazner and Schmeidler. Again we start by considering the set of all possible efficient allocations. According to the second basic theorem of welfare economics, we can associate with each one of these a set of *market prices*—marginal products if you will—which will support these allocations as market equilibria. These prices represent the 'market' evaluation of the value of each good, including of course the particular goods which are the labour contributions of each agent. Thus at each efficient allocation we can associate with each agent an implicit evaluation of his consumption bundle, which includes an evaluation of his leisure (i.e. nonlabour) time. In this way, we can associate with each agent a number, representing his *implicit income* at each efficient allocation. A possible criterion of fairness in this situation is to choose the allocation that gives *equal* implicit incomes to each agent. This allocation is called an income-fair allocation.

Will such an allocation always exist? Again the answer is yes. This can be shown by considering another way of dividing society's original bundle. Now we give each agent an equal division of all goods and an equal share of *each* other agent's labour. This could be done by giving everyone a ticket that would give him complete control over, say, one hour of every other person's time during some period. Given this initial endowment, the agents trade to a market equilibrium. Each agent's initial endowment has the same value since each agent holds an identical bundle—and therefore the final allocation must give everyone the same value bundle. It is this concept of equity that Nozick attacks on pages 68 and 69. Here the relationship between equal incomes and ownership of property rights in other agents is very explicit. Nozick contends that such a redistribution of 'natural assets' is grossly unjust. (See especially pp. 107–26.)

Regardless of the desirability of such a scheme, it clearly is also immune to Nozick's Wilt Chamberlain example. For when Wilt Chamberlain reaches maturity, all of the agents can decide how to sell his labour time. If they sell it to fans of Wilt Chamberlain, fine; if they sell it to Wilt, fine. Either way, all agents' *incomes* will be the same. The allocation will still be income-fair.

We now have three candidates for a just allocation when production is allowed: the original notion of the fair allocation, which has the defect that it might not always exist; the notion of the wealth-fair allocation; and the notion of the income-fair allocation. The last two concepts are especially interesting in that they make the central problem of justice in the production context very explicit: I refer to the problem of rewarding ability.

The wealth-fair allocation says that society will take the responsibility for an equal distribution of *goods* but that each person is entitled to complete control over his own time. Whether he is able or not, he is entitled to choose when, where, and how much he works, regardless of the social consequences. In a sense one can say that this concept favours the able at the expense of the nonable.

The income-fair allocation does exactly the reverse. It asks for a total correction for differences due to ability; it does this by ensuring that each agent has an equal share of *labour power*. If an agent is very able, his wage will be high, and consequently he will find it expensive to purchase his own leisure. In a sense, one might say that at this allocation, the able are exploited by the unable.

My own ranking of the desirability of the concepts is as follows: first, the fair allocation. Even though there may not exist a fair allocation in a productive economy, there *might* be one. And if there is, it seems ethically satisfying—no agent prefers any other agent's position, and the economy is efficient. (It is possible to show that a fair allocation *does* exist when all agents have the same testes, even though they may have different abilities. It is not hard to see that this is simply an equal division of goods and labour.)[11]

If, however, a fair allocation is impossible, which of the two other allocations, the wealth-fair or the income-fair, is more desirable? I believe I would choose the wealth-fair allocation—not, I hasten to add, for exclusively moral reasons but rather because it is so easy to organize. The income-fair allocation seems rather impractical by comparison.

Finally, I wish to point out an important fact about the fairness approach

[11] See Varian, 'Equity, Envy, and Efficiency', p. 72, for a nonconstructive proof.

to distributive justice: it is quite compatible with the *form* of Nozick's entitlement theory. Let us specify each of the three principles of acquisition, transfer, and rectification for the concept of wealth-fairness.

(1) Agents acquire at birth (upon reaching maturity?) an initial endowment of an equal share of society's resources. Upon death, each agent's property reverts to the state to be distributed equally to new generations. Agents are entitled to their own endowments of natural assets, whatever they may be.

(2) Agents can transfer ownership of goods and services only through the market mechanism. If necessary, the state should serve as a watchdog to prevent monopolistic interference with the market. Other transfers, at least those of appreciable magnitude, are disallowed. Each good which an agent desires to sell is thus made available to all interested purchasers; there are no 'private deals'.

(3) We know that under such a competitive market arrangement, the resulting allocation should be wealth-fair—no agent will prefer any other agent's consumption–output bundle to his own. If some agent does prefer some other agent's consumption–output bundle to his own, he has a legitimate complaint about the allocation, and thus there are possible grounds for rectification.

Each of these principles needs to be explained in greater detail in order to provide a satisfactory theory of distributive justice. What are we going to do about acts of God, children, mistakes, small gifts, lies, malicious envy, and so on? If these questions can be answered in a satisfactory way, the idea of fairness may provide a very attractive theory of justice that combines the considerations of both procedural justice and distributive justice.

X

EQUITY, ARROW'S CONDITIONS, AND RAWLS'S DIFFERENCE PRINCIPLE[1]

PETER J. HAMMOND

An Arrow social welfare function was designed not to incorporate any interpersonal comparisons. But some notions of equity rest on interpersonal comparisons. It is shown that a generalized social welfare function, incorporating interpersonal comparisons, can satisfy modifications of the Arrow conditions, and also a strong version of an equity axiom due to Sen. One such generalized social welfare function is the lexicographic form of Rawls's difference principle or maximin rule. This kind of generalized social welfare function is the only kind satisfying the modified Arrow conditions, the equity axiom, and a condition which underlies Suppes's grading principle.

1. INTRODUCTION

ARROW [1] investigated the problem of how to amalgamate the personal welfare orderings of the members of a society into a social welfare ordering. His approach was deliberately designed to avoid making any kind of interpersonal comparison. He was then able to show that such an approach must fail as long as one insists on certain other apparently appropriate conditions.

It would therefore seem that an obvious way around Arrow's impossibility theorem is to make interpersonal comparisons and to use them in the construction of a social ordering. Moreover, some considerations of equity which many people would think relevant for making social choices are specifically excluded by Arrow's approach.

From *Econometrica*, vol. 44, no. 4 (July 1976), pp. 793–800 (i.e. without the technical appendix).

[1] This is an expanded and subsequently revised version of a paper presented to the European Meeting of the Econometric Society, Grenoble, September, 1974. Some results along very similar lines have been independently discovered by Steven Strasnick of Harvard University. I am grateful to Kenneth Arrow for bringing this work to my attention, and to Louis Gevers and the referees for their most helpful comments.

This paper shows how, if interpersonal comparisons are made in a certain way, one can construct a social welfare ordering by a method which satisfies suitably modified forms of Arrow's 1963 conditions. Moreover—as is just as well, given that the interpersonal comparisons are deliberately based on a notion of equity—it is also possible to satisfy an extra condition, which is a kind of equity axiom. The lexicographic extension of Rawls's difference principle, or maximin rule, satisfies all these conditions. In addition, it is the *only* rule or principle which satisfies a condition which underlies Suppes's grading principle, together with these conditions.

Section 2 presents preliminary definitions and notation, and shows how some considerations of equity are excluded by Arrow's approach to social choice. Section 3 shows how these considerations of equity may be represented by ordinal interpersonal comparisons of the kind discussed in Sen [6], how they are related to an equity axiom due to Sen [7], and how Sen's equity axiom may be generalized. Section 4 defines generalized social welfare functions (GSWFs) and shows how Arrow's conditions can be modified to apply to GSWFs. Section 5 considers a particular form of Suppes's grading principle which can be applied to GSWFs. Section 6 discusses Rawls's difference principle (or the maximin rule) as a particular GSWF. Section 7 looks at the lexicographic extension of Rawls's difference principle. Section 8 contains concluding remarks. The proofs of results are presented in the Appendix.

2. ARROW SOCIAL WELFARE FUNCTIONS

Let X denote the set of potentially feasible social states: the *underlying set*. Each member of X is a (social) *option*. An *ordering* on X is a binary relation R which is reflexive, connected, and transitive, e.g. a transitive weak preference relation. A *strict partial ordering* is a binary relation which is irreflexive and transitive. Corresponding to an ordering R is a strict partial ordering P defined by:

$$xPy \quad \text{iff} \quad \text{not } yRx.$$

But there may not be an ordering corresponding to a strict partial ordering. Let $\mathcal{R}(X)$ denote the set of orderings on X. Let N denote the set of *persons*. For each $i \in N$, assume that there is a *welfare ordering* R_i on X. Let $\mathcal{R}_i(X)$ ($\subseteq \mathcal{R}(X)$) be the set of welfare orderings which person i may have. Let:

$$\mathcal{R}^N(X) = \underset{i \in N}{\times} \mathcal{R}_i(X)$$

be the set of allowable lists of personal welfare orderings.

An *Arrow social welfare function* (ASWF) is a mapping $f: \mathcal{R}^N(X) \to \mathcal{R}(X)$.

Given the list of personal orderings $\langle R_i \rangle_{i \in N}$, the image $f(\langle R_i \rangle_{i \in N})$ is the *social welfare ordering*.

Note that an ASWF takes no account of some considerations of equity. If there are two societies in which all the personal welfare orderings R_i are identical, then the social ordering is the same. Yet it might be that one person in one of the societies is especially deserving—for example, a seriously disadvantaged person. There is no way in which an ASWF can take account of such special deserts. And, in particular, since, on at least one view, equity demands that the disadvantaged receive especially favourable treatment, an ASWF does not allow for such considerations of equity.

3. THE EQUITY AXIOM

A full discussion of notions of equity and how they can be represented by means of interpersonal comparisons would take us far beyond the scope of this paper. But the notion mentioned at the end of the previous section, the notion that the specially disadvantaged should receive favourable treatment, can be captured by interpersonal comparisons in a fairly obvious way.

The type of interpersonal ordering which one can use has been considered by Suppes [9], Arrow [1], and Sen [6]. It is an ordering $\tilde{R}$ over the product space $X \times N$ of pairs (x, i), where x is a social option and i is a person in the society. To say that $(x, i) \tilde{R}(y, j)$ is to make an ethical judgement of the form: 'being i in state x is no worse than being j in state y'.[2]

Given the ordering $\tilde{R}$ on $X \times N$, for each social state $x \in X$, an interpersonal ordering $R(x)$ on the set N can be defined by the following: for all $i, j \in N : iR(x) j$ means $(x, i) \tilde{R}(x, j)$. Then $iP(x) j$ can be interpreted as saying that person i enjoys more advantages than person j in state x.

What equity demands is that the more disadvantaged should be given especially favourable treatment. This demand is acknowledged, to some extent, in Sen's 'weak equity axiom':

Let person i have a lower level of welfare than person j for each given level of individual income. Then, in distributing a given total of income among n individuals, including i and j, the optimal solution must give i a higher level of income than j [7, p. 18]'[3]

Suppose that y denotes an equal distribution of income, and x an alternative distribution in which i's income has risen and j's income has

---

[2] Arrow, apparently after Suppes, has labelled a particular form of such comparisons 'extended sympathy' (see [1, pp. 114–15]). Note too, that, whereas Arrow, Suppes, and Sen allow each person i to have his ethical views reflected in an ordering $\tilde{R}_i$ on the space $X \times N$, I am considering a single ordering $\tilde{R}$. For further discussion of this point, see the concluding section.

[3] A weakened version of Sen's equity axiom, which is in some ways a little closer to the condition (E) I shall state later, is in [8, Section 5].

fallen, with all other incomes remaining the same. Then Sen's axiom effectively requires that, if x is close enough to y, then x is socially preferred to y. This is assuming that i has a lower level of welfare than j in state y, i.e., that i enjoys fewer advantages than j.

One might now try to extend this principle to social choices which are more general than choices of income distribution. Then, the obvious and essential features of the social choice examined in the previous paragraph are as follows: (i) $xP_i y$, $yP_j x$, and, for all $k \notin \{i, j\}$, $xI_k y$; (ii) $jP(y)i$; and (iii) x is close to y. Only condition (iii) is imprecise. There are a number of ways one might try to make it precise. One way is to insist that x must redistribute income so that i, who enjoyed fewer advantages than j in state y, still enjoys fewer advantages than j in state x, i.e., (iii)$'$ $jP(x)i$.

An axiom in the spirit of Sen's would be to require that if conditions (i), (ii), and (iii)$'$ are satisfied, then x should be socially preferred to y. But in fact one can weaken this slightly to require that if conditions (i), (ii), and (iii)$'$ are satisfied, then x should be weakly preferred to y by society. So the equity axiom used in this paper is as follows:

AXIOM (E): *Suppose that* $jP(x)i$, $jP(y)i$, $xP_i y$, $yP_j x$, *and for all* $k \in N - \{i, j\}$, $xI_k y$. *Then* xRy *(where R denotes the social preference ordering)$'$*

The equity axiom (E) is an attempt to capture the principles of Sen's weak equity axiom within a general social choice context. It turns out to be a very strong axiom, as will be seen later.[4, 5]

4. GENERALIZED SOCIAL WELFARE FUNCTIONS

A *generalized social welfare function* (GSWF) is a mapping from the set of orderings on $X \times N$ to the set of orderings on X. So, if $\tilde{R}$ is the ordering on $X \times N$ which represents both personal and interpersonal comparisons of welfare, then $f(\tilde{R})$ is the social welfare ordering on X.

Arrow's 1963 conditions on ASWFs were (U) (unrestricted domain), (I) (independence of irrelevant alternatives), (P) (the Pareto criterion), and (ND)

---

[4] It should perhaps be remarked that the sense in which 'equity' is used here differs from that which has been used by, for example, Foley [2], Schmeidler and Vind [5], and Varian [11]. Their alternative definition of 'equity', or of 'fairness', does not rest on any kind of interpersonal comparison. Also, assuming that there is only one good, 'real income', and that everybody prefers more of it to less, the only equitable distribution (in the sense that all envy is avoided) is an equal distribution. In Sen's sense, however, an equal distribution of income may not be equitable. It is Sen's use of the term 'equity' which this paper adopts.

[5] A stronger equity axiom, more in keeping with Sen's original axiom, is the axiom (E*) which is obtained from (E) by replacing the second sentence with: 'Then xPy, where P denotes the social strict preference relation'.

(no dictatorship). A strengthening of (P) is (P*) (the strict Pareto criterion) and a strengthening of (ND) is (A) (anonymity).

To save writing, write R and R' for $f(\langle R_i \rangle_{i \in N})$ and $f(\langle R'_i \rangle_{i \in N})$ respectively. Also, given any ordering R on X, and any subset $A \subseteq X$, define the *restriction of R to A* as the ordering $R : A$ on A for which: for all $x, y \in A : xR : Ay \Leftrightarrow xRy$.

Now the conditions (U), (I), (P*), and (A) for ASWFs can be stated as follows:

CONDITION (U): $f(\langle R_i \rangle_{i \in N}$ is defined for every list of orderings $\langle R_i \rangle_{i \in N}$ on X.

CONDITION (I): For each $A \subseteq X$, if $\langle R_i \rangle$, $\langle R'_i \rangle$ are two lists of personal orderings on X with the property that $\forall i \in N : R_i : A = R'_i : A$, then $R : A = R' : A$.

CONDITION (P*): If $\langle R_i \rangle$ is a list of orderings on X such that $\forall i \in N : xR_i y$, then xRy. If, too, $\exists j \in N : xP_j y$, then xPy.

CONDITION (A): If $\langle R_i \rangle$, $\langle R'_i \rangle$ are two lists of orderings on X with the property that there exists a permutation σ on N such that $\forall i \in N : R_i = R'_{\sigma(i)}$, then $R = R'$.

Again, to save writing, for any GSWF f, and any interpersonal orderings $\tilde{R}$ and $\tilde{R}'$, write R and R' for the orderings $f(\tilde{R})$ and $f(\tilde{R}')$, respectively. And, given the ordering $\tilde{R}$ on $X \times N$, and any subset $A \subseteq X$, define the restriction of $\tilde{R}$ to $A \times N$ as the ordering $\tilde{R} : A$ on $A \times N$ for which:

$$\forall x, y \in A; \quad \forall i, j \in N : (x, i)\tilde{R} : A(y, j) \Leftrightarrow (x, i)\tilde{R}(y, j).$$

Now the corresponding conditions for GSWFs can be stated as follows:

CONDITION (U) (Unrestricted domain): $f(\tilde{R})$ is defined for every ordering R on $X \times N$.

CONDITION (I) (Independence of Irrelevant Alternatives): For any $A \subseteq X$, if $\tilde{R}$ and $\tilde{R}'$ are two orderings on $X \times N$ with the property that $\tilde{R} : A = \tilde{R}' : A$, then $R : A = R' : A$.

CONDITION (P*): If $\forall i \in N : (x, i)\tilde{R}(y, i)$, then xRy. If, too, $\exists j \in N : (x, j)\tilde{P}(y, j)$, then xPy.

Before stating (A), it is helpful to introduce yet a further piece of notation. Given any permutation σ on the set N, and given any ordering $\tilde{R}$ on $X \times N$, define the ordering $\sigma(\tilde{R})$ on $X \times N$ so that:

$$\forall x, y \in X; \quad \forall i, j \in N : (x, i)\sigma(\tilde{R})(y, j) \quad \text{means} \quad (x, \sigma(i))\tilde{R}(y, \sigma(j)).$$

Now one can state the following:

CONDITION (A) (Anonymity): If $\tilde{R}$ and $\tilde{R}'$ are two orderings on $X \times N$, and if σ is a permutation on N, such that $\tilde{R}' = \sigma(\tilde{R})$, then $R' = R$.

5. SUPPES'S GRADING PRINCIPLE[6]

Suppes [9] has considered a notion of justice, which relies on each person $i \in N$ having an ordering $\tilde{R}_i$ over the set $X \times N$. In this paper, only one ordering $\tilde{R}$ on $X \times N$ is being considered. Sen sees this as the case of complete identity, when $\tilde{R}_i = \tilde{R}$ (each $i \in N$) (see [6, p. 156, Axiom 9*2]). The use of a single ordering will be further considered in the conclusions. For the moment, it is sufficient to realize that the Suppes rule gives rise to the strict partial ordering J ('is more just than') defined by: xJy means there exists a permutation σ on N such that (i) $\forall i \in N : (x, i)\tilde{R}(y, \sigma(i))$ and (ii) $\exists j \in N : (x, j)\tilde{P}(y, \sigma(j))$. (See [9] and [6, p. 153, Definition 9*3].)

The relation J is clearly related to the Pareto relation. The difference is that one can permute individuals before making comparisons. This can be brought out further. Suppose we accept that, if permuting individuals leaves everybody just as well off as before, then two social states are socially indifferent. Formally, let us introduce the following condition:

CONDITION (S): If there exists a permutation σ on N such that $\forall i \in N : (x, i)\tilde{I}(y, \sigma(i))$, then xIy.

Now we have the following theorem:

THEOREM 5·1: *Suppose that X has at least 3 members, and that f is a GSWF satisfying (U), (I), (P^*), and (S). Then, whenever xJy, it follows that xPy.*

So (S) does underlie the Suppes rule, in a sense which Theorem 5·1 makes precise. It also leads to the anonymity condition, because of the following:

THEOREM 5·2: *Suppose that X has at least 3 members, and that f is a GSWF satisfying (U), (I), and (S). Then f also satisfies (A).*

Condition (S) plays an important role in Theorem 7·2 below.

6. RAWLS'S DIFFERENCE PRINCIPLE

The *difference principle*, or maximin rule (see [4, pp. 76–83]) can be defined as follows:

$$xP^Dy \quad \text{means} \quad [\forall j \in N : (y, j)\tilde{R}(y, i)] \Rightarrow [\forall j \in N : (x, j)\tilde{P}(y, i)].$$

[6] I am most grateful to Louis Gevers for suggesting the relevance of this principle.

Here, i is a person who is worst off in state y; xP^Dy if and only if everybody is better off in state x than i is in state y.[7]

Obviously, P^D is irreflexive and asymmetric. If R^D is the corresponding weak preference relation, then it is easy to show that R^D is an ordering. Moreover, if $\tilde{R}$ is represented by $u(.,.)$ on $X \times N$ (so that $(x, i)\,\tilde{R}(y, j)$ iff $u(x, i) \geqslant u(y, j)$), then R^D is represented by $\min_i u(x, i)$ in the sense that $xR^Dy \Leftrightarrow \min_i u(x, i) \geqslant \min_i u(y, i)$.

Given any ordering $\tilde{R}$ on $X \times N$, define the ordering $R^D = f^D(\tilde{R})$. Then we have a GSWF f^D. It is obvious that f^D satisfies conditions (U), (I), and (S). From Theorem 5·2, it follows that f^D satisfies (A). It is also easy to show that f^D satisfies (P) but need not satisfy (P*). Finally we have the following lemma:

LEMMA 6·1: f^D satisfies (E).[8]

PROOF: Suppose that $jP(x)i$, $jP(y)i$, $xP_i\,y$, $yP_j x$, and that, for all $k \in N-\{i, j\}$, $xI_k\,y$. Define $l \in N$ so that, for all $k \in N$, $(x, k)\,\tilde{R}(x, l)$. Then $l \neq j$. So $(x, l)\,\tilde{R}(y, l)$. It is therefore false that, for all $k \in N$, $(y, k)\,\tilde{P}(x, l)$. So it is false that yP^Dx, from the definition of P^D. Therefore xR^Dy, which confirms (E).

7. THE LEXICAL DIFFERENCE PRINCIPLE

The strict Pareto criterion (P*) will be satisfied as well if the difference principle is strengthened, and replaced by Sen's lexical difference principle (see [6, p. 138]). This can be defined as follows.

For each social state $x \in X$, give each person $i \in N$ a ranking number $r(i, x)$, so that persons who are less advantaged have smaller numbers than those who are more advantaged. The numbers rank persons in order of precedence; those of smaller rank receive greater precedence; the person of first rank receives the greatest precedence of all.

Thus, for each $x \in X$ and each $i \in N$, define $r(i, x)$ as an integer between 1 and n so that $(x, i)\,\tilde{P}(x, j) \Rightarrow r(i, x) > r(j, x)$. Where there are ties—where there are two individuals $i, j \in N$ such that $(x, i)\,\tilde{I}(x, j)$—these ties can be broken arbitrarily. As will se seen later, the tie-breaking rule will not affect the social ordering.

In any social state x, there exists for each integer r between 1 and n a unique individual $i(r, x)$ whose rank in state x is r. Write x_r for $(x, i(r, x))$, the position

---

[7] This could be simplified to the equivalent statement: xP^Dy means $\exists i \in N\ \forall j \in N : (x, j)\,\tilde{P}(y, i)$. See Sen [6, p. 157, Definition 9*5].

[8] It is *not* true, however, that f^D always satisfies (E*), the stronger axiom set out in Footnote 5 as the reader should be able to confirm using an example with at least three persons in the set N.

of being the rth ranked individual in state x. Thus $x_{r(i, x)}$ is, by definition, (x, i). It follows from the definition of $r(i, x)$ and of x_r that, for each $x \in X : x_{r+1} \tilde{R} x_r$ ($r = 1$ to $n-1$).

Define the binary relation P^L on X so that $xP^L y$ means $\exists m \geqslant 1 : x_r \tilde{I} y_r$ ($r = 1$ to $m-1$) and $x_m \tilde{P} y_m$.

Then, if R^L is the corresponding weak preference relation, and I^L is the corresponding indifference relation, $xI^L y \Leftrightarrow x_r \tilde{I} y_r$ ($r = 1$ to n).

Clearly, R^L is an ordering. If f^L is defined by $R^L = f^L(\tilde{R})$ for all orderings $\tilde{R}$ on $X \times N$, then f^L is a GSWF, called the *lexical difference principle*. It is a strengthened difference principle, because it is evident that $xP^D y \Leftrightarrow x_1 \tilde{P} y_1 \Rightarrow xP^L y$. It is evident too that f^L satisfies (U), (I), (S), and so (A).[9] That is also satisfies (P*) and (E) is shown as follows:

THEOREM 7·1: *The GSWF f^L satisfies conditions* (P*) *and* (E).

This has shown that f^L satisfies (U), (I), (P*), (E), and (S). Conversely, we have the following theorem:

THEOREM 7·2: *If X has at least three members, f^L is the only GSWF satisfying* $(U), (I), (P^*), (E),$ *and* (S).

8. CONCLUSIONS

I have shown that, if interpersonal comparisons of a certain kind are introduced, it is possible to construct a generalized social welfare function (GSWF) satisfying appropriately modified forms of the Arrow conditions. Moreover, if the interpersonal comparisons reflect equity judgements, the GSWF can also be equitable, in the sense that condition (E) (Section 3) is satisfied. Rawls's difference principle is one GSWF of this kind (Section 6). Suppes's grading principle can be derived from a condition (S) together with the modified Arrow condition (Section 5). If one imposes both (E) and (S), as well as the modified Arrow conditions, the only GSWF satisfying all these conditions is the lexicographic extension of Rawls's difference principle (Section 7).

Of course, condition (E) is just one way of ensuring that the GSWF is, in a sense, equitable. Alternative weaker conditions may not lead so directly to the difference principle.

The social ordering was constructed from a *single* interpersonal ordering $\tilde{R}$. This ordering $\tilde{R}$ incorporates the welfare preference orderings R_i ($i \in N$) of all the persons in the society; it also incorporates interpersonal comparisons of welfare levels, in effect.

---

[9] It should be noted that the tie-breaking rule used to define the ranks $r(i, x)$ cannot lead to a violation of condition (S). And, because of Theorem 5·2, f^L must then also satisfy (A).

An alternative, more general, situation is one where *each person i* in the society has an interpersonal ordering $\tilde{R}_i$ on the set $X \times N$. Each person makes interpersonal comparisons. I have considered a special case, in which either the interpersonal comparisons are those of a single ethical observer, or else one assumes unanimity, with $\tilde{R}_i = \tilde{R}$ (all $i \in N$). The latter alternative appears to be what Rawls has in mind (see [4, pp. 263–4]). It is also closely related to Kolm's assumption that there are 'fundamental preferences'.[10]

The harder, perhaps more interesting, problem of reconciling conflicting interpersonal orderings $\tilde{R}_i$ ($i \in N$) over $X \times N$ into a single social ordering R over X has been left for other work.[11]

REFERENCES

[1] ARROW, K. J.: *Social Choice and Individual Values*, 2nd edn. (New Haven: Yale University Press, 1963).

[2] FOLEY, D. K.: 'Resource Allocation and the Public Sector', *Yale Economic Essays*, 7 (1967), 45–98.

[3] KOLM, S. C.: 'Sur les Conséquences Économiques des Principes de Justice et de Justice Pratique', *Revue d'Économie Politique*, 84 (1974), 80–107.

[4] RAWLS, J.: *A Theory of Justice* (Cambridge, Mass.: Harvard University Press, 1971).

[5] SCHMEIDLER, D., and K. VIND: 'Fair Net Trades', *Econometrica*, 40 (1972), 637–42.

[6] SEN, A. K.: *Collective Choice and Social Welfare* (San Francisco: Holden-Day, 1970).

[7] ——: *On Economic Inequality* (Oxford: Clarendon Press, 1973).

[8] ——: 'Informational Bases of Alternative Welfare Approaches: Aggregation and Income Distribution', *Journal of Public Economics*, 3 (1974), 387–403.

[9] SUPPES, P.: 'Some Formal Models of Grading Principles', *Synthese*, 16 (1966), 284–306.

[10] TINBERGEN, J.: 'Welfare Economics and Income Distribution', *American Economic Review, Papers and Proceedings*, 47 (1957), 490–503.

[11] VARIAN, H.: 'Equity, Envy and Efficiency', *Journal of Economic Theory*, 9 (1974), 63–91.

[10] See Kolm [3]. As Kolm suggests, the idea of 'fundamental utility' in connection with 'justice' seems due to Tinbergen [10].

[11] A problem which was first suggested to me by Alastair McAuley.

XI

THE CONCEPT OF JUSTICE IN POLITICAL ECONOMY

JOHN RAWLS

My aim in this chapter is to see how the two principles* work out as a conception of political economy, that is, as standards by which to assess economic arrangements and policies, and their background institutions. (Welfare economics is often defined in the same way.[1] I do not use this name because the term 'welfare' suggests that the implicit moral conception is utilitarian; the phrase 'social choice' is far better although I believe its connotations are still too narrow.) A doctrine of political economy must include an interpretation of the public good which is based on a conception of justice. It is to guide the reflections of the citizen when he considers questions of economic and social policy. He is to take up the perspective of the constitutional convention or the legislative stage and ascertain how the principles of justice apply. A political opinion concerns what advances the good of the body politic as a whole and invokes some criterion for the just division of social advantages.

From the beginning I have stressed that justice as fairness applies to the

From *A Theory of Justice* (Oxford: O.U.P., 1972), Section 41.

* [of Justice as Fairness, defined in section 46 thus:
'*First Principle*   Each person is to have an equal right to the most extensive total system of equal basic liberties compatible with a similar system of liberty for all.
Second Principle   Social and economic inequalities are to be arranged so that they are both
(*a*) to the greatest benefit of the least advantaged, consistent with the just savings principle, and
(*b*) attached to offices and positions open to all under conditions of fair equality of opportunity'.
(eds.)]

[1] Welfare economics is so defined by K. J. Arrow and Tibor Scitovsky in their introduction to *Readings in Welfare Economics* (Homewood, Ill.: Richard D. Irwin, 1969), p. 1. For further discussion, see Abram Bergson, *Essays in Normative Economics* (Cambridge: Harvard University Press, 1966), pp. 35–9, 60–3, 68f; and A. K. Sen, *Collective Choice and Social Welfare* (San Francisco: Holden-Day, 1970), pp. 56–9.

basic structure of society. It is a conception for ranking social forms viewed as closed systems. Some decision concerning these background arrangements is fundamental and cannot be avoided. In fact, the cumulative effect of social and economic legislation is to specify the basic structure. Moreover, the social system shapes the wants and aspirations that its citizens come to have. It determines in part the sort of persons they want to be as well as the sort of persons they are. Thus an economic system is not only an institutional device for satisfying existing wants and needs but a way of creating and fashioning wants in the future. How men work together now to satisfy their present desires affects the desires they will have later on, the kind of persons they will be. These matters are, of course, perfectly obvious and have always been recognized. They were stressed by economists as different as Marshall and Marx.[2] Since economic arrangements have these effects, and indeed must do so, the choice of these institutions involves some view of human good and of the design of institutions to realize it. This choice must, therefore, be made on moral and political as well as on economic grounds. Considerations of efficiency are but one basis of decision and often relatively minor at that. Of course, this decision may not be openly faced; it may be made by default. We often acquiesce without thinking in the moral and political conception implicit in the *status quo*, or leave things to be settled by how contending social and economic forces happen to work themselves out. But political economy must investigate this problem even if the conclusion reached is that it is best left to the course of events to decide.

Now it may seem at first sight that the influence of the social system upon human wants and men's view of themselves poses a decisive objection to the contract view. One might think that this conception of justice relies upon the aims of existing individuals and regulates the social order by principles that persons guided by these aims would choose. How, then, can this doctrine determine an Archimedean point from which the basic structure itself can be appraised? It might seem as if there is no alternative but to judge institutions in the light of an ideal conception of the person arrived at on perfectionist or on *a priori* grounds. But, as the account of the original position and its Kantian interpretation makes clear, we must not overlook the very special nature of that situation and the scope of the principles adopted there. Only the most general assumptions are made about the aims of the parties, namely, that they take an interest in primary social goods, in things that men are presumed to want whatever else they want. To be sure, the theory of these goods depends on psychological premises and these may prove incorrect. But the idea at any rate is to define a class of goods that are normally wanted

---

[2] For a discussion of this point and its consequences for political principles, see Brian Barry, *Political Argument* (London: Routledge and Kegan Paul, 1965), pp. 75–9.

as parts of rational plans of life which may include the most varied sorts of ends. To suppose, then, that the parties want these goods, and to found a conception of justice on this presumption, is not to tie it to a particular pattern of human interests as these might be generated by a particular arrangement of institutions. The theory of justice does, indeed, presuppose a theory of the good, but within wide limits this does not prejudge the choice of the sort of persons that men want to be.

Once the principles of justice are derived, however, the contract doctrine does establish certain limits on the conception of the good. These limits follow from the priority of justice over efficiency and the priority of liberty over social and economic advantages (assuming that serial order obtains). For as I remarked earlier (§ 6), these priorities mean that desires for things that are inherently unjust, or that cannot be satisfied except by the violation of just arrangements, have no weight. There is no value in fulfilling these wants and the social system should discourage them. Further, one must take into account the problem of stability. A just system must generate its own support. This means that it must be arranged so as to bring about in its members the corresponding sense of justice, an effective desire to act in accordance with its rules for reasons of justice. Thus the requirement of stability and the criterion of discouraging desires that conflict with the principles of justice put further constraints on insitutions. They must be not only just but framed so as to encourage the virtue of justice in those who take part in them. In this sense, the principles of justice define a partial ideal of the person which social and economic arrangements must respect. Finally, as the argument for embedding ideals into our working principles has brought out, certain institutions are required by the two principles. They define an ideal basic structure, or the outlines of one, toward which the course of reform should evolve.

The upshot of these considerations is that justice as fairness is not at the mercy, so to speak, of existing wants and interests. It sets up an Archimedean point for assessing the social system without invoking *a priori* considerations. The long range aim of society is settled in its main lines irrespective of the particular desires and needs of its present members. And an ideal conception of justice is defined since institutions are to foster the virtue of justice and to discourage desires and aspirations incompatible with it. Of course, the pace of change and the particular reforms called for at any given time depend upon current conditions. But the conception of justice, the general form of a just society, and the ideal of the person consistent with it are not similarly dependent. There is no place for the question whether men's desires to play the role of superior or inferior might not be so great that autocratic institutions should be accepted, or whether men's perception of the religious practices of others might not be so upsetting that liberty of conscience should not be allowed. We have no occasion to ask whether under reasonably favourable conditions the economic gains of technocratic but authoritarian institutions might be so great as to justify the sacrifice of basic freedoms. Of course, these remarks assume that the general assumptions on which the principles of justice were chosen are correct. But if they are, this sort of question is already decided by these principles. Certain institutional forms are embedded within the conception of justice. This view shares with perfectionism the feature of setting up an ideal of the person that constrains the pursuit of existing desires. In this respect justice as fairness and perfectionism are both opposed to utilitarianism.

Now it may appear that since utilitarianism makes no distinctions between the quality of desires and all satisfactions have some value, it has no criteria for choosing between systems of desires, or ideals of the person. From a theoretical point of view anyway, this is incorrect. The utilitarian can always say that given social conditions and men's interests as they are, and taking into account how they will develop under this or that alternative institutional arrangement, encouraging one pattern of wants rather than another is likely to lead to a greater net balance (or to a higher average) of satisfaction. On this basis the utilitarian selects between ideals of the person. Some attitudes and desires, being less compatible with fruitful social co-operation, tend to reduce the total (or the average) happiness. Roughly speaking, the moral virtues are those dispositions and effective desires that can generally be relied upon to promote the greatest sum of well-being. Thus, it would be a mistake to claim that the principle of utility provides no grounds for choosing among ideals of the person, however difficult it may be to apply the principle in practice. Nevertheless, the choice does depend upon existing desires and present social circumstances and their natural continuations into the future. These initial conditions may heavily influence the conception of human good that should be encouraged. The contrast is that both justice as fairness and perfectionism establish independently an ideal conception of the person and of the basic structure so that not only are some desires and inclinations necessarily discouraged but the effect of the initial circumstances will eventually disappear. With utilitarianism we cannot be sure what will happen. Since there is no ideal embedded in its first principle, the place we start from may always influence the path we are to follow.

By way of summing up, the essential point is that despite the individualistic features of justice as fairness, the two principles of justice are not contingent upon existing desires or present social conditions. Thus we are able to derive a conception of a just basic structure, and an ideal of the person compatible with it, that can serve as a standard for appraising institutions and for guiding the over-all direction of social change. In order to find an Archimedean point it is not necessary to appeal to *a priori* or perfectionist principles. By assuming certain general desires, such as the desire for primary social goods, and by taking as a basis the agreements that would be made in a suitably defined initial situation, we can achieve the requisite independence from existing circumstances. The original position is so characterized that unanimity is possible; the deliberations of any one person are typical of all. Moreover, the same will hold for the considered judgements of the citizens of a well-ordered society effectively regulated by the principles of justice. Everyone has a similar sense of justice and in this respect a well-ordered society is homogeneous. Political argument appeals to this moral consensus.

It may be thought that the assumption of unanimity is peculiar to the political philosophy of idealism.[3] As it is used in the contract view, however, there is nothing characteristically idealist about the supposition of unanimity. This condition is part of the procedural conception of the original position and it represents a constraint on arguments. In this way it shapes the content of the theory of justice, the principles that are to match our considered judgements. Hume and Adam Smith likewise assume that if men were to take up a certain point of view, that of the impartial spectator, they would be led to similar convictions. A utilitarian society may also be well-ordered. For the most part the philosophical tradition, including intuitionism, has assumed that there exists some appropriate perspective from which unanimity on moral questions may be hoped for, at least among rational persons with relevantly similar and sufficient information. Or if unanimity is impossible, disparities between judgements are greatly reduced once this standpoint is adopted. Different moral theories arise from different interpretations of this point of view, of what I have called the initial situation. In this sense the idea of unanimity among rational persons is implicit throughout the tradition of moral philosophy.

What distinguishes justice as fairness is how it characterizes the initial situation, the setting in which the condition of unanimity appears. Since the original position can be given a Kantian interpretation, this conception of justice does indeed have affinities with idealism. Kant sought to give a philosophical foundation to Rousseau's idea of the general will.[4] The theory of justice in turn tries to present a natural procedural rendering of Kant's

[3] This suggestion is found in K. J. Arrow, *Social Choice and Individual Values*, 2nd edn. (New York: John Wiley and Sons, 1963), pp. 74f, 81–6.

[4] See L. W. Beck, *A Commentary on Kant's Critique of Practical Reason* (Chicago: University of Chicago Press, 1960), pp. 200, 235f; and Ernst Cassirer, *Rousseau, Kant and Goethe* (Princeton: Princeton University Press, 1945), pp. 18–25, 30–5, 58f. Thus among other things, Kant is giving a deeper reading to Rousseau's remark: 'to be governed by appetite alone is slavery, while obedience to a law one prescribes to oneself is freedom'. *The Social Contract*, bk. I, ch. viii.

conception of the kingdom of ends, and of the notions of autonomy and the categorical imperative (§ 40). In this way the underlying structure of Kant's doctrine is detached from its metaphysical surroundings so that it can be seen more clearly and presented relatively free from objection.

There is another resemblance to idealism: justice as fairness has a central place for the value of community, and how this comes about depends upon the Kantian interpretation. I discuss this topic in Part Three. The essential idea is that we want to account for the social values, for the intrinsic good of institutional, community, and associative activities, by a conception of justice that in its theoretical basis is individualistic. For reasons of clarity among others, we do not want to rely on an undefined concept of community, or to suppose that society is an organic whole with a life of its own distinct from and superior to that of all its members in their relations with one another. Thus the contractual conception of the original position is worked out first. It is reasonably simple and the problem of rational choice that it poses is relatively precise. From this conception, however individualistic it might seem, we must eventually explain the value of community. Otherwise the theory of justice cannot succeed. To accomplish this we shall need an account of the primary good of self-respect which relates it to the parts of the theory already developed. But for the time being, I shall leave these problems aside and proceed to consider some further implications of the two principles of justice for the economic aspects of the basic structure.

NOTES ON THE CONTRIBUTORS

KENNETH J. ARROW is James Bryant Conant Professor at Harvard, where he has been Professor of Economics since 1968. He is author of *Social Choice and Individual Values* (1951) and *The Limits of Organisation* (1974) among many other writings. He was awarded a Nobel Prize in 1972.

MILTON FRIEDMAN has been Paul Snowden Russell Professor of Economics at the University of Chicago since 1962. Since *Essays in Positive Economics* (1953), he has published a wealth of work and also been adviser to several governments. He was awarded a Nobel Prize in 1975.

PETER HAMMOND is a Lecturer in Economics at the University of Essex.

LUDWIG VON MISES was a leading economist of the Austrian School and critic of state intervention in economic affairs. Fifty years of publications extended from *The Theory of Money and Credit* (1912) to *The Ultimate Foundation of Economic Science* (1962).

EDWARD J. NELL is Professor of Economic Theory at the New School for Social Research, New York.

JOHN RAWLS has been Professor of Philosophy at Harvard since 1962. He is author of *A Theory of Justice* (1971).

LIONEL ROBBINS was Professor of Economics at the London School of Economics from 1929 to 1961. Since then he has held various offices in public life and continued to publish work on economic subjects.

A. K. SEN is Professor of Economics at Nuffield College, Oxford and author of *Collective Choice and Social Welfare* (1971) and *On Economic Inequality* (1973).

HERBERT SIMON has been Richard King Mellon Professor of Computer Sciences and Psychology at Carnegie-Mellon University, Pittsburgh, since 1965. The books which have attracted most philosophical interest are perhaps *Administrative Behavior* (1947) and *Models of Man* (1950).

HAL R. VARIAN is Professor of Economics at the University of Wisconsin.

BIBLIOGRAPHY

(See also the bibliographies at the end of some articles in this volume.)

BOOKS

K. J. ARROW, *Social Choice and Individual Values* (New York, 1951).

K. J. ARROW and F. H. HAHN, *General Competitive Analysis* (Edinburgh, 1971).

J. CHIPMAN, L. HARWICZ, M. RICHTER, and H. SONNENSCHEIN (eds.), *Preferences, Utility and Demand* (Harcourt Brace, 1971).

M. H. DOBB, *Theories of Value and Distribution Since Adam Smith* (Cambridge, 1973).

F. Y. EDGEWORTH, *Mathematical Psychics* (London, 1881).

P. C. FISHBURN, *The Theory of Social Choice* (Princeton, 1973).

M. FRIEDMAN, *Essays in Positive Economics* (Chicago, 1953).

N. GEORGESCU-ROEGEN, *The Entropy Law and the Economic Process* (Harvard, 1971).

F. H. HAHN, *On the Notion of Equilibrium in Economics* (London, 1973).

J. C. HARSANYI, *Essays on Ethics, Social Behaviour and Scientific Explanation* (Dordrecht, 1976).

M. HOLLIS and E. J. NELL, *Rational Economic Man: A Philosophical Critique of Neo-Classical Economics* (Cambridge, 1975).

T. W. HUTCHISON, *The Significance and Basic Postulates of Economic Theory* (London, 1938; 2nd edition 1960).

T. C. KOOPMANS, *Three Essays on the State of Economic Science* (McGraw-Hill, 1957).

J. KORNAI, *Anti-Equilibrium* (Amsterdam, 1971).

S. LATSIS (ed.), *Method and Appraisal in Economics* (Cambridge, 1976).

I. M. D. LITTLE, *A Critique of Welfare Economics* (Oxford, 1950).

A. LOWE, *On Economic Knowledge* (New York, 1965).

L. VON MISES, *Epistemological Problems of Economics* (Princeton, 1960).

—— *Human Action* (London, 1949).

P. K. PATTANAIK, *Voting and Collective Choice* (Cambridge, 1971).

A. C. PIGOU, *The Economics of Welfare* (London, 1920).

L. ROBBINS, *An Essay on the Nature and Significance of Economic Science* (London, 1932; 2nd edition 1935).

J. ROBINSON, *Economic Philosophy* (London, 1962).

A. ROSENBURG, *Microeconomic Laws: A Philosophical Analysis* (Pittsburgh, 1976).

A. RYAN (ed.), *The Philosophy of Social Explanation* (Oxford, 1973).

A. K. SEN, *Collective Choice and Social Welfare* (San Francisco, 1970).
—— *On Economic Inequality* (Oxford, 1973).
G. L. S. SHACKLE, *The Years of High Theory* (Cambridge, 1967).
—— *Epistemics and Economics* (Cambridge, 1973).
H. A. SIMON, *Models of Man* (John Wiley and Sons, 1957).
—— *Administrative Behaviour* (New York: 1945; 2nd edition 1957).
E. R. WEINTRAUB, *Conflict and Co-operation in Economics* (London, 1975).

ARTICLES

J. AGASSI, 'Testability and Tautology in Economics', *Philosophy of the Social Sciences* (1971).
D. BEAR and D. ORR, 'Logic and Expediency in Economic Theorising', *Journal of Political Economy* (1967).
G. S. BECKER, 'Irrational Behaviour and Economic Theory', *Journal of Political Economy* (1962).
L. BOLAND, 'Conventionalism and Economic Theory', *Philosophy of Science* (1970).
K. BOULDING, 'Economics as a Moral Science', *American Economic Review* (1969).
M. BROUFENBRENNER, 'The "Structure of Revolutions" in Economic Thought', *History of Political Economy* (1971).
A. W. COATS, 'Is there a "Structure of Scientific Revolutions" in Economics?', *Kyklos* (1969).
A. CODDINGTON, 'Positive Economics', *Canadian Journal of Economics* (1972).
—— 'The Rationale of General Equilibrium Theory', *Economic Inquiry* (1975).
G. GARB, 'Professor Samuelson on Theory and Realism: Comment', *American Economic Review* (1965).
F. H. HAHN, 'The Winter of our Discontent', *Economica* (1973).
R. F. HARROD, 'Utilitarianism Revisited', *Mind*, vol. xlv (1936).
—— 'The Scope and Method of Economics', *Economic Journal* (1938).
J. C. HARSANYI, 'Cardinal Welfare, Individualistic Ethics and Interpersonal Comparisons of Utility', *Journal of Political Economy* (1955).
—— 'Rule Utilitarianism and Decision Theory', *Erkenntnis* (1977).
R. L. HEIBRONNER, 'Is Economic Theory Possible?', *Social Research* (1966).
S. J. LATSIS, 'Situational Determinism in Economics', *British Journal for the Philosophy of Science* (1972).
W. LEONTIEF, 'Theoretical Assumptions and Nonobserved Facts', *American Economic Review* (1971).
R. G. LIPSEY and K. LANCASTER, 'The General Theory of the Second Best', *Review of Economic Studies* (1956–7).
F. MACHLUP, 'Professor Samuelson on Theory and Realism: Comment', *American Economic Review* (1964).
—— 'The Problem of Verification in Economics', *Southern Economic Journal* (1955).
J. MELITZ, 'Friedman and Machlup on Testing Economic Assumptions', *Journal of Political Economy* (1965).
E. NAGEL, 'Assumptions in Economic Theory', *American Economic Review* (1963).
B. PELEG and M. YAARI, 'On the Existence of a Consistent Course of Action When Tastes are Changing', *Review of Economic Studies* (1973).
R. RADNER, 'Aspiration, Bounded Rationality and Control', Berkeley Discussion Paper (1975).

P. A. SAMUELSON, 'Parable and Realism in Capital Theory: the Surrogate Production Function', *Review of Economic Studies* (1962).

—— 'Problems of Methodology—Discussion', *American Economic Review* (1963).

—— 'Theory and Realism: A Reply', *American Economic Review* (1964).

—— 'Professor Samuelson on Theory and Realism: A Reply', *American Economic Review* (1965).

—— 'Some Notions of Causality and Teleology in Economics', in P. D. Lerner (ed.), *Cause and Effect* (New York, 1965).

THOMAS SCHWARTZ, 'Rationality and the Myth of the Maximum', *Nous*, vol. 5 (1972).

A. K. SEN, 'Liberty, Unanimity and Rights', *Economica*, 43 (1976).

—— 'Social Choice Theory: A Re-examination', *Econometrica*, 45 (1977).

H. R. VARIAN, 'Equity, Envy and Efficiency', *Journal of Economic Theory* (1974).

—— 'Distributive Justice, Welfare Economics and the Theory of Fairness', *Philosophy and Public Affairs* (1975).

—— 'Two Problems in the Theory of Fairness', *Journal of Public Economics* (1976).

C. C. VON WEIZSÄCKER, 'Notes on Endogenous Changes in Tastes', *Journal of Economic Theory*, iii, 4 (1971).

S. WONG, 'The "F-Tuist" and the Methodology of Paul Samuelson', *American Economic Review* (1973).

G. D. N. WORSWICK, 'Is Progress in Economic Science Possible?', *Economic Journal* (1972).

AUTHOR INDEX

11 Radson
66 Coats
92, 93 McFadden

Philosophy + Public Affairs